Flight from Eden

Flight from Eden

*The Origins of Modern
Literary Criticism and Theory*

Steven Cassedy

UNIVERSITY OF CALIFORNIA PRESS
Berkeley · Los Angeles · Oxford

University of California Press

Berkeley and Los Angeles, California

University of California Press, Ltd.
Oxford, England

© 1990 by Steven Cassedy

Library of Congress Cataloging-in-Publication Data

Cassedy, Steven.
    Flight from Eden : the origins of modern literary criticism and
theory / Steven Cassedy.
        p.   cm.
    Includes bibliographical references and index.
    ISBN 0–520–06863–7 (cloth)
    1. Literature—Philosophy.   2. Philosophy, Modern—19th century.
3. Philosophy, Modern—20th century.   4. Aesthetics, Modern—19th
century.   5. Aesthetics, Modern—20th century.   I. Title.
PN45.C34   1990
801—dc20   90–39013
                                                                                CIP

Printed in the United States of America

1 2 3 4 5 6 7 8 9

The paper used in this publication meets the minimum requirements of
American National Standard for Information Sciences—Permanence of
Paper for Printed Library Materials, ANSI Z39.48-1984. ♾

To the memory of
Sylvia B. Cassedy,
1930–1989

Contents

A Note on Translation and Transliteration

Except where I have indicated otherwise, all translations are my own. In some cases I have given my own translation but have cited a published English translation. I have indicated this in the notes.

For Russian terms and for titles of books and articles I have used the international scholarly transliteration style favored in Slavic studies. For personal names I have either used the Library of Congress system or given the form that is likely to be most familiar to English speakers.

Introduction

How Literary Criticism Came into Its Own in This Country and How the Poets Got There First

WE ARE THE REAL TEXT

Books about books about books. About books. It's become an old joke by now in humanities departments. First there are books. Then literary critics come along and write books about those books. Then more literary critics come along and write books about *those* books, and the whole process can go on forever. Before too long, the critics writing books about other critics writing books about other critics writing books step back and take a look at what they're doing. They quip about how no one pays any attention to "literature" any more, and then they go back to writing books about books about books. Literary criticism has always meant writing about writing, and literary criticism has been around for a very long time. But never until recently in this country has the discipline seemed so self-reflecting, so circular, and at the same time so self-assertive.

Something extraordinary happened to American academic literary criticism in the late 1960s and early 1970. Before, the activity of reading literary works and commenting on them had been a relatively uncomplicated affair for professional scholars. At least that's the way it seems if you compare the literary criticism of earlier generations with what we see today and what we have seen in the past twenty years or so. The most radical idea the previous generation of literary scholars had encountered was that a literary work should be studied in isolation from its author. This idea was a favorite of the New Critics, who proclaimed in the late 1940s that an author's intention in writing a literary work was irrelevant to an understanding of that work. The result in literary studies was a shift in emphasis from historical and biographical criticism to criticism that was centered in the literary text itself.

But even this shift seems minor compared with what happened a generation later. Take a look at any of the standard literary journals, and you'll see what I mean. In the 1960s academic critics are still writing about traditional "literary" subjects: the themes in an author's work, the influence of one author on another, historical events that shaped the literary vision of an author. In the early 1970s, however, strange things begin to happen. More and more, literary scholars are writing about things that appear at first glance to have nothing to do with literature. New, outlandish-sounding terms creep into their writing. The titles of their articles often do not give a clear indication of what the articles are about. One has the increasing sense that literary criticism is declaring its independence from "literature" and is setting itself up as an autonomous discipline.

The titles of articles tell an entire story all by themselves. Consider, for example, a fairly traditional journal like the *PMLA*. In the 1960s we see titles like these: "Hazlitt on the Poetry of Wit," "Emerson and White-head," "Hermann Broch's Early Writings," "Hawthorne's Fair-Headed Maidens: The Fading Light." By 1970 things have begun to change ever so slightly. Critics no longer feel they must stick to the sober tone of earlier titles. Now we find, for instance, " 'Wanna Go Home, Baby?': *Sweeney Agonistes* as Drama of the Absurd." A penchant for abstraction and a concern for literary craft arrive on the scene: "The Structure of *Platero y Yo*" and "The Four Narrative Perspectives in *Absalom, Absalom!*" Still, there is nothing too striking here, and things remain fairly stable for the next couple of years. In 1973 we still see titles like "Poe and Tennyson," "Perception and English Poetic Meter," and "Proust and the New Novel in France."

But starting in 1974, we read "The Nature of Picaresque Narrative: A Modal Approach" (March 1974), "Narrative Discourse in Calvino: Praxis or Poiesis?" (May 1975), and "Risk and Redundancy," which, the author tells us, analyzes the act of reading (March 1975). This last article is only one of a great many over the following few years that focus on "text" in the abstract sense, language, and the act of reading. In October 1975 *PMLA* publishes an article with a title typical of the new style in criticism: "UNITY IDENTITY TEXT SELF." In the abstract published in the table of contents the author of this article tells us that "understanding the receptivity of literature, how one work admits many readers, begins with an analogy: *unity* is to *text* as *identity* is to *self.*" In January of 1976 *PMLA* prints an article called "Talking in James," in which the author seeks to demonstrate that in James's late fiction "talk becomes a process of imaginative collaboration, and language virtually creates the conditions under which perception is possible." " 'Reading' in *Great Expectations*," also in 1976, is about how Dickens's novel "reveals the complex metaphorical nature of the terms 'reading' and 'reader.' " And again in 1976 "T. S. Eliot's Raids on the Inarticulate" " shows how the "failure of speech" and the "weaknesses of language" are themes in Eliot's poetic works.

By the end of the decade all the stops are out. "Letters to the Self: The Cloistered Writer in Nonretrospective Fiction," we read, or "A Phenomenological Approach to the *Theatrum Mundi* Metaphor." Everything seems to be about "text," language, and the act of reading: "Language, History, and Text in Eliot's 'Journey of the Magi' " (October 1980), "Samuel Beckett, Fritz Mauthner, and the Limits of Language" (March 1980). The title has become an art form in itself in many cases, as critics use alluringly mystifying formulations to announce (and in many cases to obscure) their subject. "Rich Text / Poor Text: A Kafkan Confusion" (March 1980) is actually one of the more lucid titles in this genre. In the abstract to this article the author says that a particular "text" by Kafka "is a skeletal, or 'poor,' text in that one code of reading—the referential—dominates it, while other codes present in a classic, or 'rich,' text are almost absent. Using a method freely adapted from Roland Barthes's *S/Z*," the author continues, "my article closely examines the referentiality of Kafka's text, juxtaposing the proverbial (or common-language) response evoked by the text with the personal reactions of a single reader. Kafka's theme, the inability of common, proverbial language to make real communication possible, is allegorized in the brief tale of A and B, whose comings and goings are mirrored, and at times interfered with, by the language in which these events occur."

Other journals follow a similar pattern. In 1965 *MLN*, published at Johns Hopkins, was running articles with titles like "Death and History in Poliziano's *Stanze*" and "The Function of the Theater in the Work of Nerval." As early as 1966, however, we begin to see glimmerings of what is to come—"Beyond Formalism" and "Topology and Critical Method"—and in 1967 "Of Structuralism and Literature" appears. By the early 1970s, although there continue to be a great many articles on traditional topics, we find titles like these: "Language, Vision, and Phenomenology: Merleau-Ponty as a Test Case" (1970), "The Shape of Fiction: Notes toward a Possible Classification of Narrative Discourses" (1971), "Les sources de Valéry. Qual, Quelle" (1972), " 'Literature' / Literature" (1971), "Text, Pretextuality and Myth in the *Folie Tristan d'Oxford*" (1973), and "The Text as Practice and as Idea" (1973). Nothing could be more representative of literary criticism in the mid-1970s than this title: "Little Red Riding Hood's Metacommentary: Paradoxical Injunction, Semiotics and Behavior" (1975). For the new style in *MLN* 1976 is a banner year: "Vico on the Discipline of Bodies and Texts," "Writers Reading: James and Eliot," "Saussure and the Apparition of Language: The Critical Perspective," "Remarques critiques sur l'énonciation: La question du présent dans le discours," "Cognitive Networks and Literary Semantics," "How To Do Things with Austin and Searle: Speech Act Theory and Literary Criticism," "Structuralist Homiletics," "The Fiction of Self-Begetting," "Presupposition and Intertextuality," "Wittgenstein on Consciousness and Language: A Challenge to Derridean Literary Theory," and on and on. After this, each issue of *MLN* contains numerous articles showing the same concerns and emphases as the ones you see in the titles I've just cited.

In the 1970s, as older journals like *PMLA* and *MLN* slowly responded to the emergence of the latest styles in criticism, new journals were founded to offer literary scholars a forum more exclusively given over to the increasingly independent field of literary criticism and theory. *Critical Inquiry,* established in 1974, was one such journal. It immediately became the most authoritative and intimidating forum for theoretical discourse on literature (in fact, in a contemporary spirit of catholicity, it published articles on other arts as well). In its first year *Critical Inquiry* served up a diet representative of what was to become standard fare in its pages: "Fact, Theory, and Literary Explanation," "Reductionism and Its Discontents," "Stylistics and Synonymity," "Narrative Structure and Text Structure: Isherwood's *A Meeting by the River,* and Muriel Spark's *The Prime of Miss Jean Brodie*," "On the Margins of Discourse," and "Visual Rhetoric in *The Autobiography of Alice B. Toklas.*" In the next few years *Critical Inquiry* consistently published articles on topics that would have been completely incomprehensible to the reader of only a few years before. Titles like these are typical: "Formalism, Savagery, and Care; or, The Function of Criticism Once Again" (1975), "The Limits of Pluralism: The Deconstructive Angel" (1976), "Supposition and Supersession: A Model of Analysis for Narrative Structure" (1976), "Composition Discomposed" (1976),

"(Nonsymbolic) Motion / (Symbolic) Action" (1977), "Normal Circumstances, Literal Language, Direct Speech Acts, the Ordinary, the Everyday, the Obvious, What Goes without Saying, and Other Special Cases" (1977), "Noise" (1976), and "Culture and Modeling Systems" (1977).

Another journal that appeared on the scene in the 1970s bore the forbidding title *Diacritics*. *Critical Inquiry* is described on its front page as "a voice for reasoned inquiry into significant creations of the human spirit" and therefore presents critical articles about artworks and a certain number of articles about criticism itself. *Diacritics,* subtitled *A Review of Contemporary Criticism,* is given over exclusively to writing *about* theory and criticism. Most of its articles are reviews of books by other critics, but each issue also contains a few articles on more general subjects relating to theory and criticism. Either way, the title of an article in *Diacritics* clearly indicates a piece of writing that stands on its own, even if it is only a book review: for example, "Must One Be Metacritical?" (1972), "Sade, or Text as Fantasy" (1972), "Narrative Signs and Tangents" (1974), "Phonetics, Phonology and Impulsional Bases" (1974), "Under the Sign of Symbols: Losey and Hartley" (1974), "The Narratee and the Situation of Enunciation" (1977), and "Puss-in-Boots: Power of Signs—Signs of Power" (1977).

Now I've intentionally omitted the names of the authors of all the articles whose titles I've listed, just as I've omitted any discussion of what these articles actually contain, because to a considerable extent the titles speak for themselves and for the change in criticism I'm referring to. It's easy to see what some of the new trends are: the obsession with "text" and language is probably the most obvious. The use of a difficult, technocratic terminology is another. The quest for obscurity in all those clever, playful, and incomprehensible titles is a third. But perhaps the most basic thing of all is how the art of criticism, traditionally viewed as the handmaiden of "literature," has staked out its own territory. The articles in *Diacritics,* articles in which critics write about critics writing about either literary texts or still other critics, are a perfect illustration.

Anyone who saw the cynical film *Broadcast News* (1987) will remember the character of Aaron Altman, the earnest and principled television news reporter who, partly because he is earnest and principled but mostly because he lacks style, never achieves the kind of success that his colleagues do. In one scene he and his coworkers have gathered in the studio to preview a tape of a particularly slick report by a handsome but vacuous new anchorman. The anchorman has pushed journalistic manipulation to the limit by dramatically beseeching the tight-lipped army general he is interviewing to open up and tell his story. Naturally, the anchorman becomes the center of attention at this moment, and the camera moves in close to show his face; meanwhile the general's head, seen from behind, becomes a mere shadow at the side of the screen. When a dizzy young woman in the studio effusively praises the new anchorman for his performance, Altman cuts in and says sarcastically, "Yes, please, let's never forget—*we*'re the real story, not them."

Translated into the idiom of modern criticism: Let's never forget—*we*'re the real text.

FOUR THEMES OF MODERN CRITICISM
AND HOW THE POETS GOT THERE FIRST

And so literary theory and criticism at some point in the mid-1970s set itself up as a discipline that enjoyed equal standing with "literature." Graduate education came to focus more and more on knowledge of literary theory and less and less on an acquaintance with a standard body of literary texts. The common joke as the trend increasingly took hold was that graduate schools were turning out an entire generation of literary scholars who could discuss dozens of critics, social scientists, and contemporary philosophers but who didn't know what century Balzac lived in.

As it happens, the view that criticism is entitled to the same kind of respect as literature was given explicit formulation by the critic who more than anyone else in the United States embodied the principles of the era I've been characterizing: Paul de Man. In an essay written in the late 1960s and published in the collection *Blindness and Insight,* de Man at one point says, "The relationship between author and critic does not designate a difference in the type of activity involved, since no fundamental discontinuity exists between two acts that both aim at full understanding; the difference is primarily temporal in kind. Poetry is the foreknowledge of criticism. Far from changing or distorting it, criticism merely discloses poetry for what it is."[1]

This may sound like an arrogant and arbitrary appropriation of power by a practitioner of a discipline that always has been, and always should be, a subservient one. After all (we're tempted to think), the literary theorist or critic needs literature to theorize about or criticize, whereas the literary artist can get along just fine without any help from the critic. This, in fact, may be what de Man means when he says that the difference between the two activities is "primarily temporal in kind": poetry comes first. But, he'd like to add, that doesn't make it primary in any other sense.

We can accept this view or reject it. What is important in the passage is something that de Man may not realize he's saying, and if he does, it's certainly not what he means to emphasize in a context heavily laden with terms and concepts from Martin Heidegger. "Poetry is the fore-knowledge of criticism" actually has a much more ordinary meaning, even and especially for de Man himself, than the Heideggerian context suggests, and that meaning is that de Man learned many of the fundamental principles of his own criticism, above all the idea that theory and poetry are equal (if not equivalent), *from poets* (something Heidegger would have approved of, by the way), from the very poetry to which he was most fond of applying his own critical principles. Mallarmé figures heavily in the writing of de Man, for example, and so does Rilke. In fact, as I'll show at the end of this book, Rilke is the subject of a whole circular chain of reasoning in de Man that starts from the poet and then uses the poet's work as an example of principles that have their source precisely in that work.

This book is not about the new styles of criticism. Too many other books have been written about that (no surprise, since one of the chief characteristics of criticism in the last few decades is its concern with criticism). This book is about the intellectual origins of the new styles in criticism, and by "the new styles in criticism" I mean those of the 1960s and early 1970s, when theory and criticism established themselves firmly in our universities. I am not talking about the latest styles of the 1980s, especially the various types of "leftist" criticism that have attracted attention in the last few years. Criticism of this sort has been around for a long time, but I am not persuaded that it has really come into its own in this country until recently. Even Duke University professor Frank Lentricchia, one of the most visible representatives of this movement, thinks that the writers usually identified as the forebears of his style of criticism were not "shaping influences" in American criticism through the 1970s.[2] But the 1960s and 1970s were when the generation of scholars and teachers that have now begun to fill senior positions in institutions of higher learning, members of the new "establishment" (including, incidentally, many practitioners of contemporary political criticism), was being trained in graduate school. We usually refer to this era as the era of structuralism and poststructuralism, a time in which

French names—like Roland Barthes and Jacques Derrida—figured so prominently that many academics in this country complained of the "colonization" of the American humanities department. In an era when the most influential humanities faculty in the country, the one at Yale University, was archly called an outpost of Paris's Left Bank, it began to look as though you could locate the origin of every trend in the United States by simply looking at what had happened in France five years earlier. If you were interested in knowing where the French fashions came from (and there's a good chance you weren't, because it wasn't important), then a shadowy collection of figures—many of them German, like Heidegger, Husserl, and Nietzsche—would present itself. A few of the braver literary types in the 1970s actually wrote about these thinkers (another instance of the flight of literary criticism into more sophisticated and respectable fields). But to most it seemed that if it was possible to speak of a "modern consciousness" in literary criticism and theory, that consciousness had sprung forth fully armed from the head of Jacques Derrida (or Roland Barthes, or some other contemporary French thinker).

I believe we have to look back farther than that. If it is legitimate to speak of a modern consciousness at all, then I think we need to talk about the one that's been around for the last hundred years or so, and not only in France. If we are interested in the origins of that consciousness, we will find it not in writers who were primarily professional critics and philosophers but in those who were known first as poets and novelists. That's where we first see the combination of interests that motivated contemporary criticism and theory in the late 1960s and the 1970s, and that's undoubtedly why critics of that recent era were so often drawn to these poets. The period of origins lasts from about 1885 to about 1920.

What is this modern consciousness that has found its way into literary criticism? From the chaos of methods, systems, and forbidding terms that we encounter in criticism of this era there emerge four basic, often overlapping themes: (1) the idea of *language* as an object of interest in its own right; (2) an approach to literary texts that is *theological* in style; (3) a belief that works of art are *relational* systems; and (4) the idea of *being*. Hence I've divided this book into four parts, called "Language," "Theology," "Relationalism," and "Ontology." Each of these four themes holds out to the early modern poet and the modern critic the promise of an irreducible essence at its center, a myth, something whose existence can be accepted only after a mystical leap of faith. But the early modern poet and the modern critic characteristically confront this mystical essence with an attitude of neurotic ambivalence. It is always there as a fundamental principle, and yet poet and critic bend their energies to escaping it. The flight from Eden curiously follows a path that is circular, but some who travel it don't know this. "You can't do without Eden," said Mallarmé. For a poet so dedicated to the flight into the airy reaches of abstraction and impersonal nothingness, these are profound words indeed. As one of Mallarmé's modern-day commentators sees it, these words show Mallarmé's ultimate commitment to *belief* in a world (including his own poetic world) increasingly threatened and characterized by the forces of skepticism.[3] As I see it, they show that the path from Eden is circular.

LANGUAGE

In the 1970s it became almost routine in American criticism to analyze the style of a particular writer and then arrive at the conclusion that, when it came right down to it, the writer's work was really about language. Everything was "text," "discourse," "code." Critics were fond of talking about language, and they came to think that the poets they analyzed felt the same way. A perfect example is Paul de Man. *Blindness and Insight,* which came out in 1971, was a collection of essays that were meant to demonstrate that literary critics owe their greatest insights precisely to the areas where they are most "blind." I'm not sure this is what the book really proves, and I'm not sure de Man knew it was going to prove this when he originally wrote the various essays that are collected in it. If there is a theme in *Blindness and Insight,* however, it is that everything in a text always comes back to language and that language is indeterminate. "If we no longer take for granted that a literary text can be reduced to a finite meaning or set of meanings," he says in the foreword, "but see the act of reading as an endless process in which truth and falsehood are inextricably intertwined, then the prevailing schemes used in literary history . . . are no longer applicable (p. ix). And in an essay in the book called "Criticism and Crisis" we read this: "It is the distinctive privilege of language to be able to hide meaning behind a misleading sign, as when we hide rage or hatred behind a smile. But it is the distinctive curse of all language, as soon as any kind of interpersonal relation is involved, that it is forced to act this way. The simplest of wishes cannot express itself without hiding behind a screen of language that constitutes a world of intricate intersubjective relationships, all of them potentially inauthentic" (p. 11). De Man sees his own lonely theory of language everywhere. It is in Rousseau's *Essay on the Origin of Languages,* in which, de Man thinks, "what stands under indictment is language itself" (p. 140). It is in Rilke's poetry, which de Man discusses in his later book *Allegories of Reading* (1979). In another passage he abruptly announces that a certain line of verse in Rilke "designates the impossibility for the language of poetry to appropriate anything, be it as consciousness, as object, or as a synthesis of both."[4] It is there even in Oedipus. Everyone is familiar with the end of the Oedipus myth, and most people probably assume Oedipus's blinding himself had something to do with the guilt he learned of after performing the actions that made him guilty. But for de Man, incredibly, the meaning of Oedipus's blindness at Colonus is that he "has learned that it is not in his power to solve the enigma of language."[5]

Many critics were not content just to write about language and say that the poets they wrote about were also writing about language. Critics are not linguists, and when they write about language, they usually write about a certain kind of language—not "ordinary" language, but the language we find in poems and other kinds of "literature." And so they have to try to account for the specific, distinctive qualities of that language, which means trying to account for the difference between poetic or literary texts and other forms of writing. In the past the issue has generally been formulated as a distinction between the language of poetry and the language of prose. No one seems to escape the belief that the difference lies somehow in language itself, that if you want to isolate what distinguishes a sonnet from a grocery list, you should look at the language, where you are sure to discover some essential, inherent quality. You are also likely to decide that the inherent quality is the way the language of the sonnet calls attention to itself as language. You then use a term like "poeticity" or "literarity" for that quality. Even de Man, with all his talk of the indeterminacy of language (language in general), is incapable of abandoning the ancient myth that poetic language (he calls it literary language) is inherently different from other kinds. The only difference between de Man's version and the older versions of this myth is that de Man has updated the terminology. In a passage from *Blindness and Insight* that he hoped would be safely ambiguous, he defines the quality of the literary by saying that it refers to "any text that implicitly or explicitly signifies its own rhetorical mode and prefigures its own misunderstanding as the correlative of its rhetorical nature; that is, of its 'rhetoricity.' " Then in a footnote to this passage he

attempts to clarify his statement: "The criterion of literary specificity
does not depend on the greater or lesser discursiveness of the mode but
on the degree of consistent 'rhetoricity' of the language" (pp. 136–37).
"Rhetoric" is a key term for de Man, for reasons I don't need to go into
here. Apart from the density of de Man's style and his use of the word
rhetoricity, this passage is not substantially different from a great many
other accounts of the specificity of poetic or literary language. In the
area of language the specificity of poetic or literary language is the Eden
to which modern criticism always returns. In Part I, I will show how modern critical attitudes toward language—like de Man's—were formed at
the end of the nineteenth century and the beginning of the twentieth.

THEOLOGY

The poetry-prose distinction is only one example of a mystification that
operates in modern criticism. But virtually every school of criticism rests
on a principle or set of principles that must be accepted simply on faith
in order for the entire system to stand. The English Marxist critic Terry
Eagleton has cleverly demonstrated this point in an introductory book
on literary theory.[6] In many systems of criticism, Eagleton maintains,
the critic speaks by authoritarian pronouncement instead of logically
proving the truth of an argument.

The idea we get from Eagleton's account, even though he doesn't
express it quite like this, is that the very style of thinking in most modern
criticism is theological. For instance, it was part of the faith of American
New Criticism in the generation before the 1960s and 1970s that a
literary text was a sacred and hermetic object to be worshiped like an
idol. Two of the most famous books in this school have titles that show
what I mean: *The Well Wrought Urn*, by Cleanth Brooks, and *The Verbal
Icon*, by W. K. Wimsatt. Even de Man, the chief skeptic of the post–
New Critical era, speaks with the voice of a religious visionary. Eagleton
doesn't spend much time on de Man, but Frank Lentricchia, in a book
on American criticism between 1957 and 1977, devotes an entire chapter
to showing that the principle of authority plays the central role in de
Man's criticism. De Man "does not argue in any formal sense for the
logic and truth of his position," Lentricchia says. Instead, he engages
in clever rhetorical strategies designed to take the reader into his confidence, mystify the reader, and thus silence any opposing argument.[7]

When we look closely at the early modern poets, we find that their thinking about literature was often driven by theological ideas, that in fact their theories are often a form of theology thinly disguised. This is particularly true of Russian thinkers, who never seem to escape the patterns of theological thought that have remained so tenacious in their culture over the centuries. They will elaborate a view of the artwork that is founded on principles borrowed from the Russian Orthodox theology of icons. And French poets like Mallarmé seem perpetually engaged in a delicate minuet with the Catholic theology they have been brought up on and seek to escape from. This theology impels them, like their Russian contemporaries, to adopt religious objects and practices as models for literary artworks. There is thus a fair amount of evidence to suggest that much of modern criticism is theological not only in its character but in its origin, too. This is the subject of Part II.

RELATIONALISM

The term *relationalism* applies to structuralism more than to anything else. Consider a book by French structuralist critic Claude Bremond called *Logique du récit* (The logic of narrative).[8] Bremond's purpose is to analyze stories into a determinate number of "functions," that is, roles played by the characters in stories. The idea is that an overarching logic governs the events of all stories and that the critic with sufficient scientific acumen can find it and thus show its universality. So Bremond spends most of his book listing the different roles and the various directions that the action of a story can take. There are beneficiary and victim, voluntary agent and involuntary agent, informer and dissimulator, seducer and intimidator, obligator and interdictor, improver and worsener, and so on. To get a sense of where all this goes, take a look at one of Bremond's many diagrams (see page 13). He is talking about the "frustrator," and the diagram he offers us is meant to show the relations between this and other roles. Criticism for this school often becomes something like an exercise in algebra, and that's not surprising since algebra is one source of structuralist thought. Some of the books and essays produced in this movement look like something out of a mathematics or logic textbook, filled as they are with symbols and arrows and plus signs and minus signs. The diagram is the structuralist's favorite tool because it conveniently reduces the object (a novel, a story, a poem) to a visual network, far removed from the literary work it started out as.

But isn't this just another form of mystical essentialism in a secular-

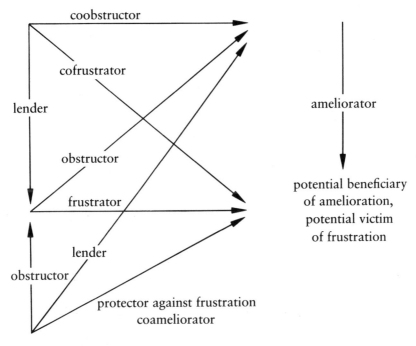

From Claude Bremond, *Logique du récit* (Paris: Seuil, 1973), p. 292.

ized form? The structuralist retrieves abstract networks of relations in literary texts, with the result that the text is often reduced to a relational structure, as the name *structuralism* suggests. The characteristic mode of reading is thus one that involves a mystical penetration behind the "text" to something insubstantial, invisible, or abstract, like the essence that hides in a sacred object. When we look back at the turn of the century and right afterward, we see that much of this thinking is prefigured in the poets I'll be discussing. We also find an important link between overtly theological thought and modern relationalism in the figure of Roman Jakobson. He will provide the transition between Part II and Part III, and relationalism will be the subject of Part III.

ONTOLOGY

"What is a text?" we asked ourselves in the first graduate seminar I ever attended. We weren't the first to pose the question. Lots of critics and philosophers had wondered about it—not only how you tell a literary text apart from an "ordinary" one, but just exactly what the thing *is,* where it exists, what the nature of its being is. The study of being is called ontology, and in the twentieth century there came to be an ontology of artworks, in which the ontology of literary artworks had its own niche. Criticism of the last few decades has grown tired of asking this question explicitly, but it is implicitly posed in the inquiries into language I've mentioned. When language continues to call attention to itself *as such,* it can't help focusing our attention on the question of what it is. And when what it is is something as indeterminate and untrustworthy as what so many modern critics make it out to be, then it has a way of reducing itself to an opaque substance, the way words do if you repeat them over and over again. The whole New Critical attention to texts and the close scrutiny of them was, in a sense, a way of ontologically isolating them. The following generation continued the trend.

There are other questions of ontology, too. The 1987 best-seller by Allan Bloom, *The Closing of the American Mind,* was a sweeping indictment of higher education in this country, and one of the author's favorite ideas was that the ugly moral wasteland of the contemporary American university has its origin in German thought, starting with Nietzsche in the nineteenth century. The worst culprit in the twentieth century, Bloom thinks, is Heidegger. In one of his less measured statements Bloom asserts that the entire field of comparative literature today has "fallen largely into the hands of a group of professors who are influenced by the post-Sartrean generation of Parisian Heideggerians, in particular Derrida, Foucault and Barthes. The school is called Deconstructionism, and it is the last, predictable, stage in the suppression of reason and the denial of the possibility of truth in the name of philosophy."[9] I don't think I'd describe Michel Foucault and Roland Barthes as "Parisian Heideggerians," nor do I think the Heideggerian strain in modern criticism is quite the all-determining force that Bloom suggests. Still, there is no doubt that Heidegger's presence in modern criticism is pronounced. Heidegger's chief philosophical purpose was to investigate the nature of being, particularly *human* being. For him, poetry raised ontological questions with peculiar force since, as he saw it, language is the "house of Being."[10] Bloom is right to mention the French "deconstructionist" philosopher Jacques Derrida when he speaks of Heidegger's influence on recent French literary theory. Heidegger's legacy in modern criticism is the critique of language that we find not only in Derrida but in Paul de Man, too. For Derrida, the big issue is what he calls the metaphysics of presence, the notion in Western thought that oral language enjoys a kind of priority over written language because it makes things present. Derrida thinks this is wrong since language never makes anything present but only "defers" meaning endlessly beyond the horizon. De Man has basically the same notion, although he expresses it slightly differently. Both owe their idea to something in Heidegger called the hermeneutic circle, which has to do with the way we can never interpret anything without already having understood it, which implies already having interpreted it, which implies already having understood it, and so on. The question is profoundly ontological in Heidegger because it involves the notion of human existence in a human world. It is ontological in Derrida and his American disciples because it involves the notion of making present. One of the biggest ideas among literary scholars in the 1970s was Derrida's conquest of Western metaphysics, which left everything in a state of indeterminacy and ambiguity. It's the very thing Bloom decried in *The Closing of the American Mind*, and it, too, was anticipated by our turn-of-the-century poets.

One of Heidegger's best-known commentators, the Anglican theologian and translator of *Being and Time* John Macquarrie, believes that Heidegger's thought is a form of theology, in which "Being" is virtually synonymous with "God."[11] There's a lot of truth to this notion, although doctrinaire Heideggerians would disagree. In fact, it is easy to see ontology as yet another quest for mystical essence, for Eden. This time instead of being called God, or a network of relations, or poeticity, the indwelling essence is called Being.

These are the ideas that directed the study of literature in many of our prestigious institutions of higher learning in the late 1960s and the 1970s, especially at the graduate level. And since the graduate students of those years are professors today, these ideas to a considerable extent still direct the teaching of books at the university. This is not to suggest that every professor of literature is some sort of wind-up toy, blindly acting out the patterns that were laid down by demonic, all-controlling professors from his or her graduate-school days. It just means that these ideas are bound to be prevalent. Nor does it mean that professors do not change their views and teaching methods during their teaching careers. They do, and that is how the latest generation of leftist scholars has come to integrate a politically oriented criticism into its teaching even though few of its members were formally schooled in anything like political criticism.

But even where such changes have taken place, certain beliefs seem to subsist among the scholars who teach in the universities, and so our students continue, in one way or another, to be indoctrinated in these beliefs even when they are at the same time being indoctrinated in an overtly political system of thought. To begin with, our students have been taught that literary criticism and theory is an independent field with its own cast of star characters. They have been taught to focus their attention on language and, in many cases, to abandon their childish trust in its ability to communicate concrete meanings. They have been taught that books and poems can be quantified, measured, diagramed, and reduced to airy structures of pluses and minuses. They have been taught to reflect on issues of being, presence, and absence, in a way that often leads to the same lonely worldview as their reflections on language. But at the same time they have been taught, even by the most cynical and sacrilegious enemies of meaning and morals, to approach their books and poems unquestioningly as objects of value that contain inherent, distinctive essences. They have been taught, often unwittingly, that "you can't do without Eden," that all paths return to it.

Of course, not every single one of these ideas by itself was brand-new either for modern critics or for the poets who preceded them. It's the conjunction that makes this "modern consciousness" what it is. And this modern consciousness was already present in the late nineteenth and early twentieth centuries, in the poets.

THE CAST OF CHARACTERS AND WHAT'S NOT HERE

The cast of characters: the French poet Stéphane Mallarmé (1842–1898) and his disciple Paul Valéry (1871–1945); the Czech-born Austro-German poet Rainer Maria Rilke (1875–1926); the Russian symbolist poet Andrei Bely (1880–1934); and the Russian avant-garde poet Velimir Khlebnikov (1885–1922). There are others, too. Roman Jakobson (1896–1982), probably the most renowned linguist of the century, figures as an important historical link between the early twentieth century and more recent literary criticism and theory in Western Europe and the United States, though he is not a poet. Writers and thinkers of an earlier era put in an appearance, including philosophers, linguists, and theologians. Two names come up more often than others: Mallarmé and Bely. They had nothing to do with each other, and Bely has remained a relatively obscure figure both in his native country and outside. To show Bely's "influence" on succeeding generations of literary critics would be tricky, especially because almost no one has acknowledged any sort of intellectual debt to him. But in chapter 6, when I come to talk about the pivotal role Jakobson played in exporting theology from Russia to the West, I will show that Bely did play a role of the sort that can be characterized as "having an influence."

Mallarmé's "influence" is another story, at least according to some observers. In a taped conversation with English critic Stephen Heath in 1970, Roland Barthes said that "in France there is a certain way in which since Mallarmé everything is repetition. Since Mallarmé there have been no new mutatory texts in French literature [texts, that is, that produce lasting changes in history]. We in France have invented nothing since Mallarmé, and it is very fortunate too when it is Mallarmé we repeat!"[12] Barthes uses the word *literature,* but it is clear from the context (he mentions Marx as the author of a mutatory text) that he is speaking of a historical process that embraces more than just "literary" texts. Barthes is speaking at a time when French imperial control of American humanities departments had almost reached its height (with Barthes and others like him as colonial viceroys in absentia), so to say that everything in France since Mallarmé is a repetition of Mallarmé is effectively to say that everything in American criticism since the late 1960s is a repetition of Mallarmé. In fact, all we need to do is show that Mallarmé was a shaping force in the thought of Derrida, as a number of writers have done, and we will already have shown his importance for modern American criticism.[13]

This book is not an influence study in the simple sense of the term *influence.* I have not set out to show that the poets I discuss from the early modern era directly "caused" the critics of more recent times. Something like this happened in certain cases, it is true. For example, Mallarmé's ideas on language had an impact on later thinkers, and it is part of the reason those thinkers use Mallarmé as an example of theories they propose as their own. There are connections and exportations, but no individual figure I talk about can be identified as personally and directly responsible for a whole range of things that happened later.

That's not really the purpose of my book, anyway. Rather, it is to show that the same basic set of assumptions and beliefs that have informed recent criticism in the United States, and that have thus helped to shape the way we teach and read in higher education, were already there in the early modern era. Bely is a dominating figure because, more than almost anyone else, he combines the issues of modernism in one consciousness. Did he "give" us modern criticism all by himself? I doubt it. Instead, he represented a style of thinking of an entire era that has been passed on to succeeding generations in a way that probably can't be scientifically described.

Since I was not attempting to establish a complete list of the "sources" of modern literary criticism, I did not feel compelled to speak of every figure that might be relevant to a subject like this. I thought it would be much better to choose a limited number of figures that were truly representative and to focus on them—again and again. With the notable exception of Rilke, whom I mention at the end of the book, they are mostly French and Russian. Naturally, my selective method means that certain persons—in fact, a great many—are not here at all.

I said that my four themes overlap. This overlapping has the effect of making my book into something like the relational structures I'll be talking about in Part III since members of the cast return at various moments in contexts that are sometimes only slightly different from the ones in which they previously appeared. Different scenes thus evoke other scenes and subvert the narrative progression of my "text." And, of course, like the path from Eden, the end brings us back to the beginning.

PART I

Language

CHAPTER ONE

Flight from Eden

Myths about Myths about
Language in Modern Times

It's an age-old problem with language: since it has never done what it was meant to do, since no one has ever established a lasting notion of what it was meant to do, and since it has never submitted to any plausible account of why it functions in the inadequate way it does, the only way out has been to resort to myths. Most of these myths are myths of origin: language today is imperfect in performing its assigned task, but in the beginning it was different in a way that can be ideally hinted at but not fully described. This is the way Rousseau sees it. "The first language of man," he says, "the most universal, the most energetic language, and the only one he needed before it became necessary to persuade men in an assembly, is the cry of Nature."[1] In those early days "people spoke only in poetry."[2] Man had not yet learned to reason, but that was fine since his life was an unspoiled vision of simplicity and his needs were few.

Some myths are not quite like this one. The myth about language that has served as a point of reference for almost all philosophy of language in the West is a myth of the present, and it belongs to Cratylus in the dialogue of that name by Plato. Cratylus is a naive etymologist who thinks that language is meant to name things and that names conse-quently bear a necessary connection with the things they designate. But even Cratylus's argument requires an appeal to an unknowable and ideal past, a past when the words of language sprang into existence by a kind of natural necessity.

The distance of the myth, whether it's a distance in time or just a distance in thought, a sense of distinctness from the way things are today, is essential. It is a correlate to the present inadequacy of language: if language is imperfect today, it must be that it has fallen from grace, from some distant Eden where it did all the things it no longer does. But language is inadequate only in relation to a standard that has been assumed, often without any explicit argument, from the outset. Thus the pure, natural language that Rousseau's primitive man spoke—or sang—in that idyllic landscape of uncorrupted, precivilized virtue was ideal because Rousseau expects from language a perfect medium for the expression of man's passions. Love, hate, pity, and anger are the things that first raised men's voices, and this is why the first languages were "singing and passionate" rather than "simple and methodical."[3] The birth of language in the passions has to be accepted before the myth makes sense. And the pure language that Cratylus sees in operation in the present is pure because he expects from language a perfect medium for the transmission of things in nature. The primacy of this function of language has to be accepted before *his* myth makes sense.

We can see what makes myths about language so valuable. It is not at all important to ask whether the authors of these myths (if there is such a thing as the author of a myth) really believe them to be plausible, historical accounts of the emergence or origin of language. It is important only to ask what the myths tell us about their authors' notions of language in the present—for instance, that Rousseau saw the unity of speaker and speech as a fundamental obligation of human language, whereas Cratylus saw the unity of name and thing (signifier and signified) as an equally fundamental obligation.

Why does this need to be said? Because the history of the theory of literary language in modern times is a history of the attempted flight from Eden and the subsequent, irresistible pull of Eden. This history parallels, in fact is intertwined with, the history of modern linguistics, a distinctly modern product that is modern precisely because it has tried to be "scientific" and dispense with disobedient, metaphysical ideas like myths of the origin of language. But modern linguistics, for all its efforts to demythify, hasn't resisted the temptation of the traditional myths any more than Rousseau or Cratylus did; or any more than the visionary poets of the late nineteenth and early twentieth centuries who dared, in what appeared to be a last, desperate appeal for the metaphysical integrity of the human spirit in a scientific and skeptical age, to propose their own myths about the nature and origin of language. It wasn't really a last, desperate appeal, because the myths were carried on—by even the scientifically inclined literary theorists. And it wasn't an appeal for the metaphysical integrity of the human spirit either, because the myths served the same function for the visionary poets as for the theorists. The myths were there to be rejected in favor of a far lonelier view of language. At least that's what they all thought. The only problem was that the myths never really went away.

THE MYTH OF THE FRACTURED MYTH

The curious thing is that there is more than one myth—or more than one level of myth. There are the various myths about language, its primeval unity, its innate expressiveness, its state of perfection in some other time and place than now and here. But there is also the myth of how these myths came to be abandoned. For modern criticism not only has perpetuated many of the myths of its predecessors but also has told its own story with a pretty fair mythical imagination of its own.

The story of one of the most fundamental and "radical" tenets of modern criticism and linguistics is a perfect illustration of this point. The lost unity of language in the early modern era was most forcibly asserted by the Swiss linguist Ferdinand de Saussure, who used the expression *l'arbitraire du signe* (the arbitrariness of the sign). This cardinal concept, *the* concept of Saussure's *Cours de linguistique générale* (Course in general linguistics, published in 1916), the frontal assault on the myth that the sign, or word, bears a motivated connection with the thing it designates, has been seen as a necessary condition for modern linguistics and criticism. It is the cornerstone of the "lonelier" modern view of language.

The myth of modern criticism is that this concept was new. It was not. Eugenio Coseriu, a Romanian linguist teaching at Tübingen, wrote an article in the 1960s in which he demonstrates first, how pervasive the belief is that the theory of *l'arbitraire du signe* originated in the twentieth century and, second, how far this belief is from the truth. In fact, Coseriu shows, the notion has to be traced back to Aristotle. For one thing, Aristotle sees language from a purely functional rather than a Cratylic point of view, rejecting the Cratylic idea of any sort of motivated or necessary connection between words and the things they stand for. For another, the very concept of arbitrariness and the expressions in Latin, French, German, and English to convey it can themselves be traced back to Aristotle and a troublesome little two-word phrase he used in his treatise *On Interpretation*. The phrase in Greek is *kata syn-theken*, and in Coseriu's understanding it means something like "through what is already established." In a famous passage from *On Interpretation* Aristotle defines language as "sound that is meaningful *kata syntheken*," which is to say that the words of language have meaning not through any kind of natural necessity, as Cratylus believed, but through historical necessity, through tradition, through what is already established.

Next, Coseriu says, the concept of *kata syntheken* is adopted by a long line of Western philosophers and translated into various modern languages by a number of different phrases. What is striking is that if one is willing to accept Coseriu's idea that the various words and phrases (*ad placitum, institutio,* and *conventio* in Latin, *arbitraire* in French, *Willkür* in German, *arbitrary/arbitrariness* in English) are equivalent, a great many thinkers steadily from the seventeenth century up until Saussure had already proposed the notion of the arbitrariness of the sign. In fact, many of them had done so without any particular claim to originality, in some cases treating the idea as a self-evident truth. Coseriu lists about twenty philosophers, among them Hobbes, Locke, Leibniz, Christian Wolff, Berkeley, Condillac, Lessing, Fichte, and Hegel.[4]

Coseriu, whose business it is to know the facts about the history of language philosophy, expresses shock and indignation at this common oversight. And who can blame him? After all, Hobbes, Locke, and Leibniz are not insignificant thinkers. The writers whose ignorance is in question are not insignificant in their fields either; they are prominent linguists and historians of linguistics. Is the problem that Coseriu's list of names is largely restricted to philosophers who were known less for language philosophy than for other things? This may well be part of it. The twentieth-century philosopher and historian of philosophy Ernst Cassirer devotes a brief section of his monumental work *The Philosophy of Symbolic Forms* to the history of language philosophy, mentioning a good many of the same names as Coseriu does. But then Cassirer is hardly a standard to measure others by, since he was enormously erudite and saw everything in such broad terms as only his uncannily vast learning permitted. The fact remains that Coseriu's list does not look like the list of figures one would include in a history of language philosophy, linguistics (to the extent that these two are different), or modern literary theory.

But something else is going on here, something that Coseriu doesn't mention and that he really has no reason to mention. Look at the writings of the literary theorists who wrote in the years right after Saussure and to whom the notion of the arbitrariness of the sign (to choose just this one concept of "modern" language theory) may be attributed, of any theorist who is committed to undermining the notion that language functions because of a mystical unity between sign and world (or sign and speaker, or sign and national spirit). What about the Russian Formalist critics, for instance, who in the 1910s and the 1920s were so intent on rejecting the old myths and retaining only the most functional, "scientific" view of language? (Never mind, for the moment, that they didn't really abandon the myths; we'll get to that shortly.) How many of them cite Hobbes, Locke, Leibniz, Wolff, Berkeley, Condillac, Lessing, Fichte, or Hegel as their models and predecessors? These names almost never appear in the writings of the Formalists or in writings about them.

The names that do appear are either from the tradition that still entertained the old myths, and are thus cited antagonistically, or from a new, revolutionary tradition, and are thus cited favorably. Viktor Shklovsky, one of the most famous members of this group, in his early writings uses a critique of the nineteenth-century philologist Aleksandr Potebnia to launch his own theory of poetic language, citing the contemporary Russian Futurists as illustrations of the "new" ideas he is advocating.[5] When the renowned linguist Roman Jakobson, whose early career is an integral part of the history of Russian Futurism and Formalism, comes to talk about the formative influences in his early linguistic theories—the principle of relativity and the belief that everything in language "is based on relationship"—he mentions not the linguists or philosophers of language but "the great men of art born in the 1880's": Picasso, Joyce, Braque, Stravinsky, Khlebnikov, and Le Corbusier. It was in studying Khlebnikov's poetry, Jakobson says, that he first tested one of his most basic concepts, that of the phoneme.[6]

Is this preference for recent thinkers just a manifestation of the cult of the new that is a trademark of modernism, a bold refusal to acknowledge any predecessors except either the latest ones or those who are to be discarded for having old, worn-out ideas? Maybe. Is it simple ignorance? Possibly in some cases, though certainly not in the case of Jakobson. But two things are clear. One is that the ideas of the Formalists (to take just this one example) were not as new as the Formalists' mythical account of their own ideas made them out to be. The other is that the Formalists, while perpetuating the myth of the novelty of their own ideas (the myth of the rejection of myth in favor of functionalism and science), were still holding on to precisely those myths they claimed to be rejecting.

L'arbitraire du signe is only one idea that the twentieth century has canonized, and canonized as specifically new. The Russian Formalists are only one group of critics and did not, besides, explicitly propose a doctrine of the arbitrariness of the sign. It would be wrong to suggest that their failure to recognize predecessors in this doctrine is by itself evidence of much of anything. Still, there is a pattern here. Modern literary theory and criticism has always promoted its own novelty in cases where it is not completely novel. It has defined itself by a relation of antagonism with its past while continuing a great many of the myths it rejects. The whole process appears to be one vast evolutionary rejection of the myths. When Shklovsky criticizes Potebnia for overlooking the formal elements of language in his distinction between poetic and prosaic language, for ignoring the "facts" of sound and rhythm and thus being unscientific, there are two things he doesn't realize (apart from the circumstance that what he says about Potebnia isn't really true): first, that Potebnia, like Shklovsky himself, is engaged in a valiant attempt to reject the old, unscientific myths about poetic language and, second, that he, Shklovsky, was just as unsuccessful as Potebnia. Both merely perpetuated the myths they sought so earnestly to overturn.[7]

And that is pretty much the story of this chapter. Over and over again modern criticism, like a neurotic lover foolishly, ridiculously vowing every day to escape the clutches of the abusive and overbearing tyrant who was once a source of tenderness and security, seeks a radical break with the myths of the past, only to find itself helplessly drawn back to them. The poets I've chosen as characters in this story define the terms of the whole ritual. They supply the idea of the break, and they sustain the myths to run back to. One of the most prominent myths is precisely that there is no myth, that we have finally made that break. We haven't.

THE FRACTURE

Before we describe this history, we need to have a sense of where it goes. How will this struggle for freedom from the old myths play itself out in twentieth-century criticism? I've used the word *break* to describe the desired liberation from mythical forms of thought. As it happens, the notion of a break or fracture comes to be an integral part of the very theories that seek that break with the past. Now, however, the break has to do with language itself, not just the relation of theorists and poets to their past.

The late French philosopher Michel Foucault has described the modern view of language in *Les mots et les choses* (Words and things, translated into English for some reason as *The Order of Things*) in a way that is useful, although his context is different from ours. For Foucault, a view of language is part of an *episteme*, by which he means an entire way of understanding and knowing in a given epoch. An *episteme* is different from a worldview or *Weltanschauung* in that it has as its specific object the human, social world. The three broad classifications into which the objects of a single *episteme* can be divided are life, work, and language.

Foucault is interested in three *epistemai*, the most recent of which extends from shortly before the beginning of the nineteenth century to the present. The big change that begins to occur in the thinking about language early in this period is the change from a view of language as a representational medium to a view of language as functional. In the period of Foucault's first *episteme*, roughly corresponding to the sixteenth century, the prevailing notion of language is of a medium that operates through a principle of resemblance between words and designated objects. In the period of the second *episteme*, comprising approximately the seventeenth and eighteenth centuries, the notion of resemblance is rejected in favor of a binary notion of language. That is, language is seen as a neutral and conventional means for representing—rather than imitating—the world, and the emphasis is on the split between representing word and represented world. In the modern period representation gives way to a notion of pure function, as philologists discover laws of similarity among the Indo-European languages, particularly those laws that show resemblances among such purely grammatical attributes of languages as inflectional endings. "Language is no longer composed only of representations and sounds that, in turn, represent these representations and order themselves as strings of thought require. It is instead composed of formal elements that are grouped in a system and that impose on the sounds, the syllables, and the roots an order that is not that of representation." This is how there comes to appear in the modern age a "dimension of the pure grammatical."[8]

As a result, language in the modern age takes on a kind of opacity and becomes an object in its own right, instead of being merely a transparent, representational medium. It "folds back on itself, acquires its own density, displays a history, laws, and an objectivity that belong to it alone." Language exists now only in a "dispersed mode." "For the philologists, words are like so many objects composed and passed on by history; for those who wish to formalize, language must rid itself of its concrete content, leaving only the universally valid forms of speech to appear. If one wishes to interpret, then words have become a text to be fractured in order that one can then see the emergence of this other meaning they hide."[9]

Foucault's presentation of the modern *episteme* goes a long way toward describing the status of language in the writings of twentieth-century literary critics, theorists, and aestheticians. But critics, theorists, and aestheticians are not Foucault's subject, at least not exclusively or even prominently. Foucault speaks largely of the professional philosophers— in addition to speaking of authors and poets from time to time—and thus provides a perspective similar to the one we find in Coseriu's article on the arbitrariness of the sign. When Foucault speaks of Mallarmé, saying that with him (and Nietzsche) "thought was led, and violently so, back towards language itself, back to its unique, difficult being," thus making Mallarmé a crucial figure in the twin processes of the "fracturing of language" and its transition to a state of "philological objectivity,"[10] he speaks almost as though the whole question had been settled with Mallarmé. It had not. But the value of Foucault's discussion of language for us lies in its capacity to describe the limits of the trend he is talking about, to describe a view of language that has come to dominate much twentieth-century thinking.

The term *fracture* is apt, and it certainly gives a good idea of the situation in which language finds itself in the twentieth century. The fracture operates on levels that Foucault does not enumerate (this is not his purpose). But one may classify a great many twentieth-century theories of language according to the terms in which they formulate a fracture. Its most basic sense may be found in the Saussurian doctrine of *l'arbitraire du signe,* in which the fracture severs the sign from its referent. Any aesthetics that is formalist in the general sense—any aesthetics emphasizing functions and relations over elements (in this case words)—will accept this doctrine as a self-evident truth.

Other schools of criticism, aesthetics, and language theory have seen the fracture as operating at a higher level than sign and referent, namely the level of the extended utterance. Theorists loosely grouped under the rubric of phenomenology tend to see the problems of language arising not out of the relation between words and things, or signs and referents, but instead out of the relation between larger signifying units and a

newly problematized entity called meaning. Edmund Husserl, the founding father of this movement in philosophy, had initiated this trend in his
Logische Untersuchungen (Logical investigations, 1900–1901) by referring to meanings as an independent class of ideal objects that don't
need to have anything to do with the signs associated with them.[11] In
fact, the nature of this association is far less simple than has commonly
been supposed, Husserl thinks. Signs may well be signs for something,
he says, but they do not in all cases possess a meaning or sense that is
"expressed" by them.[12]

When Roman Ingarden, a Polish pupil of Husserl, comes to talk specifically about literary texts in the late 1920s, he organizes language
into what he calls meaning units, or unified utterances. Like Husserl
before him, Ingarden distinguishes sharply between meanings, which are
created by subjective acts of consciousness, and the units of language
associated with those meanings. The meaning function of language—
the function, that is, that associates a meaning with a particular meaning
unit—is conferred on that meaning unit from without by a subjective
act of consciousness and can therefore in no way be considered as au-
tomatic or absolute.[13] The very premise of Ingarden's theory is thus that
there is no necessary, simple, or natural relation between language and
its meanings. Three decades later the French phenomenologist Maurice
Merleau-Ponty also was to insist on the lack of a necessary and direct
relation between utterances (by which Merleau-Ponty understands units
larger than individual words) and their associated meanings. For him,
meanings are ideas that cannot be directly expressed but can only be
approached through a series of "adumbrations" (*Abschattungen,* a Husserlian term). In his essay "On the Phenomenology of Language" (1951)
he describes how the adumbrations in a given utterance suddenly "con-
tract into a single meaning" by a process that can't even be described.
For Merleau-Ponty, there can never be any question of a direct signified-
signifying relation because the signified always "surpasses" the signifying.[14]

A much more radical fracture, however, is the one we find in the
work of Jacques Derrida and his many American epigones. In fact, the
whole trend known as postmodernism, which helped set the tone for
literary studies in the 1970s, is dedicated to an idolatrous fascination
with the lonely, nihilistic worldview that is implicit in Derrida's fractured
theory of language. For Derrida, language can be characterized only as
a play of differences among an intricate network, or "tissue," of signs.
Language is marked by the "impossibility for a sign, for the unity of a

signifier and a signified, to occur in the plenitude of a present and an absolute presence."[15] There is no present or absolute presence in any sign other than the divine logos, and the logos is a purely metaphysical, "infinitist" notion.[16] In the language of man, meaning is always in flight, always beyond the horizon; there is no presence, no unity, only the trace of what was just there. Thus language is not only the differences at play in a tissue of signs; it is also *différance* (with *a* instead of *e*), a word Derrida invented to combine the two principal senses of the French verb *différer*, "differ" and "defer." In the intricate complex of differences that is language, meaning is always deferred, put off, scattered. Derrida introduces the concept of the trace to describe the way in which language is never fully present (as we would like to think it is) but exists instead in a state that looks back to something that was already there. The trace, always flitting ahead of the presence that it leaves behind, thus describes a double process of "retention" (since it *retains* what has been present) and "protention" (since it *tends* forward, away from that present). Signification is born at this juncture of retention and protention, and Derrida finds in the French language a word that happily combines the notion of juncture and rupture he sees united in the trace—*brisure,* which means "hinge," as in the hinged articulation between two parts of a shutter (this definition, of course, allows Derrida to exploit the double sense of "articulation"), and "fracture."[17]

There is another kind of fracture that at one time had become canonical in literary aesthetics, and that is the fracture that separates speaker from language. This fracture is the premise of any objectivist literary aesthetic, any aesthetic that regards the word as independent of its speaker and the literary work of art as independent of its creator. Such a view had become virtually an article of faith in the teaching of literature in many of the most respected American universities in the 1960s and 1970s, when it was fashionable for professors to shock undergraduate students by telling them that inquiries into an author's life or into the author's avowed understanding of his or her own work were irrelevant to a true understanding of that work—hence the license to throw lecture notes away and spend hours of class time in an exercise known as close reading, wherein students, with their instructor's minimal participation, take a piece of writing, like a bit of organic tissue, pick it into tiny bits, and comment on how those bits interact either with each other (the bits) or with them (the students).

Objectivist criticism became entrenched in the 1950s, when many of the next decade's academics were still in graduate school. Cleanth

Brooks published *The Well Wrought Urn* in 1947, proposing a view of literary artworks as organic structures whose constituent parts were to be understood and judged only in terms internal to the artwork as a totality.[18] In "The Intentional Fallacy," first published in 1946 and then again as a chapter of *The Verbal Icon* in 1954, W. K. Wimsatt and Monroe Beardsley had argued that consulting an author to discover the meaning of that author's words was illegitimate. "Critical inquiries are not settled by consulting the oracle," the essay ends.[19] And in *Aesthetics: Problems in the Philosophy of Criticism* (1958), a work designed as an introductory college textbook in aesthetics, Beardsley forcefully espoused objectivism as a principle of all art criticism.[20]

Wimsatt and Brooks, in their *Literary Criticism: A Short History*, published in 1957, trace the origins of the objectivist aesthetic, or "impersonality," as they put it (since the author's "person" does not appear in his works). Credit goes to T. S. Eliot, they say, not because he was the first to come up with the idea but because it was he who "brought this matter of impersonality squarely to the attention of his generation." Eliot's position in separating the personal experience of the poet from the poem itself is stated in 1919 "with almost shocking emphasis," as Wimsatt and Brooks put it.[21]

The idea of severing the speaker from his words is by no means restricted to such New Critics as Wimsatt and Brooks. Nor am I persuaded that Eliot is the one who brings it into the open. It is implicit in any formalist or structuralist view of language (in the general sense of those terms), where the emphasis is on relations between words rather than on their expressive qualities. And it emerges in the phenomenological views of language I mentioned a moment ago, since for thinkers like Ingarden and Merleau-Ponty the meanings of language escape and surpass the speaker as much as they escape and surpass language. But no matter what the specifics of the view are, language is a long way from the organic unity it enjoys in the myths—unity with man in Rousseau and many of the romantics, unity with God in the Gospels.

Many of the relativizing tendencies in the twentieth century are evidence of a fracture in the primitive unity of language. This notion is true of any theory asserting that the meanings of language are determined by a context of some sort. It is essential to the thought of Mikhail Bakhtin, the Russian philosopher and literary theorist whose works became immensely fashionable in the 1980s. One of Bakhtin's central notions is *raznorechie* (translated as "heteroglossia"), which describes the necessary interaction in verbal utterances between the fixed system of a given language and the context of a particular utterance.[22] It is certainly there in E. D. Hirsch, who, some twenty years before he gained notoriety for his *Cultural Literacy* (a kind of companion best-seller to Allan Bloom's *Closing of the American Mind* in 1987), wrote a book in which he gave a theory of literary interpretation. Hirsch distinguishes between the "meaning" of a literary work as a fixed thing established in the context of its writing, and the "significance" of a literary work as something that changes over history as a function of the contexts of future generations of readers.[23] It is there in so-called reception theories, which see the meaning of language as largely determined by characteristics of the listener (or reader). And it is there in Marxist theory, which views consciousness and, consequently, language as determined by social existence.

The twentieth century is not responsible for inventing the skepticism necessary to produce language theories as lonely and unsettling as some of these. The fracture is there, at least in germinal form, in the early modern period I am discussing. But it is never asserted wholeheartedly. Instead, the old myths dwell side by side with the fractured notion of language. And the forum that allows for this cohabitation is the one where the distinction between poetic language and ordinary, or prosaic, language is investigated. The typical symptom of the surviving neurotic attachment to the old myths is the tendency to distinguish between two types of language, the language of poetry and the language of prose (or whatever you want to call language that is not poetic), and to assign a privileged, Edenic status to poetic language.

THE MYTH OF THE POETRY-PROSE DISTINCTION . . . AND THE MYTH THAT THERE IS NO MYTH

Maybe it would be most accurate to say simply that the whole poetry-prose distinction is a myth, at least as it is framed in this period. Whether or not this is true, the distinction presents a problem since so much of modern literary criticism and language theory has been intent on fostering an image of itself as the product of rational reflection, of a carefully, thoughtfully elaborated "methodology" (a buzzword of literary study today). It has in many cases sought to earn itself a place next to the other "human sciences," which are also a product of modern times and whose central obsession has been with their place next to the methodologically more secure natural sciences. The scientifically inclined schools of literary criticism, the formalisms and the structuralisms, have ridden the coattails of twentieth-century linguistics, something that is evident not only because modern criticism has often borrowed the methods and terminology of linguistics but above all because it has focused on the same object of study, namely language. Even where the notion of science and scientificity has not had an overriding appeal, the concern has been with detachment, with sober and impassive judgment—hence the preference for a spirit of objectivism in so much twentieth-century criticism.

But literary criticism is of necessity either implicitly or explicitly an aesthetic. Its object of study is not language in general, signifying objects in general, or meaning in general; it is specifically *literary* language, *literary* signifying objects, *literary* meaning. The problem has been, then, to account for the specific "literariness" of literary language (what Jakobson called *literaturnost'*), but to do so without abandoning the highly esteemed posture of scientificity. It is questionable whether modern criticism or modern linguistics has successfully done this, though both have certainly tried. The task presents some significant difficulties. For to set aside a certain body of written texts and call them literary is to assume the existence of an aesthetic value, some quality that mysteriously places these texts in an entirely different category from the ones in which we place "ordinary" written texts. And the minute we start talking about values, we are talking about murky, essentialist, metaphysical qualities whose existence is suspect and whose functioning is hopelessly obscure, at least from a "scientific" viewpoint.

Nonetheless, modern thinking has had trouble abandoning the romantic notion that literary texts are somehow the object of reverence and awe. It has also not quite been able to abandon the notion that poetic literary texts are more literary than prose texts and that they are, consequently, more the object of reverence and awe. And there is an assumption, usually unwritten, that literary works of art owe the specificity they possess as works of art to qualities in the language that composes them. It follows that there must be a difference between literary language and "ordinary" language and that this difference accounts either entirely or in part for the difference between, say, a poem by Blake and a paragraph from a car repair manual. Even deconstructionist thinkers like Derrida and Paul de Man, for all their skepticism about language and meaning, retain a faith in the specificity of poetic language. Derrida drew a clear distinction between literary and philosophical texts, and de Man, as I mentioned in my introduction, used the term *rhetoricity* for his version of the specificity of poetic language.[24]

And so we see in modern criticism the complicated situation I described earlier. The myth subsists that there is an intrinsic distinction between poetic and prosaic language. I use the word *myth* not because I wish to assert that the poetry-prose distinction is false in all of its versions (although I do happen to believe it is false when it is expressed as a distinction between two types of *language*); I use it because belief in the poetry-prose distinction is framed as a myth, usually a Rousseauistic myth of original purity. But as literary aesthetics and its corresponding philosophy of language grow increasingly "scientific," there is an increasing tendency toward formalism in philosophy of language, and with formalism comes a tendency to demythify. Hence the coexistence, in the early modern period, of the myth itself (that is, the myth of the poetry-prose distinction) and the myth that there is no myth.

The idea of poetry (a term that can mean anything from imaginative writing to specifically lyrical verse) as a distinctive form of verbal expression that stands in natural opposition either to other forms of expression or to whole ways of apprehending the world is an idea of long standing. Aristotle, in the *Poetics,* had opposed poetry (understood in its broadest sense as what we might call today simply literature) to history, saying that poetry is more philosophical, indeed is "greater" than history, because poetry expresses universals whereas history expresses particulars.[25]

The more familiar distinction since Aristotle has been between poetry and prose, poetry being understood in a more specific sense than the one it has in Aristotle. This distinction is standard in the poetics of romanticism. Rousseau sets the tone for the entire era in his "Essay on the Origin of Languages," where poetry is identified as the earliest and, of course, most natural of languages. The English and German romantics return again and again to the same theme: poetry, specifically as distinguished from prose, is the purest, the most original (in the sense of being close to the origin) form of verbal expression. The German romantic critic Johann Gottfried von Herder, in his essay on the origin of language, asserts, like Rousseau before him, that poetry is older than prose and that in its capacity to express passions in all their immediacy lies the primitive source of all verbal communication.[26]

By the late romantic era in England something new has happened: the poetry-prose distinction has given way in a great many instances to a distinction between poetry and science. M. H. Abrams, in his classic work on English romanticism *The Mirror and the Lamp*, documents this transition, citing Thomas Babington Macaulay's 1825 essay on Milton as evidence that Aristotle's poetry-history distinction had been converted into the distinction between poetry and science.[27] But the poetry-science opposition does not arrive directly from a rejection of Aristotle; it comes along instead to replace the distinction that was dominant at the time, namely the distinction between poetry and prose. This, at least, is how Wordsworth sees it. As early as 1800, in the preface to the *Lyrical Ballads,* he goes so far as to say that "there neither is, nor can be, any essential difference between the language of prose and metrical composition." Then, in a footnote, he says that "much confusion has been introduced into criticism by this contradistinction of Poetry and Prose, instead of the more philosophical one of Poetry and Matter of Fact, or Science."[28] The poetry-science opposition in most cases does not represent an abandonment of the poetry-prose distinction; it represents merely a clarification, in epistemological terms, of the perceived province of prose, since science in the new opposition corresponds to prose as the vehicle exclusively suited to its methods and worldview. Thus poetry is to prose as feeling is to intellect, or as expression is to description, or as emotion is to scientific cognition.

This view is taken over in the work of Wilhelm von Humboldt, author of the highly influential *Über die Verschiedenheit des menschlichen Sprachbaues und ihren Einfluß auf die geistige Entwicklung des Menschengeschlechts* (On the diversity of human speech structure and its influence on the spiritual development of the human race, published 1827–29) and in many ways a pivotal figure both for the history of language philosophy and for our story here. Humboldt divides the territories of poetry and prose in a manner similar to that of the romantics. Poetry apprehends reality in its sensible (*sinnlich*) manifestations; it is "inseparable from" music and is thus more appropriately the vehicle of aesthetic beauty than is prose. It is given to the rendition of "individual moments" in human experience rather than to universals. Prose, by contrast, is concerned with facts and concepts rather than with ideas or sensation. Since it is suited to the rendition of ordinary life, it is the province of the objective, of science and scientific terminology; and where poetry "belongs to the individual moments of life," prose accompanies man "in all the expressions of his spiritual activity."[29]

But there is a significant difference between the opposition that Humboldt makes and the one the romantics made, and that is that for Humboldt the opposition does not of necessity entail the privileging of poetry over prose. Humboldt's distinction is simply descriptive, and this is because his approach to language is in certain fundamental respects different from that of the romantics. Humboldt sees language above all as a function of our inner being. It is an organic medium, representing the perpetual spiritual activity of an entire nation (not the individual). As Humboldt put it in his famous formulation, language is not a mere dead created thing (*ein totes Erzeugtes*) but an ongoing creation (*eine Erzeugung*); it is not (finished) work (he uses the Greek word *ergon*) but ceaseless activity (*energeia*).[30] Any definition of language must, then, be a genetic one, that is, one that sees language not as the product of an act of genesis in some distant, mythic past but as a continuing genesis in the present. Thus Humboldt has taken the romantic myth of origin, by which language is a creature fallen from the grace it had "in the beginning," and replaced it with a myth of origin where that origin is always *now*.

The secret to the creative, perpetually generative force of language in the present is what Humboldt calls the inner form of speech, a notion that will be taken over by the Russian philologist Potebnia, with lasting consequences for the Russian tradition. Inner form is the thing that makes language what it is. It is the key to the connection between language production and the sound of language. It is what allows language to express those thoughts that the greatest minds entrust to it.[31] Language deals not with objects but with concepts.[32] Its principal task is to mediate between objective reality and subjective inwardness, and it successfully accomplishes this task when sound and inner form are harmoniously joined. At that moment the process of language production and the external sound qualities of language work together to form a language that is living and rich, particularly in metaphorical content. This happens especially in the works of poets and philosophers, who contribute to the development of a nation's language by infusing its words with spiritual content. The success of a language for Humboldt is always measured by the progress of that language through history, and this notion leads him to mention a phenomenon that Potebnia and the entire Russian tradition later canonize. Harmony of inner and outer form is lost when a language stagnates. At that moment metaphors that had previously had a "youthful sense" become, through daily use, "worn out" so that they are "barely perceived anymore."[33]

Why is Humboldt a pivotal figure? To begin with, he has sought to abandon all forms of naive Cratylism and romantic primitivism in his approach to language. If Humboldt believes in the specificity of poetic language, it is not because he sees poetry as based in some mystical unity of either word and object or word and speaker. For him, poetic language is distinguished from prosaic language more by its function, by the way it is used, than by any intrinsic properties. The nonexistence of a necessary or motivated connection between signs and the things they designate in language *in general,* whether that language is poetic or prosaic, is already implied in the subject of Humboldt's work. Humboldt's point of departure, as the title of his work suggests, is precisely the fact of the diversity (*Verschiedenheit*) of human speech, the obvious fact that, owing to the existence of a multitude of human languages, there is no single, universal, and necessary way of saying any one thing.

The flight from Cratylism or natural-sign language is further signaled by Humboldt's insistence that language has to do not with things but with concepts. This is because language does not spring into existence ready-made to serve poets as a vehicle for the expression of their feelings; on the contrary, we ceaselessly create language for the purpose of meaningfully organizing our own experience. And since Humboldt was a good Kantian, believing that conscious beings can never "know" things in and for themselves, to him language, like any activity that generates meaning, cannot deal directly with objects.

Humboldt's Kantianism is another reason for his status as a pivotal figure. Ernst Cassirer writes about it in the brief history of language philosophy that he includes in the first volume of the *Philosophy of Symbolic Forms.* As Cassirer sees it, Humboldt betrays his underlying Kantianism in at least two ways. The first is in the notion of language as a subjective medium whose function is to objectify sensory impressions, thus serving as a kind of bridge between subjectivity and the objectivity that, according to Kant, we can never know in and for itself. The second is in the distinction between the matter (namely sound) of language and its form. In Cassirer's reading of Kant form is "the truly objectifying principle of knowledge" because it is the source of unity in our apprehension of objects. The function of form in Humboldt is entirely analogous since inner form for him is exactly what serves as a mediating function between subjectivity and the objective world of phenomena. Humboldt's entire conception of language thus appears in Cassirer's eyes to be founded in the "basic principle of the transcendental method" (the method in Kant by which the philosopher logically deduces the categories that the mind uses to order experience). Cassirer calls this principle "the universal application of philosophy to science." Humboldt's innovation consists in making language the object of that "universal application" rather than mathematics and mathematical physics, as Kant had.[34]

The Russian tradition that is central to the development of language theory in modern literary aesthetics begins precisely in the context of the transition that Cassirer identifies in the work of Humboldt. It is important to keep in mind that the period in question is transitional and that the notion of the perpetuation of myths remains fully in force. Humboldt certainly has his own myths, in spite of any Kantian formalism that Cassirer sees in his thinking. The notion of inner form is scarcely an empirically scientific one; even less scientific is Humboldt's concept of nationhood and the way in which some vaguely defined and almost mystical national character finds itself expressed in language. The Russian tradition begins in the shadow of Humboldt, with a bow to Humboldt, but also, strangely enough, with a reassertion of some of the older myths Humboldt had apparently rejected—the myth of origin, for instance, which now shows itself in a slightly new form.

The Russian Tradition from Potebnia to Shklovsky, with Some Poets in Between

The history of the modern tradition in Russia can safely be said to begin with the Ukrainian-born philologist Aleksandr Potebnia (1835–1891). Until the 1980s few people in the West paid much attention to Potebnia's role in the history of modern language theory and criticism. He customarily received a few pages in historical accounts of Russian Formalism and even Russian symbolism. Victor Erlich mentioned him decades ago in the book that introduced the English-speaking world to Russian Formalism.[1] A voluminous, more recent study of Russian Formalism, in German, contains one fairly long discussion of Potebnia and numerous brief references to him.[2] There have been sporadic articles on him both in the Soviet Union and in the West,[3] though generally not in widely read journals, and there have even been a few books on him published in the Soviet Union.[4] In the 1980s, however, Potebnia began to attract some attention in the West, owing in large part to the surge of interest in early twentieth-century Russian language theory and psycholinguistics, and in 1986 a full-length book in English on Potebnia was published.[5]

The work that established the outline of Potebnia's thought for his entire career was a collection of articles called *Mysl' i jazyk* (Thought and Language). It was published in 1862, the year Potebnia turned twenty-seven. His purpose in this book was to take Humboldt's work as a point of departure, correct certain of Humboldt's misconceptions, and explore an area left unclear in Humboldt, namely, the relation between thought and language. As Potebnia sees it, a satisfactory account of this relation is precisely where his contemporaries and immediate predecessors are most deficient. Potebnia devotes the second and third articles of his collection to the work of Humboldt and two of his successors, Karl Friedrich Becker (1775–1849) and August Schleicher (1821–1868), showing how the system of each of these linguists collapses on this point. Both Becker and Schleicher focus on the problem of whether thought precedes language or language precedes thought, but, as Potebnia sees it, both assert one position only to contradict it unwittingly later on.[6] Humboldt is not much better on this count, in Potebnia's estimation, because although he does not actually contradict himself, he certainly leaves the matter confused. Thought and language simply do not coincide in any simple formula, Potebnia points out, and Humboldt does not seem to have been aware of that.[7]

The thought-language problem itself is not exactly the point here since Potebnia's impact on succeeding generations had little to do with this issue. It has more to do with the progress of the myths I have been talking about. But there is a matter of chronology in Potebnia's discussions of his immediate predecessors that is fascinating because it partially explains why his impact on Bely and subsequent thinkers was what it was. Potebnia reduces the flaws in Becker's thinking to a contemptuous phrase, referring to the German linguist's "fruitless formalism."[8] The whole problem in Becker and Schleicher appears to be a lack of logical and scientific rigor, as the contradictions in their arguments demonstrate.

If Potebnia had waited another ten years or so, however, he would have been much less likely to fault Schleicher for lack of methodological rigor. Schleicher's most important contribution to the history of linguistics was his *Darwinian Theory and Linguistic Science,* published in 1873. Ernst Cassirer assigns this book a cardinal position in the same transitional phase of the history of linguistics that Humboldt belongs to. Schleicher's book, in Cassirer's view, represents the last step needed after Humboldt "to dissolve linguistics completely into natural science and linguistic laws into pure natural laws."[9] Schleicher's book was a vigorous assertion of positivism in the study of languages and resolved the earlier thought-language issue by proposing a doctrinaire monism that denied the independence of thought or spirit from matter.

Potebnia formed his theory in the late 1850s largely in response to

recent developments in language philosophy and did not change it substantially for the rest of his career. The date is crucial because ten years
later the picture would have been very different, and chances are that
his thought would not have taken the direction it did had he started
writing then. If Potebnia's view of language is infused with a particular
type of mythic thinking, it is no doubt partly because of this circumstance. Later thinkers like Bely owed their conception of language in no
small measure to this accident in the history of linguistics.

The most important impulse Potebnia gave to modern literary aesthetics was his redefinition of inner form, which profoundly affected his
own version of the poetry-prose distinction. The notion of inner form
arises in the context of a psycholinguistic distinction that is central to
Potebnia's doctrine. In a section on "the language of feeling and the
language of thought" Potebnia distinguishes between the two cognitive
processes of understanding and association. Understanding of language
takes place when sound precedes meaning; association takes place when
meaning precedes sound. Understanding is thus a sort of immediate,
necessary apprehension of the meaning of language, whereas association
promotes only an indirect apprehension through the assignment of
purely conventional meanings to signs. Inner form is relevant only to
understanding, not to association, because it is directly tied to human
thought. "The inner form of a word," says Potebnia, "is the relation of
the content of thought to consciousness; it shows how man's own
thought represents itself to him."[10]

What does this statement mean? Potebnia tells us in the most concrete
terms, by making yet another distinction. A word whose inner form is
in evidence is one whose meaning is *objective,* as opposed to one whose
meaning is *subjective.* Words accessible to the understanding have objective meanings since the meaning is simply *there,* whereas words ap-
prehensible only through association are subjective since listeners must
rely on their own subjective faculties to supply a meaning. What, then,
is an objective meaning? Easy: it is the "closest etymological" one. Thus
the Russian word for table, *stol,* has an objective meaning because it
contains the Slavic root /STL/, "to spread." The presence of this root
confers on the word *stol* a kind of immediate meaningfulness and thus
makes it objectively understandable to a speaker of Russian.[11] In a word
like this the inner form is successfully joined to the outer form, or the
sound of the word.

Of course, this theory sounds glib and naive today. But Potebnia has
done something extraordinary: he has attempted to take the Humbold-

tian notion of inner form and bolster it firmly on a "scientific" foundation of philology, thus making concrete what had been vague and intangible in his German predecessor. But at the same time, apparently without knowing it, he has replaced Humboldt's truly original contribution to the philosophy of language, namely the *energeia* concept, with the old myth of origins. Potebnia thus claims the existence of a state of primeval purity and thinks that because it has been identified with scientifically established etymological roots, it won't be seen as mystical or mythical.

But mystical and mythical is just what it is, and the person who noticed this was Andrei Bely. In a review article of Potebnia's *Thought and Language* published in 1910, Bely pointed to the most prominent paradox of Potebnia's system. He shows how Potebnia's notion of the relation between inner and outer form leads to a view of the ideal word that privileges the artistic over the ordinary, since the ideal word for Potebnia, containing as it does an inherent, objective meaning, must necessarily be an autonomous entity, a symbol. "This conclusion," Bely says, "again and again brings [Potebnia] back to the poet-romantic's dream of an unexpressed, fluid, momentary, and rationally incommunicable meaning that shines through as if from the depths of every word. Behind the cover of its ordinary sense the word conceals inside itself a primeval-elemental, magical-active force. . . . From linguistics, grammar, and the psychology of verbal symbols Potebnia arrives at the assertion of a mysticism of the word itself."[12]

Bely's comment is valuable for two reasons. The first is simply the shrewdness he shows in calling attention to a pitfall in Potebnia's thinking. The second is the light he sheds, perhaps unwittingly, on Potebnia's historical role. Bely finds it shockingly contradictory that Potebnia should take as a point of departure the supposedly scientific disciplines of linguistics, grammar, and psychology and arrive from them at a position as mystical as his doctrine of inner form.

But from our perspective this contradiction is exactly what is so important in Potebnia. Potebnia was apparently convinced that his emphasis on the thought-language problem and his psycholinguistic foundation were a timely corrective to the least scientific aspects of Humboldt's theory. He was not willing to consider himself a part of the romantic legacy in language philosophy that unabashedly espoused mystico-mythical ideas. And if, as Bely accurately noticed, Potebnia ended up regressively asserting a mythical tradition even older than Humboldt's, this is only an indication to us that he is a transitional figure.

He is a perfect example of the process I have described because he sub-scribes at once wholeheartedly and unwittingly to one of the oldest myths in existence but views himself as rejecting all myth. To a signifi-cant extent for Potebnia, the myth—beyond the actual myth of origins—is that there is no myth.

THE POETRY-PROSE DISTINCTION

Since there is no myth and, consequently, no murky, unscientific con-ceptual framework, Potebnia blithely makes his way from his conception of inner form to a poetry-prose distinction that will be adopted in many significant respects by even the most formalistic of subsequent Russian linguists, critics, and aestheticians. In the last article in *Thought and Language* Potebnia systematizes his conception of inner form and gives it more clarity. He now speaks of words as containing three elements: outer form, which is defined as the "articulate sound"; content; and inner form, which he unabashedly defines as the "closest etymological meaning" (*Mysl' i jazyk,* p. 134). What does this system have to do with poetry? The successful unity of sound and meaning is the "form" of poetic production, Potebnia says. The force responsible for creating this unity, the "third link," is none other than inner form (p. 138). Now inner form is also the symbolic meaning of a word, by which Potebnia means the meaning that is directly accessible. Symbolic meaning, or "symbolism," is the province of poetic language, as Potebnia says at the beginning of the article. "Poeticity," he had said, is the symbolism of language, whereas "prosaicity" is the "oblivion of inner form" (p. 134).

There are profound analogies, according to Potebnia, between words and art. Art, like language, is a means for the creation of thought, and its goal, like that of the word, is to produce a certain subjective mood (*nastroenie*) in both creator and perceiver. Art, because it is an active, creative force, is a form of *energeia,* just like language (p. 143). But not all language, of course: only poetic language enjoys the privileged status that makes it analogous to art. There is an excellent reason for this, too. The privileging of poetry does not arise from an arbitrary decision that judges it superior to prose. Poetry is privileged because it is *earlier.* We have here the myth of origins all over again, and Potebnia easily slips into a Rousseauistic mode of evocation to make his point. Everything is "first," "in the beginning," back in a mythic past of perfect linguistic transparency. "The first word is poetry," says Potebnia; this is why poetry precedes all the other arts. "The most perfect words of folk poetry date back to a time when people would not have been in a condition either to conceive of or to produce anything worthy of the name of paintings or statues." "In the beginning the word and poetry concentrated within themselves the entire aesthetic life of the people" (p. 150).

Poetry precedes not only all other forms of art but all other forms of speech as well. So primal is poetry, in fact, that the "late" division between poetry and prose can be said to arise from poetry itself (p. 152). The distinction comes about as a result of a gradual process of loss over time. Poetic language is language still imbued with inner form, whereas prosaic language develops in proportion to the loss of inner form. Inner form is lost as the objectivity of language (that is, objectivity understood in Potebnia's sense) gives way increasingly to abstraction. With the rise of abstraction in a word comes its increasing distance from sensual perception. This distance, incidentally, is why prosaic language tends to be the domain of science: prose is given to analyzing reality, whereas poetry seizes reality directly in its sensible manifestations, says Potebnia, loosely translating from Humboldt (p. 152).

Potebnia's opposition thus not only sets up poetry in a favored position of mythic purity but also specifically ties aesthetic value to poeticity and, by extension, to the myth of origin. A poetic word is valued in direct proportion to its symbolism, which means its inner form, which means its proximity to a primal state, which means its proximity to its own etymological root. And the corollary is that the more abstract a word, the more detached from its origin, the more intellectual effort required to discern its meaning, the less poetic and, consequently, the less aesthetically valued it is.

THE WORD IS THE WORK

Since primal language is poetry, and since poetry is at the root of art, it follows that there is a fundamental analogy between art and language, artworks and words.[13] Put one way, in fact, there really is no difference between a word and an artwork, since the word (poetic, of course) *is* art. But the analogy works on the level of specifics, too: the artwork in general contains the same three moments as the word, namely outer form, inner form, and content, and these three moments interact in the name of the same function for the artwork as for the word, namely the creation of thought.[14]

Thus the word, in its strict sense as a discrete lexical unit of meaning, is a kind of microcosm of the larger artwork of which it might form a part. As long as the word is a poetic one, the same propositions that are true of the word are true of the artwork. The artwork, by implication, functions like a symbol in the way the word does. And it stands in the same relation to the world as the word does: like the word, it creates something that was not there before, it is *energeia* rather than *ergon*, and, as a consequence, it contains more than what the speaker or artist put into it.

In one way this kind of thinking sounds perfectly trite and entirely unworthy of anyone's attention. After all, isn't the lack of distinction between individual lexical units and the broader units of meaning in language more a regressive idea than a progressive one? Ancient cultures did not distinguish sharply between the individual word, of the sort that we expect to find listed in a dictionary, and speech or utterance. In those days (and in oral cultures today, I'm told), the only parts of language that really are perceived as intrinsically discrete are proper names.

But Potebnia is pointing to something that really is new and something that will be prominently featured in the following generation or two. Apart from the mythic aspects of Potebnia's theories, apart from the silly idea that the inner essence of a word is nothing more than the word's Slavic or Indo-European root, Potebnia's conception carries a level of philosophical complexity that merits attention. He sees the act of speaking as a deeply relational act, one that touches each of a complex of coordinates without actually rendering any one of them or being identical to any one of them. These coordinates are things like the word (as lexical item, "articulate sound"), the image or concept, the speaker, and the world, with inner form as a kind of pure (but only vaguely defined) mediating function. That is to say, the word is a structure of relations, and this is the source of its analogy to the larger units of language and, ultimately, to works of art composed of language. Words, phrases, language, poems—all these things are there in our perception as relational complexes. In a literal sense they are nowhere, and yet they truly have the power to create a "somewhere."

The notion of symbol will serve to designate this class of things for Andrei Bely. When he comes along to define symbols, he does so in a way that makes it impossible to determine whether he is talking about words, poems, specific figures of poetic speech, or, for that matter, signifying objects in the very broadest sense of the term. This is not only because Bely has decided to return to an archaic notion of language as logos, where logos can mean, as it did in Greek, a range of things from discrete utterances to language broadly conceived. It is also because Bely's interest transcends the limited philological subject of words as lexical items. He is concerned with a much more modern subject, and that is meaning, specifically its structure and function. But it is Potebnia, standing on the border between the realm of linguistic myth and the realm of modern science and functionalism, who had set the stage. And to judge from what he had to say about his predecessor, Bely knew it.

BELY: THE VALUE OF FORMALISM
AND THE FORMALISM OF VALUES

Everything came together for Bely in 1909, if you can call what happened that year "coming together." It came together in the sense that Bely wrote most of his greatest theoretical works in a stupendously concentrated period of activity. He claims to have written his crowning article on the theory of symbolism, "The Emblematics of Meaning," in a week (the article is close to a hundred printed pages long). After writing his trend-setting article on metrics, "Lyric Poetry and Experiment," Bely wrote three accompanying pieces on metrics and his famous "Magic of Words" in a single month, then in two additional months dashed off the two-hundred-odd pages of commentary to his collection *Symbolism* and reread Potebnia.[15]

Bely's concern for the previous twelve years or so had been a theory of symbolism, something to define the cultural and philosophical era of which he was a part. *Symbolism* is the monument to this whole period since in it are collected Bely's most important theoretical pronouncements. But the book has a strangely schizoid character that would appear to make nonsense of any superficial attempt to find a unified vision in the different things Bely says. Bely himself knew this and wrote about it toward the end of his life in his memoirs. This "heap of screamingly contradictory articles," he says of *Symbolism,* was a reflection of his "stormy and agonizing personal life" at the time.[16]

It's true that the articles are "screamingly contradictory." There are articles proposing purely formalistic and scientific systems of aesthetics; there are the articles on metrics, which rely on the extensive use of statistics for verse analysis; and there are the difficult idealist articles on theory of symbolism, like "The Emblematics of Meaning" and "The Magic of Words." It's not true, however, that all these contradictions are simply the reflection of Bely's personal life. They are the reflection of a deep division in Bely's thinking, one that arguably lasted his entire adult life.

Less self-conscious remarks that Bely made about his theoretical writings will show what I mean. For both in the period when the essays were written and later on, in his memoirs, Bely seems confused about the true orientation of his studies. One moment he appears to think that the secret to a theory of symbolism lies in the direction of Kantian epistemology, or what he calls criticism (since Kant arrives at his epistemology through a *critique* of pure reason), and the next moment he appears to think that it is some sort of religion. In the introductory footnote to "The Emblematics of Meaning," for example, Bely states that the theoretical foundation for a theory of symbolism (a foundation, incidentally, that has not yet been established, he says) is to be found "in the context of a critical reappraisal of the basic epistemological premises concerning reality."[17] In his memoirs he speaks of the "epistemology of symbolism" and how he had wanted his theory to be critical (in the Kantian sense) rather than mystical.[18] But in the preface to *Symbolism* Bely unabashedly writes that symbolism is "a certain religious creed, having its own dogma," that this is the positive side of a doctrine of symbolism whose negative side alone he has given in "The Emblematics of Meaning." He then goes on in a bizarre and rambling paragraph to explain that theory and dogma are irreconcilable because "dogma is the Word become Flesh." About this, he continues, it is best to read in the Gospel according to John (S, p. ii).

Bely has good reason to be confused. His readers have been confused for more than half a century. It is at least to his credit that he later recognized just how chaotic the contents of this book were in subject, method, and, most of all, ideological orientation. My own view, however, is that there is a great deal less confusion in it than even Bely thought. To be sure, it is difficult to reconcile the contradictory things Bely says about his aims in approaching a theory of symbolism. But that difficulty assumes one takes him seriously when he characterizes his own work. As it happens, in spite of the breadth of knowledge that came from his desultory nature and amazing eclecticism, Bely showed an extraordinarily narrow understanding of what he himself did. His theory of symbolism can't be completely defined by being identified as a form of religion any more than it can be completely defined by being described as critical. It has the ability to encompass both forms of knowledge, because for Bely a theory of symbolism is a universal theory of meaning. It accounts for all types of signifying objects and thus can be used to analyze, say, religious icons as well as words in a poem.[19]

This universality has to be recognized before any sense can be made of Bely's theory of symbolism. But once it is, then that theory takes on a tremendous number of implications for our study of the theory of language, for a theory of language necessarily becomes a subset of a theory of symbolism. Bely's confusion then falls into place as another symptom of a transitional age. Like Potebnia, Bely was in the process of abandoning the traditional myths but was unwilling to let go entirely.

The essay where Bely presents what might plausibly be characterized as a theory of language is "The Magic of Words." Bely's rhetoric sounds as if he had lifted it directly from the pages of Potebnia, and this is not especially surprising since Bely had reread Potebnia (whom he mentions repeatedly) and written his review of *Thought and Language* in the same period when he wrote "The Magic of Words." He evokes the myth of origin, for instance, in terms largely reminiscent of Potebnia. "In the beginning (*pervonačal'no*), poetry, the process of cognizing, music, and speech were all one and the same," he says in a passage strikingly similar to the one in *Thought and Language* where Potebnia asserts that poetry is the first expression of the aesthetic life of a people (*S*, p. 431).[20] He refers at one point in the essay to inner form, without mentioning either Potebnia or Humboldt, and speaks freely of representations, images, contents, and all the other terms that Potebnia had established as integral parts of his theory. The entire second part of "The Magic of Words," in fact, is borrowed (in this case with appropriate attribution) from a posthumously published work by Potebnia called *Notes on the Theory of Literature*.[21]

The central concern of the essay is Bely's poetry-prose distinction. Poetic speech for Bely is "living" speech, and the thing that distinguishes it from prosaic, or "dead," speech is that it is generative, creative. "The word creates a new, third world: a world of sound symbols by means of which both the secrets of a world located outside me and those imprisoned in a world inside me come to light," Bely says. "The aim of communication is to kindle, through contact made between two inner worlds, a third world that is indivisible for those communicating and that unexpectedly deepens the individual images of the soul. . . . The original victory of consciousness lies in the creation of sound symbols. For in sound there is recreated a new world within whose boundaries I feel myself to be the creator of reality" (*S*, p. 430; *SE*, p. 94).

But only the poetic word is creative in this sense. In opposition to it stands the dead and deadly "word-term." Such is "the common prosaic word," which "has lost all its sound and pictorial imagery." It is a "fetid, decomposing corpse," says Bely. Word-terms come about as the result of a process of abstraction like the one Potebnia describes. As in Potebnia, the process begins in the mythical era with the poetic word and ends with the abstract term. In fact, Bely outdoes Potebnia by presenting the process as a kind of genesis of human knowledge: "The word begot myth; myth begot religion; religion begot philosophy; and philosophy begot the term" (*S*, p. 440; *SE*, p. 103).

Although Bely's rhetoric sounds a great deal like Potebnia's, and many of the terms of his discussion are borrowed from Potebnia, there is a significant difference of emphasis. Bely has restored to Potebnia's philosophy of language the geneticist orientation of Humboldt, but with a modification that firmly establishes Bely's modernity. Language is certainly an organic and creative force for Bely, just as it had been for Humboldt. But Bely is concerned more immediately with the individual act of speech; Humboldt had seen the creative force of language at the level of a whole people and a whole language. And because Bely focuses on the individual act of speech, his interest is attracted to the ontological dimension of language and speech. He even uses this term at one point in a discussion otherwise lifted from Potebnia. Speaking of the creation of a metaphor, Bely says that in a metaphor, which joins two images into one figure of speech, a new, third image is generated from the combination of the two original images. This third image, he says, is independent of the two images that "engendered" it because "creation endows it with ontological being independently of our consciousness" (*S*, p. 446; *SE*, p. 109). Where Potebnia had sought to account for the representational powers of language, Bely seeks to account for language's ability to generate being.

Even Bely's reformulation of Potebnia's derivation of the poetry-prose distinction shows this difference in orientation. For Bely, it is not enough to point to a historical (or mythico-historical) process that begins with poetry and ends with prosaic abstraction. He insists that the steps of this progress are linked by the generative force of the word: each step begets the next.

Another aspect of Bely's essay shows a reorientation that is distinctly Belyan if not specifically modern. Bely repeatedly uses the word *cognition* without saying clearly what he means by it. In "The Emblematics of Meaning" he develops at great length a polarity between cognition, by which he essentially means ordinary scientific understanding, and creation, by which he means the sort of power he attributes to speakers of poetic language in "The Magic of Words." Both are forms of knowledge; hence language for Bely is a form of knowledge. This is why he says at the beginning of "The Magic of Words" that "cognition is impossible without words" (*S*, p. 429; *SE*, p. 93). Words are the vehicles of knowledge—word-terms for scientific knowledge (cognition) and poetic words for creation.

Recognizing that Bely's orientation in "The Magic of Words" is toward issues like ontology and theory of knowledge has the effect of knocking the wind out of his visionary rhetoric. In fact, one can easily come around to the view that the magic Bely talks about and the myths he evokes are meant in a figurative sense. Words have the power to generate being by a process analogous to that by which a magician would generate being, if there were such things as magicians. The analogy, of course, is limited to the idea of generating being and does not suggest that the being that is generated is material, as it is in magic.

Why, then, does Bely write in the style he does, and why does he insist on invoking the same old myths of origin as Potebnia? Something strange is certainly happening, and it all looks even stranger in the light of what Bely says about Potebnia in his critique of *Thought and Language*. There Bely accuses Potebnia of practicing a form of mysticism. He refers to the distinction between geneticist theories of language like Humboldt's, according to which language is always being created in the present, and nativist theories, according to which language was already handed down in perfect form at some point in a mythic past. Because of his regressive reinterpretation of inner form, Potebnia was not the Humboldtian geneticist he considered himself to be, Bely says, but had returned to a mystical, nativist conception of language.

But Bely offers an explanation for this shortcoming on Potebnia's part, and it confirms the view that Bely is using Potebnia's rhetoric in "The Magic of Words" for some other purpose than to propose a mysticism of his own. What Potebnia is really presenting in disguise, according to Bely, is a theory of the value of the word in which the word is considered "from the point of view of its irrational content." The problem for Potebnia was that he allowed himself to become entangled in all kinds of contemporary psychological theories, thus losing sight of what he was really doing. He lacked an understanding of values as an epistemological problem; but then that was not his fault, Bely says, because the problem had not been articulated at the time Potebnia wrote.[22]

Bely doesn't articulate it here either, but he had made it the basis for his most extensive statements on the theory of symbolism in "The Emblematics of Meaning." That essay too, like "The Magic of Words," is filled with mystico-mythical rhetoric, but in the end it proposes a formalistic theory of meaning. What are values, and why is their presence in a theory of meaning an indication that that theory is formalistic rather than mystical?

In "The Magic of Words" the emphasis is on the creation of meaning. In "The Emblematics of Meaning" the emphasis is on epistemology, which is to say the reception of meaning. I will speak at length of "The Emblematics of Meaning" in chapter 5. For now, all that needs to be said is that Bely uses the analogy between objects of meaning (a generic category that includes words) and religious icons. Religious icons in the Russian theological tradition are seen as embodying an essence that we might refer to as divine grace. What Bely does is to replace the theological conception of the icon with a secularized conception by substituting "value" for the essence that is embodied in an icon. Value is a term that had gained currency in the recent writings of neo-Kantian philosophers like Heinrich Rickert (1863–1936). In a book called *Der Gegenstand der Erkenntnis* (The object of cognition) Rickert had sought to redefine Kantian epistemology by asserting that every act of ordinary cognition, instead of merely proceeding according to rules prescribed by the structure of the mind (Kant's Categories, or Pure Concepts of Understanding), contains an element of will, a kind of positive, ethical affirmation of truth.[23] The object of this affirmation is a value, and a value is simply something that the human subject, again by will, esteems. Rickert's system thus provides a means for eliminating the strict separation that Kant had made between practical reason, which has to do with morals, and ordinary scientific understanding, which has to do with the way we organize experience in the physical world.

Rickert's philosophy served Bely particularly well because even though it blurs the boundaries between scientific understanding and something as nasty and metaphysical as morals, Rickert proposed his own system as entirely free of any metaphysical implications. The value-based theory of knowledge is a purely formal system, both because values are not metaphysical objects (according to Rickert) and because the focus is on the process of cognizing. Thus when Bely adopts the Rickertian notion of value and integrates it into an otherwise theological structure where it takes the place of divine grace, he too is adopting a formal system.[24]

Bely's assertion that Potebnia was proposing a theory of the value of the word and at the same time was considering the word "from the point of view of its irrational content" should now be clear. The problem in Potebnia is the "irrational content." Had Potebnia had the benefit of neo-Kantian value-based epistemology, he could have elaborated a theory that was free from the irrational elements that in fact contaminate what he wrote. And if we now consider Bely's theories in this light, then his own quasi-mystical and religious rhetoric appears all the more either to be the result of some sort of schizoid confusion or, more likely, to serve as an analogy in a structural description of something that resembles, but isn't quite, mysticism and religion.

Bely described the key notion of his theory of symbolism years later in a passage striking for its concreteness. The passage comes from a work with the ungainly title *Why I Became a Symbolist and Why I Never Ceased Being One in All the Phases of My Intellectual and Artistic Development,* and if ever there was evidence to support the assertion that Bely's theory of symbolism was attempting to be formalistic, it is here. The account Bely gives is credible both because it has the advantage of distance from the symbolist period (*Why I Became a Symbolist* was written in 1928) and because it was written at a moment when Bely had a spiritual commitment different from the one he professed to have during his earlier period. The purpose of this memoir is to show that the central idea of symbolism, what he calls here "symbolization," was a constant in his career that saw him through such ideologically diverse periods as the symbolist period and the current period, when he claimed allegiance to a system of thought known as anthroposophy.

Symbolization is the process by which a symbol comes into being. To demonstrate the universality of the process and its lifelong presence in his own life, Bely evokes a childhood experience. The whole thing begins with a state of consciousness, in this case fear. Here is how a symbol comes to be:

> Wishing to reflect the essence of a state of consciousness (fear), I would take a crimson-colored cardboard box top, hide it in the shadows, so that I would see not the object but the color, and then walk by the crimson spot and exclaim to myself, "SOMETHING PURPLE." This "SOMETHING" was the experience. The purple spot was the form of expression. The two, taken together, constituted the symbol (in the process of symbolization). The "SOMETHING" was unidentified. The cardboard box top was an external object bearing no relation to the "SOMETHING." But this object, having been transformed by the shadows (the purple spot), was the end result of the merging of THAT (imageless) and THIS (objective) into something that is neither

THIS nor THAT, but a THIRD. The symbol is this THIRD. In constructing it I surmount two worlds (the chaotic state of fear and the object given from the external world). Neither of these worlds is real. But the THIRD world exists.[25]

Bely does not use the vocabulary of value philosophy here, but the process is unquestionably the same as the one he outlines in "The Emblematics of Meaning." A vague state is embodied in a physical object, with the result that the physical object becomes a symbol, thus generating a "third" state of being that is independent from both the vague state and the physical object. This is symbolization, and Bely would have us believe that it fits all the different systems of belief (and there were many) that he adopted in his career.

Future generations of critics and poets would ridicule Bely for espousing an aesthetics, and a worldview underlying that aesthetics, that always pointed towards the otherworldly. The poets known as Acmeists, whose most famous representatives were Anna Akhmatova and Osip Mandelshtam, prided themselves on their rejection of the symbolist commitment to mystical ideals. As early as 1913 the Acmeist Sergei Gorodetsky, in his manifesto titled "Some Currents in Contemporary Russian Poetry," describes the "battle" between Acmeism and symbolism as a "battle for *this* world."[26] The characteristic attitude of antiaestheticism that so many members of the Russian avant-garde adopted in Bely's day allowed little sympathy for the supposedly mystical orientation of symbolist poets. And, of course, it was part of the polemical posture of Formalist critics like Viktor Shklovsky to reject symbolist notions of mystical and allegorical content in favor of a "scientific" pursuit of functions and techniques in language.

But to call Bely a mystic is entirely unfair because it ignores the most basic characteristic of his thought and his personality. Bely was a man of conflicting temptations, and his favorite thing seems to have been to place himself in various systems of thought, explore all their twistings and turnings, but remain at a distance from the center, where the unwary wanderer might find himself trapped into actually believing something. This is why Bely fits so neatly into our story. His spiritual diffidence, his tendency toward formalism, and his ironist's pose in his "adoption" of different religious and mystical systems of thought all indicate the struggle with myth characteristic of this age. Yet the perpetuation of these systems, even if they present themselves only as temptations, is evidence that Bely's escape is not complete. As far as theory of language goes, we can see Bely caught in the same conflict as everyone else I've mentioned. In "The Emblematics of Meaning" his theory of meaning is formalistic (this is his "fracture"), but the entire *formal* edifice of his thought is borrowed from Russian Orthodox theology. And when he comes to talk about poetry in "The Magic of Words," we find him succumbing to the alluring power of the poetry-prose myth just as Potebnia and everyone else before him had.

THE ZAUMNIKS

The word *zaum'* was coined in 1913 by Aleksei Kruchenykh (1886–1969). It is a difficult word to translate—for two reasons. The less important is that there is no English word that renders clearly what it means. "Transrational language" is often used, since *za-* corresponds to *trans-* and *-um'* has to do with mind or reason. But "transrational" has a technical, philosophical ring to it that is entirely missing in *zaum'*, and since no one has come up with a more plausible English equivalent, many writers simply use the Russian word. The more important reason is that *zaum'* was used to mean more than one thing.

The principal exponents of *zaum'* language theory are Kruchenykh and Velimir Khlebnikov, both commonly classified as members of the avant-garde Cubo-Futurist group. Kruchenykh and Khlebnikov show the transitional stage of thinking that is typical of the era. They are at home in an Edenic world of mysticism—much more than Bely is—yet we see in them a pull toward the modernist "fracture."

Their pronouncements on language can be divided into two broad categories. In both versions of *zaum'* theory the constant factor is that *zaum'* language is distinct from any existing language and is ideally referential, which is to say that it shows an ideal correlation with the things it designates. The difference between the two versions is one of orientation.

The first version of *zaum'* theory is an old-fashioned nativist theory of language. Poetic language is seen as being motivated directly by the objects it designates. There is thus an intrinsic connection between any object and a set of sounds that will express that object. In his first *zaum'* manifesto, "Declaration of the Word as Such" (1913), where the word *zaum'* was introduced, Kruchenykh invented a word for "lily" composed entirely of vowels since he felt that in this sequence of sounds the object's "original purity" was restored.[27] In an essay called "The Simple Names of Language" (1916) Khlebnikov listed words beginning with the consonants *m, v, k,* and *s,* hoping to demonstrate that the words in each group have an idea in common and that this idea is expressed by the intrinsic quality of the initial sound. Thus words beginning with *m* often signify "the smallest members of certain varieties," an initial *v* often denotes the "action of subtraction," words starting with *k* often have to do with death, and so forth.[28] If one envisions the sign-signified problem as a polarity between word and world, then in this version the point of inception is the world since objects in the world motivate the formation of words appropriate to them.

In the other version, things are reversed, and the point of inception is the word. In a manifesto called "New Ways of the Word" Kruchenykh points out that in the archaic conception of language, thought takes precedence over words. He feels this view is wrong and has undertaken to correct the error. "Until now," he says, "it has always been asserted that 'thought dictates laws to the word, and not vice versa.' We have pointed out this error and come up with a free language that is both transrational (*zaumnyj*) and universal. Previous artists have proceeded from thought to the word, but *we* proceed by means of the word to direct comprehension."[29]

If words precede thought and comprehension, it is because they *create* meaning, indeed even surpass it. As the theory comes to be elaborated in the writings of Khlebnikov, language creates its own worlds through the same necessary sign-signified correspondence that exists in a nativist conception of language, but with the obvious difference that the signified comes into being only at the moment it is named. This is where Khlebnikov's version of the poetry-prose distinction comes in. In more than one place Khlebnikov distinguishes between the function of a word when it serves reason and its function when it serves poetry. "The word lives a double life," he says in an essay titled "About Contemporary Poetry." "Either it simply grows like a plant, putting forth a cluster of neighboring sound stones, and then the principle of sound lives a self-spun life, while the portion of reason named by the word remains in shadow; or else the word goes over into the service of reason, and sound ceases to be almighty and autocratic; the sound then becomes a 'name' and obediently fulfills the commands of reason."[30] In another essay, titled simply "About Verses," Khlebnikov likens poetic language to magical invocations, saying that in the case of invocations "the demand may not be made on the word, 'Be easy to understand like a bill-board.' ''[31] The poetic word thus shows a certain density, whereas the ordinary word is transparent.

The creative power of poetic language is not exactly the same thing for Khlebnikov as it is for Bely in "The Magic of Words." Language certainly created its own worlds for Bely, but those it created were recognizable worlds marked by the subjectivity of the speaker. Bely's chief concern in asserting the creativity of language was to emphasize the existential autonomy of meaning. Khlebnikov has in mind the creation of a realm of existence that has nothing to do with the one we are familiar with. In his notion language generates objects and worlds that not only never existed before but were never even conceived of. Bely's magic is thus a form of ontogenesis, whereas Khlebnikov's *zaum'* is a form of mythopoiesis.[32]

Needless to say, when Khlebnikov and Kruchenykh put their ideas into practice and actually create transrational words, the results are predictably unrecognizable and look like little more than gibberish. But this is not really a problem for us, even if they took all their *zaum'* poetry seriously. The theory simply has to be seen as idealist, like Bely's, and not designed to produce practical results.

Why view *zaum'* theory as anything but madness or, at best, regressiveness? In both versions it is clearly mystical, as Kruchenykh himself was not ashamed to point out. In "New Ways of the Word" he characterizes the poetic word in general as transrational (*zaumnoe*) and then, by way of explaining the term, adds "mystical" in parentheses, along with other adjectives.[33] But there is something modern and even philosophically interesting about *zaum'*. The mystical leap from signifying word to signified object (an object that is actual in the first version and mythical in the second) leads to the assertion that poetic language is objective and autonomous. The phrase that the Futurists used to speak of the autonomy of language was similar to the one Bely used in his critique of Potebnia. The Futurists talked of "the word as such" (*slovo kak takovoe*); Bely had used the phrase "mysticism of the word itself" (*mistika samogo slova*).[34] The word "as such" has an existence all its own in both versions of *zaum'* theory. In the first, nativist version, word and object exist in a relation of solidarity, owing to the perfect, intrinsically motivated referentiality of the word. The word thus shares in the existential autonomy of the object. In the second version it is autonomous because it is the existential point of departure for the mythic "concrete" reality it creates, this reality itself being seen as separate and independent. This is where the modernist fracture modestly appears in *zaum'* theory.

THE EARLY SHKLOVSKY, OR HOW IT ALL BECOMES
OFFICIAL IN THE WORK OF AN ACTUAL CRITIC

What does language theory of this sort look like when it turns up in the work of a critic of the same era? Viktor Shklovsky (1893–1984) is a perfect example because he shows just how intimate the relations were between poets and critics in this age. In fact, when you place Shklovsky next to writers like Bely and Khlebnikov, you begin to wonder whether the distinction between poet and critic (or, for that matter, between symbolist, Futurist, and Formalist) is all that meaningful. Shklovsky was not a poet, but he was not exclusively a critic either (he wrote novels).

Like so many others, Shklovsky saw himself as a demystifier and a demythifier. Among his earliest writings are an article on Potebnia and one on transrational language, both published for the first time in 1916. They are probably more interesting for what they say about Shklovsky than for what they say about their subject because they both show Shklovsky implicitly defining himself in relation to the recent past and the present. The past and the present for him are exactly the intellectual context I have just been talking about.

The article "On Poetry and Transrational Language" is usually seen as Shklovsky's defense of the theories of the *zaumniki*. If defending the *zaumniki* is what Shklovsky thought he was doing, then he certainly went about his task in a strange way. More than half the article is devoted to listing examples of transrational language from traditional literature, where, Shklovsky shows, the authors in question had no intention of writing in anything like transrational language. The point is that transrational language exists (here he apparently is lending support to the Futurists' theories), but not only in its pure form. For the most part, in fact, it exists "in a hidden state, as rhyme existed in ancient verse—alive, but something one was not aware of."[35] Where it does appear in pure form is in the language of mystical sects and in glossolalia. Perhaps this assertion can be construed as validating the Futurists' idea of *zaum'* by demonstrating that it existed before the term had been invented. At the same time, however, it has the effect of devaluing their discovery. After all, the *zaumniki* were not claiming to have found something that was already in plain sight; they were claiming to have either invented or discovered something that no one else had ever known about. When Shklovsky says it was there all the time, but not necessarily in its pure form, he shows that the *zaumniki* were doing nothing more than supplying a name for an existing phenomenon.

Besides, the whole thrust of the article seems to be toward a theoretical point independent of what the *zaumniki* were doing. Shklovsky's notion is that language and poetry are mutually determining things, that one can no more say poetry is a phenomenon of language than one can say language is a phenomenon of poetry. Transrational language in its pure state demonstrates this because of the way in which its unrecognizable speech "wants to be language."[36] Shklovsky's thinking goes well beyond anything the *zaumniki* had done. In its emphasis on the perceptual aspect of language—that is, the tendency of the listener to take sound combinations that do not exist in his or her own lexicon and assimilate them into a structure that is somehow on the verge of meaningfulness—Shklovsky's article looks ahead to the psychoperceptual orientation his work will start to assume in the article "Art as Device."

The article on Potebnia is more aggressive. The curious thing about it is that Shklovsky's critique of Potebnia is based on a misunderstanding and is used to assert a position that is not much different from Potebnia's. Shklovsky outlines his predecessor's theory of the poetic word, referring to the tripartite structure of outer form, image (or inner form), and meaning. He then points out, rightly, that for Potebnia the imaginality (*obraznost'*) of a word means its symbolism, which is directly proportional to its poeticality. Shklovsky disagrees. In his opinion what distinguishes poetic language from prosaic language is not images but something he calls the palpability (*oščutimost'*) of its construction." The poetic image is only one of several means for rendering the construction of language palpable: language can be made palpable as well in its acoustical, pronunciative, or semasiological aspects.[37]

In fact, as Shklovsky saw it, Potebnia was so concerned with images that he committed a cardinal error, which was to argue away the importance of external form. "From the position that 'the clarity of a representation or its absence (that is, the imaginality of a word) cannot be made out in its sounds' and that 'imaginality equals poeticality,' " says Shklovsky, "Potebnia draws the conclusion that the poeticality of a word cannot be made out in the sounds of that word, that external form (sound, rhythm) may be left entirely out of account in a definition of the essence of poetry."[38] Victor Erlich thinks that Shklovsky may have learned about Potebnia from secondhand sources.[39] The suggestion appears to make sense, for it is difficult to recognize Potebnia in Shklov-sky's critique: no one who has read *Thought and Language* can possibly think that Potebnia ignores outer form since he devotes many pages to the subject of the relation between the outer form and the inner form of a word. Still, Erlich's statement is puzzling since in the critique of Potebnia Shklovsky cites page numbers from *Notes on the Theory of Literature*. In addition, there is evidence to show that Shklovsky in one of his earliest articles appropriated words and phrases from Potebnia (without citing his source). There is no question, then, that Shklovsky knew Potebnia firsthand; the only question is whether he knew more than a few pages of his work.

Let's return for a moment to the article on Potebnia. Shklovsky's first reproach, that Potebnia was concerned only with images and not with the palpability of language, is just as unfounded as the second, although it is much easier to see why Shklovsky thought this. In fact, it is a flaw in Potebnia's system that makes Shklovsky's statement inaccurate. For what Shklovsky really wishes to see is a doctrine of the self-valued word or word "as such," a doctrine by which poetic language distinguishes itself from prosaic because it calls attention to itself *as language*. But isn't that exactly the doctrine Potebnia has unwittingly subscribed to, as Bely pointed out in his shrewd critique? Isn't Potebnia's "mysticism of the word itself," as Bely calls it, the very thing Shklovsky would like to see, though he certainly would not like to see it called mysticism?

He also would not have liked to see it *be* mysticism. But here is where Shklovsky's critique of Potebnia is most interesting. One commentator has suggested that the most important concept of Shklovsky's early career, the concept of *ostranenie,* arose as a direct result of his misunderstanding of Potebnia.[40] The term is introduced in the 1917 article "Art as Device," where Shklovsky again brings up Potebnia, referring to his theory slightingly as one according to which art is "thinking in images," and then goes on to give a more complete account than previously of the distinction between poetic and prosaic language. Since it is the business of art to give us a perception of things that allows us to see them, not just recognize them, art must use the technique of "making strange" (*ostranenie*), showing things in a new and different way, so that the perceiver "sees" them as if for the first time. Poetic language, which is the medium of verbal art, has the responsibility of promoting this type of vision, and it does so above all if words themselves are used in surprising and different ways, so that they call attention to themselves. Thus poetic language differs from prosaic in that prosaic language has become automatized; its constituent words are not noticed in and for themselves but simply exist to point to their objects and then disappear.[41]

In "Art as Device" Shklovsky has dressed up his ideas in the garb of scientific respectability by discussing language in the context of something that sounds like perceptual psychology. But what he is presenting is not fundamentally different from what he had said three years earlier, even before the Potebnia study, in an article titled "The Resurrection of the Word." There Shklovsky had made the same distinction between recognizing and seeing as modes of perception associated, respectively, with prose and poetry. The same appeal is made to restore the word to a position of value by using words that call attention to themselves as words. Hence the "resurrection" promised in the title. What is striking about the article, however, is how much Shklovsky's style resembles that of Potebnia and Potebnia's successors. Yet this is not surprising, because Shklovsky, without telling us, has borrowed a great deal of material for his article from Potebnia and other sources close to Potebnia.

The basic ideas are the same as in Potebnia. Potebnia had seen the process by which poetic language becomes prosaic as one of increasing abstraction. So does Shklovsky. Potebnia had talked about the objectivity of poetic language, meaning its nearness to sensual perception. Shklovsky speaks of the disappearance from consciousness of everything that is habitual, including prosaic language. And, most important of all, Potebnia had based the whole thing on a myth. Again, so does Shklovsky. Here is how Shklovsky begins his article:

> The creation of words is man's most ancient [drevnejšim] form of poetic creation. Today, words are dead, and language resembles a cemetery, whereas the word that had just come into being was imaginal and full of life [živo obrazno]. Every word in its basis [osnova] is a trope. For example, the word "moon" [mesjac]: the original [pervonačal'noe] meaning of this word was "measurer." . . . And often, when one succeeds in reaching the image that had formed the basis of a word but that has been lost, obliterated, one is amazed at its beauty, a beauty that once was but is no more.[42]

Sound familiar? It should, because it is the same myth of original purity that Potebnia had found himself irresistibly drawn to. The same words and themes are there. There is talk of origins and tremendous separation in time. Shklovsky even uses the favored adjective to describe the linguistic Eden, pervonačal'nyj (from pervyj, "first," and načalo, "beginning"); Potebnia had used this word repeatedly in his own evocations of the myth of origins (as had Bely).

A great deal of the material Shklovsky uses in "The Resurrection of the Word" is borrowed, and an examination of his sources shows how dependent he was on the Potebnian myth. In one instance he borrows from exactly the same page of Potebnia's *Notes on the Theory of Literature* as Bely had done in the second part of "The Magic of Words": the introductory section to Potebnia's lengthy discussion of literary tropes. Shklovsky casually mentions the commonly used metaphor "foot of a mountain" (*podošva gory*),[43] but he does not tell us that this is the very same example that Potebnia had used to illustrate the notion of metaphor.[44] Bely's adaptation of that page from Potebnia had included an analysis of an expression containing the word *mesjac* (moon) (*S*, pp. 443–46; *SE*, pp. 106–8); *mesjac* is the first example Shklovsky gives of a word whose original (Potebnia would say etymological) meaning is more poetic than its current one. Perhaps Shklovsky was borrowing from Bely, too.

Most of Shklovsky's borrowings, however, are from another nineteenth-century linguist, a contemporary of Potebnia named Aleksandr Nikolaevich Veselovsky (1838–1906). In 1895, four years after the death of Potebnia, Veselovsky had published an article titled "From the History of the Epithet."[45] This is where Shklovsky gets a great many of the examples he uses to illustrate his point about poetic language.[46] For instance, in a discussion of poetic figures that through continued use have lost their vividness, Shklovsky mentions the epithets in the common Russian expressions *solnce jasnoe* (bright sun), *belyj svet* (white world), and *grjazi topučie* (mucky mud), all of which appear in Veselovsky's article as examples of what Veselovsky calls tautological epithets.[47] When Shklovsky then talks about epithets that have become so habitual that they are used even in contexts where they don't make sense, he uses the following examples: the "white hands" (*belye ruki*) belonging to a Moor in a Serbian epic; "my true love," used in English ballads of both faithful and unfaithful lovers; the "starry sky" to which Nestor, in the *Iliad*, extends his hands in broad daylight; and a fragment of folk poetry, which Shklovsky misquotes.[48] All examples come directly from Veselovsky.[49] This second group of examples in Veselovsky occurs in a discussion of what Veselovsky terms the oblivion of the real sense (*zabvenie real'nogo smysla*) of the epithet. Oblivion results in petrification (*okamenenie*), the phenomenon where an expression has become so hardened through habitual use that it survives in the most contradictory of contexts for the simple reason that it is no longer noticed by speaker or listener. These are really the same concepts Shklovsky is using in "The Resurrection of the Word," except that Shklovsky prefers terms like *renewal* and *rebirth*.

But there is more to this story, and it shows that something strange is going on. Most accounts of nineteenth-century Russian linguistics and philology make a great deal of the difference between Potebnia and Veselovsky. Veselovsky is usually cited as the less psychologically inclined of the two, the more inductive, the more concerned with depersonalized facts of literary production. Since he sought to deny the importance of individual creativity in literary production, viewing it as a vast, historical process definable in terms of "formulas," he is seen as the precursor to the "antipsychological" tendencies of the early Formalists.[50] And since Shklovsky has borrowed most heavily from Veselovsky, we might be tempted to think that his theoretical inclination would be toward the more sober and inductive methodology of Veselovsky rather than toward Potebnia's image-based, psychological system.

The odd thing, however, is that Veselovsky has apparently done some borrowing of his own, for in the pages Shklovsky has drawn from, virtually every example Veselovsky cites in support of his discussion appears also in precisely the same few pages of Potebnia we have been talking about. Some examples thus appear in all three writers: the passage from the *Iliad* describing Nestor, the "white hands" from the Serbian epic, and "mucky mud," to cite only three.[51]

If Veselovsky's examples are the same as Potebnia's, it seems to be because in this essay his concepts are the same, too. Potebnia, on one of the pages from which Veselovsky has borrowed examples, speaks of certain epithets that are tautological, then mentions the oblivion (*zabvenie*) of the representation (*predstavlenie*) and its renewal.[52] The next page contains Potebnia's list of permanent (*postojannye*) epithets. Veselovsky, too, refers to the permanence (*postojanstvo*) of certain epithets. The point is that the subject is the same in all three writers. All three are speaking of a central, vivid element that a word loses as it is subjected to continued use. In the pages in question Potebnia calls the element the representation (*predstavlenie*) and links it up with the word's etymological root; Veselovsky calls it the word's real sense; and Shklovsky, unabashedly using the terminology of Potebnia, calls it the word's inner form.

Thus three years after "The Resurrection of the Word," when Shklovsky comes to talk of *ostranenie* as a technique (*priem*) for restoring the vitality of language, his point of departure is the same as in the earlier essay, namely, the feeling that ordinary language has suffered the loss of a vital element. The solution is really the same too, namely, the proposal of a means for restoring the capacity of the poetic word to make things concrete and visible instead of just recognizable.

Does all this mean that Shklovsky has nothing new to say and is merely a helpless victim of an age-old mythical tradition? By no means. As for Bely and the avant-garde theorists, what is new is largely a question of emphasis. Shklovsky's insistence on the distinction between seeing and recognizing suggests a move away from grounding the old poetry-prose distinction in language itself. The Formalist critic in 1917 is distinctly uncomfortable with a theory of language that unhesitatingly ascribes the difference between an everyday form of language and an aesthetically valued one to something contained in language. Much more solid is the notion that the difference is located in the mechanisms by which the subject perceives language.

After Shklovsky the field will open up to all kinds of new methodologies purporting to help define poetic language in the most objective and nonmystical of terms. Other Formalist critics will wrestle with the problem of defining verse language. Above all, there will be Jakobson's definition of poetic language in terms of the distinction between figures of speech: metaphor, where concepts are substituted for each other along the "vertical" axis of selection, and metonymy, where the substitution takes place along the "horizontal" axis of combination.[53] The later theories are surely not free from the charge of mysticism that can be leveled at the Russian tradition inaugurated by Potebnia. But there is no doubt that for all his tendencies to move the emphasis from language itself to perceptual phenomena in the listener, Shklovsky is still very much in the grips of the old tradition. The tendencies are just that—tendencies. And Shklovsky is perfectly at home in the milieu I've been describing, just as Jakobson will be a few years later, having partially broken with the past but still perpetuating the myth about himself that there is no myth.

CHAPTER THREE

Mallarmé
and the Elocutionary
Disappearance of the Poet

To judge from what he wrote, Stéphane Mallarmé never made up his mind whether he was a mystic. There is no denying the existence of a cult of poetic art in him, nor is there any mistaking the tone of almost religious awe when he comes to speak of poetry. But there is also the persistent hint in Mallarmé's writings that he is not entirely serious, that he views his own idolatrous attitude with considerable irony.

One measure of his idolatry is his tendency to liken art to religion. The artist becomes a privileged figure enjoying powers similar to those of a priest or magus. The early "L'art pour tous" (Art for everybody) shows Mallarmé fully in the grip of this idea. "Every sacred thing that wishes to remain sacred," Mallarmé begins, "envelops itself in mystery. Religions take refuge in arcana that are revealed only to the predestinate: art has its arcana, too."[1] Of all the arts, poetry has suffered the most from a democratization that has left it unhappily accessible to the vulgar masses. Only poetry is "without mystery against hypocritical curiosities, without terror against impieties," and Mallarmé nostalgically recalls the "gold fasteners of ancient missals," the "inviolate hieroglyphs of papyrus scrolls" (OC, p. 257). "L'art pour tous" appeared in 1862, five years after the publication of Baudelaire's Les fleurs du mal, and it is not surprising to see the young Mallarmé mention that work and adopt the aggressive, antidemocratic tone of its author. The poet soars over the vulgar masses, like Baudelaire's ungainly albatross. "Man may be democratic; the artist splits in two and must remain an aristocrat" (OC, 259).

Later on, in his last years, Mallarmé takes a more cynical view of art and the artist. Perhaps it is out of despair at seeing that his ideal of a sacred art of poetry has not been realized in this life. Perhaps he has simply arrived at a more hardened, demystified view of the whole subject; it's difficult to say. But the tone is unmistakably different from what it had been thirty-odd years earlier. In one of the four pieces collected under the general title "Quant au Livre" (Concerning the Book), after a convoluted passage in which he considers and then rejects the notion of suicide or abstention from writing, Mallarmé makes these comments:

> Apart from headline news entrusted with spreading a faith in the everyday nothingness, unskilled if the scourge measures out its own period as a fragment, significant or not, of a century.
>
> So look out for yourself and be there.
>
> Poetry, consecration; that attempts, in chaste crises in isolation, during the other gestation in progress.
>
> Publish.
>
> (OC, p. 372)

This is Mallarmé at his tortuous best. What exactly does it mean? All that really concerns us now is what it means in its tone, and the tone is unquestionably less earnest than it had been in "L'art pour tous." It had become Mallarmé's custom, when he sought to portray the least exalted side of a profession in letters, to resort to wry descriptions of it as a commerce, both in the literal sense as the marketing of books and in the figurative sense as the marketing of meanings. Mallarmé enjoys depicting the man of letters as a shameless pander to the whims and financial needs of the moment. He characterizes his craft by using vocabulary drawn from the world of newspapers and money, treating the sacred side of literature with a contempt that is almost masochistic. Thus the glib mention of poetry as consecration is followed with the blunt, sarcastic command to publish, that is, to produce literature for consumption.

There is a significant analogy between Mallarmé's attitude toward art and his attitude toward language. His attitude toward art expresses itself as a tension between religious idolatry and skepticism. When Mallarmé turns to the topic of language, he shows the same tendency, but without regularly having recourse to the vocabulary and imagery of Catholicism. Instead, the tension turns up as the same one we have seen in the Russian theorists. It is the tension created by the twin temptations of linguistic mysticism—a kind of naive Cratylism, on the one hand, and modern scientific conventionalism, on the other. We can see these temptations primarily in two texts: the relatively early Cratylic fantasy called *Les mots anglais* (English words), written in 1875 and published in 1877, and the later "Crise de vers" (Crisis in verse), a patchwork of material written between 1886 and 1895.

ENGLISH WORDS AND THE GAME OF CRATYLISM

One sign that something is amiss in *English Words* is that the text is far longer than any other published work by Mallarmé. The French have a fondness for starting at the absolute beginning of a subject and proceeding by a kind of irresistible logic to the heart of the matter. Even French cookbooks open with an essay devoted to the question, Why do we nourish ourselves? But not Mallarmé. Ellipsis, truncated syntax, and a kind of twisted economy of expression were his trademarks. Few things he wrote in prose were more than several pages long. So it is with considerable suspicion that the reader must regard a treatise that opens in the following manner and then continues for almost two hundred pages in the standard edition: "What is English? A serious and lofty question: treat it in the sense in which it is posed here, that is, absolutely—one simply cannot until the last of these pages, once all has been analyzed. For the moment, it behooves us to answer, keeping in mind the external and commonly noted characters of English, that this idiom is one of those in the world that a contemporary must know" (*OC*, p. 899).

Maybe Mallarmé is simply making fun of the very tendency that leads his compatriots to write introductions to cookbooks. After all, this first paragraph doesn't give the kind of answer a reader would expect in a learned philological discussion, and in fact it doesn't really make much sense. Besides, it isn't the true logical point of origin. Mallarmé poses a more basic question two pages later, and his answer to this one is hardly more satisfying than his answer to the first: "What is Language, among scientific materials to be studied? From each of them, Language, entrusted with expressing all the phenomena of Life, borrows something; it lives: and, since (to help childhood grasp) it is unavoidable that the outside world should lend its images, any figure of discourse, relative to this or that manifestation of life, is fine to use for speaking about language" (*OC*, p. 901).

Much of what Mallarmé writes in *English Words* is borrowed from the works of various nineteenth-century linguists and philologists. The work that served as the source of the bulk of his historical observations on English is called *The Philology of the English Tongue*, written in 1873 by a man named John Earle (1824–1903). Mallarmé's "borrowings" are so extensive, in fact, that scholars today don't even speak of his text's originality; rather, they find themselves proposing explanations for the cases where Mallarmé merely altered Earle's text slightly instead of shamelessly translating it word for word. Not that he is trying to hoodwink us: any reader can easily discover Mallarmé's heavy reliance on his sources. Using an old-fashioned scholarly study for so much material undoubtedly serves the same purpose as the formulaic Cartesian opening. Both create the illusion that the author is presenting a traditional treatise on language of the sort that might contain a thesis like the one Mallarmé advances.

And what of that thesis? Here is how Mallarmé states it: "What it behooves us to realize now seems to me to be the relation that exists between the meanings of words that I will assume to be unknown to you, and their external configuration" (*OC*, p. 918). Where does this relation emerge? As he explains a little later, it emerges in the beginning of the word, in what he calls the "attack" (*OC*, p. 926). An intrinsically meaningful opening sound is common to languages of the north, Mallarmé explains. For we mustn't forget that the close sound-sense relation is something that English has in far greater measure than French: hence the need to write a book about English words and not about French, or Hottentot. Mallarmé's notion is extremely simple. It is that in a great many cases the opening sounds of an English word give an indication of its meaning—though not precisely that opening sounds contain *in themselves* a clue to a particular meaning. In other words, there is nothing magical about, say, an initial *b* sound that causes it to signify a certain thing or concept. It's just that in English certain initial sounds commonly denote the same thing or concept. Mallarmé wants us to believe that the force of his theory is in frequency of correlation, not in a mystical explanation. Thus his method: "to group and eliminate" (*OC*, p. 918).

Once the logical foundation for the essay has been established, Mallarmé can proceed to the principal task of his enterprise: to make lists. His lists are arranged by initial letter and consist first of the group of words that belong to the same "family" and then of the group of "refractory" words that do not—"isolated words," as he calls them. Are the isolated words a problem for Mallarmé's theory? Not at all. "Nothing could be more practical," he says, than to isolate the refractory words. "Nor could it be more in agreement with the theory of a Language, or with intelligent mnemonics. Separated after having so often come together since their common origin, these words now succeed in coming together once again, owing to your reflection, in a state of the Language treated with order" (*OC*, p. 922).

What this means exactly I hesitate to say, but perhaps it doesn't matter much. The essential thing in each list is the group of words belonging to the same family, and Mallarmé now offers his lists up in the section of his text called "Table." Here is where it is most difficult to take Mallarmé seriously or to believe that he took himself seriously. Under the letter *b*, for instance, we read that words in this group have meanings that are "diverse, yet secretly connected." The meanings have to do with "production and giving birth, fecundity, amplitude, swelling and curvature, boastfulness; also mass or boiling and sometimes goodness and blessing" (*OC*, p. 929); hence the common thread in *baby, back, bat, bear, beech, beck, bell, bend, bind, better, bet, bid, big, bite, black, blend, blink, bless, block, blot, blow,* and so on (*OC*, pp. 926–28). Further on we read that *m* (*may, make, mash, maze, meet, melt, merry, mid, milk, mildew, mingle, moon, moor, morn, mow*) "translates the power to do, thus joy, male and maternal; also, through a meaning that has come down to us from far in the past, measure and duty, number, meeting, melting and the middle term: and, finally, by a turnabout less abrupt than it might appear, inferiority, weakness or anger" (*OC*, p. 960). And *k* (*keg, kedge, kin, kind, king, kill, quell, knit, knot, knop, knob, knuckle*) "generally carries the sense of knottiness, knuckle, etc., but only by allying itself with *n* and becoming silent for the benefit of this nasal. Note also the group *kin, kind, king,* from which a notion of familial goodness emerges" (*OC*, p. 941).

This last group, because it is so small and because so many of the words are etymologically related to each other (as Mallarmé knows), shows better than many others the absurdity of Mallarmé's claims. He might just as well have said that *k* in English mysteriously unites the meanings of kegs, kedges, kin, kind, kings, killing, knitting, knots, knops, knobs, and knuckles. But of course Mallarmé is writing in French, which allows him to disguise what he is doing; for when he uses French words to give the common ideas from a list of English words, the French words do not resemble each other. *Keg, kedge, kin,* and *kind,* for instance, in Mallarmé's translation are *caque, flotteur d'ancre, parenté,* and *familier et bon.* Translate these French words into English, however, and you come up with a list of words for common ideas that looks suspiciously like the original list of words from which the common ideas were extracted. The list of common ideas, to be sure, is shorter than the original list of words, but usually because the original list contains words that are etymologically related. Hence there is nothing amazing in their beginning with the same letter or, for that matter, in their having a common meaning.

What do we make of Mallarmé's linguistic speculations? Certainly not that he meant to be taken at his word. Jacques Michon, who wrote a full-length book on *English Words*, says that in the debate that has been carried on since *Cratylus*, Mallarmé places himself squarely on the side of the Cratylists. But he adds that Mallarmé is "a disenchanted occultist, for whom absolute language cannot exist."[2] Edouard Gaède is a little more skeptical, but in being so he shows more faith in Mallarmé. *English Words*, he says, though it pretends to be a scientific work, is in reality "a vast poem on the nature of language." There can be no sincere talk of naivete in Mallarmé's absurd etymologies, Gaède feels, because Mallarmé's whole enterprise is a fictional one. Mallarmé "sets out to complete, *fictionally,* the jumble of scattered data that these [etymological] dictionaries offer, by placing the data in a succession that would introduce a law of continuity and thus a principle of intelligibility." In fact, Gaède says, Mallarmé's real point is to propose a theory of language that is thoroughly at odds with traditional Cratylism. The implicit theory of language that emerges from Mallarmé's classifications is one according to which language renders not objects but "a certain plan as a function of which the real takes shape." Gaède thinks that the very fact Mallarmé's work is a fiction signifies that for him language is not a representative, but rather a productive, medium.[3]

This last statement, in my opinion, is excessive. But there can be no doubt that Gaède is right about the fictional quality of the project. Whether Mallarmé is trying to be funny, or whether he is simply giving expression to a kind of Cratylist nostalgia, *English Words* is a document that exists in the moment of hesitation between an older, mythical view of language and a newer, more skeptical one.

"CRISIS IN VERSE"

The facts that shine through the irony or fiction of *English Words*—namely, that there is no necessary correspondence between the sound of a word and its meaning in French, English, or any other language, that the sound-sense relation is arbitrary and capricious—serve as the logical point of departure for the more somber and skeptical view of language that Mallarmé proposes almost two decades later in "Crisis in Verse." But if these facts show that the system in *English Words* is a lie, and if they thus precipitate the crisis that Mallarmé refers to in the title of his later essay, they also serve as the basis for a hopeful resolution to that crisis.

The section of Mallarmé's patchwork essay in which he presents his view comes from a piece he published in *Variations sur un sujet* (Variations on a subject) in 1895. The point of departure is two marvelously simple perceptions:

> Languages being imperfect in that they are several, the supreme one is lacking: since thinking is writing without accessories, or whispering but the immortal word still being tacit, the diversity, on earth, of idioms prevents anyone from uttering words that otherwise would turn out to be, by a unique stamp, materially truth itself. . . . Next to *ombre*, opaque, *ténèbres* darkens little; what disenchantment in the perversity that bestows upon *jour* as upon *nuit*, contradictorily, a timbre that is dark in the former case, light in the latter.
>
> (OC, p. 363–64)

Mallarmé is making the same point that Humboldt made in his principal work on language. Both refer to the fact of the diversity (*Verschiedenheit, diversité*) of human languages. Any theory of language that pretends to see a necessary correspondence between sound and sense is contradicted by the simple fact that there are so many languages and that each has its own word for any one thing or concept. Otherwise we would be able to utter words that "would turn out to be, by a unique stamp, materially truth itself." That is the first point. The second applies to an individual language considered apart from "the diversity, on earth, of idioms." Take a language like French, for instance, and put it to the test to see if there is a necessary connection between the sounds of its words and their meanings. You will soon come upon examples like the one Mallarmé mentions: *jour,* which has a dark sound but a light referent (day), and *nuit,* which has a bright sound but a dark referent (night). As Mallarmé well knows, this single example is sufficient to demonstrate the fallacy of supposing with Cratylus that even in a single language there can ever be an intrinsic correspondence between sound and sense. And as Mallarmé undoubtedly also knows, having demonstrated the fallacy of the sound-sense correspondence, he has demonstrated the fallacy of *English Words* as well. For even if English did show a statistically high correlation between words with certain initial letters and a small group of related concepts (and Mallarmé has not shown that it does), this would still not be enough to establish the inevitability of the correlation. Either language is magic or it's not; the existence of even a few exceptions shows that it's not. *English Words,* filled as it is with faulty methodology (intentionally, no doubt), really demonstrates the same thing as "Crisis in Verse," only ironically.

But that's only the crisis in language; the essay is about a crisis in *verse.* Here is how Mallarmé makes the transition. Immediately after the last phrase I quoted he says, "The wish for a term of brilliant splendor, or that it should be extinguished, the opposite; as for simple, luminous alternatives—*Only* know that *verse would not exist:* it, philosophically compensates for the shortcoming of languages, superior complement" (*OC,* p. 364). This appears to be Mallarmé's crabbed way of saying that if our wish for a universal match between bright words and bright ideas, dark words and dark ideas, were to come true, then we would no longer have verse. Verse owes its existence to this patent shortcoming of language. This is certainly a novel idea, particularly since other, contemporary poets and thinkers asserted the distinctness of verse by claiming for it the mythical, Cratylic condition.

But Mallarmé has a somewhat more imaginative notion of (verse) language than many of his contemporaries. In fact, what he has done is to invert the poetry-prose distinction of his contemporaries and successors by claiming a Cratylic aim for prose and a different notion of language for verse. Here is how he introduces the distinction, in a characteristically complicated and humorous passage:

> Abolished the pretension, aesthetically an error, even though it governs masterpieces, to include on the delicate paper of a volume anything other than, for example, the horror of the forest, or the silent, scattered thunder in the foliage; not the intrinsic and dense wood of the trees. A few spurts of deeply felt pride veraciously trumpeted abroad arouse the architecture of the palace, the only one fit to live in; apart from any stone, on which the pages would close with difficulty.
>
> (*OC,* p. 365–66)

It's not just that Cratylism is false in the real world; it's that, even if it were true, it would be an aesthetically wrong concept. In the privileged language of poetry, language mustn't strive to render the forest—that is, the trees themselves, or the palace—in its physical reality. After all, Mallarmé quips, we wouldn't be able to close the book on all those big stones. No, poetic language instead must strive to communicate intangible things, like the horror the forest inspires or the mute thunder—not the actual crashing thunder, but the residue of feeling it leaves behind in the trees.

Ordinary language doesn't function in this way. It functions, so Mallarmé's favorite joke goes, like money in a commercial exchange: "Narrate, teach, even describe, that's fine and even if it were enough for each of us perhaps, in order to exchange human thought, to take from or place in the hand of someone else a coin in silence, the elementary use of discourse serves the needs of universal *reportage,* of which, with the exception of literature, all the genres of contemporary writings contain elements" (*OC,* p. 368).

How is poetic language different? The key is what Mallarmé calls transposition. "What is the use of the marvel of transposing an act of nature into its vibratory almost-disappearance through the play of speech, however; if it is not so that from it should emanate, without the encumbrance of a close or concrete reference, the pure notion" (*OC,* p. 368). The most famous sentence in this essay once again stresses the non-representational functioning of poetic language. "I say: a flower! and, apart from the oblivion to which my voice relegates any contour, understood as something other than the known calyxes, musically there arises, idea itself and pleasant, the flower absent from all bouquets" (*OC,* p. 368). The result of the use of language is not the transfer of a concrete thing; the thing is "transposed" so that only the pure notion of it remains. As Mallarmé says in another famous statement, "*Divine transposition . . . goes from fact to the ideal*" (*OC,* p. 522; Mallarmé's emphasis). The "flower absent from all bouquets" is the ideal flower evoked in the sound "flower," and it is absent for the good and sufficient reason that it is ideal. Poetic language, rather than having "the function of facile, representative cash," rediscovers a prized quality: virtuality (*OC,* p. 368).

Concrete things are not all that disappears in the act of poetic speaking. "The pure work implies the elocutionary disappearance of the poet, who instead yields the initiative to words, mobilized by the clash of their inequality; they light up from their reciprocal reflections, like a trail of fire on gems, taking the place of that palpable breath in the lyric inspiration of yore or the enthusiastic personal direction of speech" (*OC,* p. 366). Meaning no longer comes from the poet; nor does it come as the result of aggregating the individual meanings of words, the way one can aggregate the individual values of coins and bills in a fistful of cash.

Instead, it emerges from the "reciprocal reflections" of the words, from the relational complex formed by the poem, which is seen as a structure, not a linear accumulation of word-references.

Mallarmé has come a considerable distance in this essay from the apparent impasse he faced in the observation that words don't mean by a "unique stamp." In fact, he has found a way out of the archaic notion of language that makes such an impasse possible. In the old notion, both for those who are confirmed Cratylists and for those who nostalgically yearn for Cratylism in an ideal past, language is a vertical medium made up of distinct units of meaning, each of which has the responsibility of transmitting a particular thing or concept. The naive Cratylists believe that this is how language really works. The skeptics realize that language doesn't work this way in the real world, but they feel that it should, that real languages represent a kind of fall from grace. Mallarmé, however, has abandoned the view of language that both groups presupposed. If there is no "unique stamp," then that is all to the good since language, at least *good* language, has a higher purpose. In this view it's not even relevant to be "materially truth itself." Truth doesn't have the rudimentary sense that the old view assumes.

Where Mallarmé's reflections lead is to a relational notion of language. But they also lead to another cardinal moment in the history of language theory. In chapter 1 I mentioned Mallarmé's role in the fracturing of language. I quoted Foucault's comment that Mallarmé played a major role in that process and in the movement of language to a state of "philological objectivity." We can now see how true Foucault's comment is, and we can see the logic by which Mallarmé arrived at those ideas. Once we have abandoned the Cratylic comfort of the sound-sense correlation, placing ourselves in a world where meaning assembles itself from the spaces between words, we have also abandoned the bond that unites poet and language. Transposition takes place in the language, not in the poet. It renders the pure notion of things. This pure notion comes to us from the clash of inequality of words; hence the "elocutionary disappearance of the poet," that is, the disappearance of the poet as a speaking presence. Because language is a system of clashing inequalities, the poet has yielded the initiative to words. When it comes right down to it, words are all there is; they are the only real thing that we encounter in language. That's why Mallarmé chooses to compare them with gems—hard, cold, objective gems. And that's why Foucault can speak of the "unique, difficult being" of language that Mallarmé leads our thought back to. Mallarmé has fractured language by separating it from the poet, and he has rendered it hard, opaque, objective, precisely *because* it is separate.

Mallarmé is not the only French poet to address problems of language in a context of literary aesthetics. Paul Valéry comes to mind, too. His "Poetry and Abstract Thought" ("Poésie et pensée abstraite") revives the old poetry-prose distinction, suggesting that the peculiarity of poetic language is that it calls attention to itself as language. Valéry also modifies the Cratylic conception of language by proposing that poetic language merely gives the illusion of a necessary harmony between sound and sense.[4] But "Poetry and Abstract Thought" was written in 1939 and doesn't form part of our history. Besides, the most interesting things Valéry had to say about language have more to do with relationalism than with Cratylism or the poetry-prose distinction, so we'll leave them for later.

The value of Mallarmé's theory of language is that it so compactly presents the whole complex of issues in modern literary aesthetics. The argument in "Crisis in Verse" leads naturally, logically, to a theory of relationalism. Mallarmé's hesitation between mysticism and skepticism shows him still in the grips of an older tradition based on faith ("You can't do without Eden") but pulled also toward the realm of the purely speculative and the thorny, characteristically twentieth-century question of aesthetic ontology. All these areas of thought are related. Poised on the edge of the twentieth century, Mallarmé conveniently bequeaths them to modernity as a system.

PART II

Theology

Introduction:
The Hidden God

One of the cleverest and funniest accounts of literary criticism in the twentieth century is Marxist critic Terry Eagleton's *Literary Theory: An Introduction*.[1] Eagleton's project is to discredit most of the major schools of twentieth-century literary criticism by exposing for each one the underlying, untested assumption that must be accepted on faith in order for the whole system to stand. Eagleton has an extraordinary gift for this kind of analysis. He shows, for instance, how T. S. Eliot's notion of a Tradition in literature is based solely on authoritarian judgments handed down by Eliot himself and then given the status of absolute, almost divine principles. Similarly, the critical program of New Criticism, with its intensive focus on the poem itself, starts by imbuing the poem "with an absolute mystical authority" (p. 49). Like Eliot's doctrine of the great Tradition, New Criticism is at bottom a religious system in disguise. Phenomenological criticism, with its habit of reducing everything to pure subjective consciousness, is authoritarian, too, because it depends heavily on intuition (p. 57).

And so it goes for virtually all schools of modern criticism: if you look closely at them, they all turn out to be authoritarian, mystical, religious. A moderately skeptical mind will find Eagleton's debunking easy to accept. But Eagleton comes close to wrecking his entire enterprise at the end of the book when having proclaimed with great satisfaction the death of literary studies, he proceeds with the blind faith of a true ideologue to outline for the reader the sole realms of criticism worthy of being practiced. These are ones that pursue the goal of "human emancipation, the production of 'better people' through the socialist transformation of society" (p. 211). What exempts socialist and feminist criticism from the charges Eagleton levels at all other types of criticism is that they are *categorically* different, and this because they "define the object of analysis differently, have different values, beliefs and goals" (p. 212). In other words, once the activity of literary criticism rests on the solid bedrock of a political program dedicated to the destruction of social inequality, it is beyond reproach from any quarter because no one can possibly question the assumption that inequality is bad (and that the elimination of privilege and private property are the solution to it). Hence the need for humanists in our day to turn their attention to areas of cultural endeavor whose worth, Eagleton feels, cannot logically be disputed, areas, that is, where "cultural and political action have become closely united" (p. 215). And Eagleton lists these areas: the culture of "nations struggling for their independence from imperialism," the women's movement, the "culture industry" (culture of minorities), and working-class writing (pp. 215–216).

Eagleton has asked us to take the skeptical line throughout his book and decry the clandestine articles of faith in each of the systems he talks about. He then asks us to regard another system as not just another system but as something different *in kind* from all the systems he disdains. But isn't there an untested, authoritarian principle here, too? "Men and women do not live by culture alone; the vast majority of them throughout history have been deprived of the chance of living by it at all, and those few who are fortunate enough to live by it now are able to do so because of the labour of those who do not. Any cultural or critical theory which does not begin from *this single most important fact,* and hold it steadily in mind in its activities, is in my view unlikely to be worth very much" (p. 214, my emphasis). Does Eagleton have any more right to tell us what the "single most important fact" is than Eliot does to tell us which are the most important texts? Eagleton is asking us to accept on faith, first, that the humanities are tools of capitalism, second, that they have an intrinsic responsibility to devote themselves to political change, and, finally, that the form of political change to which they must devote themselves is the "socialist transformation of society."

So Eagleton has his untested assumption, too, and he has introduced it with the same slippery logic as his predecessors, hoping in the end that a universal sense of social justice will persuade his readers to accept principles that in fact are merely handed down by authoritarian fiat. The social-activist theory of literary criticism begins to look a little like theology, as well. But social-activist literary criticism is not my subject. I mention Eagleton's ideas only because they leave us with the disheartening sense that no school of critical theory escapes the sort of mystical authoritarianism he talks about. After all, if a critic like Eagleton, whose basic motivating force is precisely a resistance to arbitrary expressions of authority, does not escape the cancer of mystical authoritarianism, then who can?

Eagleton says at one point that there is "no need to drag politics into literary theory. As with South African sport, it has been there from the beginning" (p. 194). This is one of his most basic beliefs. In fact, however, he has demonstrated the truth of another statement, a paraphrase of that one: There is no need to drag theology into literary theory; it has been there from the beginning, and it lives on in the theory of Eagleton himself.

That is the subject of Part II. If there is a hidden god in almost every species of twentieth-century literary theory, it is because the intellectual origins of the entire movement that has produced twentieth-century literary theory were more or less explicitly theological. Eagleton dates the beginning of this movement with the publication of Viktor Shklovsky's "Art as Device" in 1917. One could easily quibble with this choice: Shklovsky had already written other articles on literature before 1917 (we looked at some of them in chapter 2), and there were other writers, too, compatriots of Shklovsky who had already written similar things. Eagleton is certainly right, however, in saying that something is happening in this period that had not been happening, say, a generation earlier—what he calls "the transformation which has overtaken literary theory in this century" (p. vii). But we need to examine Shklovsky's predecessors and contemporaries to understand what sort of transformation had taken place. It turns out that the transformation was not so marked as we might think, that the origins of Shklovsky's type of literary theorizing go deep into the theological history of Russia, and that these origins are never entirely abandoned.

Yet even this is only part of the story, for there are two theologies. There is Russian Orthodox theology, which threads its way through a millennium of Russian culture and into the early twentieth century, when all the major Russian literary thinkers of the early modern period share its heritage. The Russian whose impact on succeeding generations was the most direct was not Shklovsky or any of the other Formalist critics; it was a linguist, Roman Jakobson. In spite of his reputation as a guiding force in the modern "science" of language, Jakobson operates in an old system of religious language philosophy that in many ways has simply been dressed up in the more modern fashion of scientific terminology. The other theology is a Western, largely Catholic one. It can be seen in French writers like Mallarmé, although the content of Catholic theology is obscured by Mallarmé's constant urge to satirize and profane the same religious principles he surreptitiously adopts.

Theology has a great deal to do with language: it is, in its root sense, "God-talk" (*theo-logos*), as the Heideggerian theologian John Macquarrie puts it in the title of his book on the subject; and, since Christian theology is talk about the Christian God, it is also talk about God's Word. In some ways this brings us back to the subject of Part I. But in this part we will move on from language to the question of artworks, specifically artworks made out of language, and see how the hidden god has affected our thinking about them in modern times.

CHAPTER FOUR

How God Didn't Quite
Die in France

A book by Sartre on Mallarmé came out in 1986, six years after Sartre's death. It includes a long, unfinished essay with the characteristically Sartrean title "L'engagement de Mallarmé" (Mallarmé's commitment) and a shorter essay called, simply, "Mallarmé (1842–1898)." Both were written in 1952.[1]

We don't usually think of Sartre as a funny man, but when he turned his attention to literary subjects, he was capable of being quite a joker. The first section of "L'engagement de Mallarmé" is called "Les héritiers de l'athéisme" (The inheritors of atheism), and it starts out like this:

> 1848: the fall of the monarchy deprives the bourgeoisie of its "cover"; with a single stroke Poetry loses its two traditional themes: Man and God.
> First God: Europe had just heard a stupefying piece of news, still contested by some today: "God dead. Stop. Intestate." When it came time to divide up the estate, panic reigned: what had the Deceased left?
>
> (p. 15)

Sartre views the whole phenomenon of Mallarmé as essentially a late reaction to the recent "death of God." "Les héritiers de l'athéisme" paints a sweeping picture of European culture in the wake of this event. Sartre then turns his attention to Mallarmé, in a section called "L'élu" (The chosen one). With the same kind of licentiously creative psychological analysis that he was to employ in his later monumental work on Flaubert, *L'idiot de la famille*, Sartre picks through the spiritual world of Mallarmé, revealing to his eager readers all the exciting details of the great artist's sexual and religious life. The sexual life need not concern us (it is largely the invention of Sartre, who was fond of doing that sort of thing). But what Sartre says about Mallarmé's religious life is extraordinarily clever, especially because it has a direct bearing on the philosophy of art that Sartre finds in Mallarmé.

Mallarmé's peculiar aesthetics, it would appear from Sartre, actually has a double source. There is the spiritual desolation in Europe caused by the death of God, something that allows Sartre to talk in general about what it means to be a poet in the late nineteenth century. And there is the personal desolation caused in Mallarmé by the death of his own mother (when he was five). The way Sartre sees it, both deaths produced in Mallarmé a strange cult of absence, negation, and nonbeing, which in turn produced a religion and an aesthetics that are intertwined.

The religion is a sort of obverse Christianity. Sartre describes Mallarmé's grief over yet another death, that of his sister, when he was sixteen. "It's the death of his mother all over again," Sartre says. "This mystery of the Disincarnation, the union of a myth and a ritual, seems to found a Christianity in reverse. It's not the Parousia, but Absence that is the hope and aim. What 'was in the beginning' was not the logos, but the vile abundance of Being, Vulgarity; it is neither Creation nor the passage of the Word into the World that we adore, but instead the passage by emaciation of Reality into the Word" (p. 113). For Mallarmé, religion had become an interrogation into being, and all the traditional absolutes had been replaced with negation and absence. The departed mother and sister become the emblems of this absence. "The young priest of the new religion does not address God; he reserves his prayers for a Great Goddess who will be the image of everything a woman can be for a man apart from carnal love, a white goddess of chastity mingling mother and sister in a single absence" (p. 114).

From the absence of God (and mother) the natural place to turn to was poetry, which is how religion and aesthetics are connected for Mallarmé. But the connection is not what we might expect. After all, wouldn't it be natural to seek in poetry a replacement for the lost God (and the lost mother's love)? This is apparently what Mallarmé did, but he faced an irreconcilable contradiction. "After having killed God with his own hands," says Sartre, "Mallarmé still wanted a divine guarantee; Poetry had to remain transcendent, even though he had eliminated the source of all transcendence" (p. 152). So poetry, too, becomes a place where strange ontological impossibilities reign, just as they do in religion; it becomes "pure Negation" (p. 141). It is "a hole bored into Being, the establishment and delimitation of an absence that, bit by bit, from one allusion to the next, turns out to be the world. Through the poem, on a single point in the world, the total absence of the world is realized" (p. 162). The poem "displays the world and everything that's in the world; not in order to *give* us things, but in order to take them away from us. . . . Meaning is a second silence in the heart of silence; it is the negation of the word-thing" (p. 160). Precisely because poetry could not be the replacement for religion, it became essentially the same thing as religion. But religion, after the death of God, had become a religion of absence, and so poetry became a poetry of absence.

There is much truth in what Sartre says. Not always, of course, in the sense of factual truth: how can Sartre pretend to know about things like Mallarmé's sexual habits? There is truth in Sartre's clever way of contextualizing Mallarmé's religious attitude, and there is truth in the way he links that same attitude with Mallarmé's aesthetics. He certainly tends to conceptualize the figure of Mallarmé in characteristically Sartrean terms (speaking of the *engagement,* or commitment, of Mallarmé, the emphasis on his existential "situation"), but he has refrained to a surprising degree from the kind of doctrinaire and heavy-handed treatment we might expect from him, especially in the early 1950s.

One comment about "man" and his situation in history, however, is worth citing. I have mentioned more than once Foucault's observation about Mallarmé's pivotal position in the modern history of the way language is seen. In an era when language was increasingly viewed as a functional system, as something with its own objectivity, Mallarmé had played a crucial role in leading thought violently "back towards language itself," Foucault said.[2] But an era for Foucault here means an entire *episteme,* which implies a certain universal way of understanding, and he credits Mallarmé with a major change in that universal way of understanding. Sartre, too, sees Mallarmé as a pivotal figure, and, like Foucault, he considers Mallarmé's view of language to be the critical thing. But Sartre is interested in it not solely for its impact on the way people think about language but also for its impact on the way people *are.* Mallarmé, as Sartre saw it, created a whole new man. "Ever since he decided to write in order to launch the Word [Verbe] on an adventure from which there is no return, there is no writer, no matter how modest, who will risk himself in a book without risking the Word [Parole] at the same time. The Word or Man: it's all the same thing. . . . With Mallarmé a new man is born, reflective and critical, tragic, whose life line reveals a decline." This new man, Sartre continues, "surpasses himself and totalizes himself in the fulgurating drama of the incarnation and the fall, he cancels himself and exalts himself at the same time, in a word, he makes himself *exist* through the realization of his own impossibility" (pp. 144–45, Sartre's emphasis).

Perhaps Sartre is just indulging in rhetorical excess. It is one thing for Foucault to say that Mallarmé was responsible for a new conception of language. But can we really assert that Mallarmé gave birth to a whole new man? This is a natural way for Sartre to think, reluctant as he was to separate art from life, the artistic calling from one's calling as a man. These days people have grown tired of Sartre's pedantic ideas about commitment in art and the greater, human vocation of the writer. Maybe Mallarmé didn't create a whole new man. Maybe he just created—or helped create—a whole new critic and reader, a whole new way of thinking about literary texts. And maybe Mallarmé's inverse theology had a great deal to do with the new critic and reader he created.

IN THE BEGINNING WAS . . . NOTHING

In almost every Dostoevsky novel, it seems, there is an exchange between two characters in which one, often without warning and always without apology, bluntly asks the other if he believes in God (or if there is a God). Every Dostoevsky character is torn between the twin temptations of faith and faithlessness. Nonetheless, the answer is almost always as blunt and unhesitating as the question: Yes, there is a God, or No, there is no God. Period. Imagine Mallarmé, arch-ironist of French letters, the man who cultivated the art of *politesse* to the point where he lavished praise on the most tasteless rubbish written by his friends; imagine this man assaulted by one of Dostoevsky's shaggy, maniacal heroes with this question: Do you believe in God, yes or no, answer at once! What would he have said? Did he believe in God?

The question of Mallarmé's religious thought is complicated. The beginnings are not entirely clear. We read that his father and stepmother were both Catholic. His maternal grandparents continued to play an important role in the boy's life after his mother had died. His grandmother appears to have been religious, whereas his grandfather was something of a skeptic. Mallarmé was sent to a boarding school run by a religious order, where he consistently received poor to passing grades in religion.

For a writer like Mallarmé, whose style is marked by such extraordinarily compulsive economy of expression, every document assumes tremendous significance. So anyone who is interested in the question of Mallarmé's religious beliefs has no choice but to examine a letter the fifteen-year-old Mallarmé wrote to his sister on the occasion of her first communion:

> My dear little sister,
>
> How could I let such a pretty day pass by without writing you a few words; I have very little time to myself, but in a case like this shouldn't I make the time? I have learned with great joy that you earned a medal for good conduct. That's proof of your fine preparation for one of the most important acts in your life. . . . I have no advice or exhortations to give you: for I am sure that you have had no lack of either these days, both from our dear mother and from those who have prepared you to receive your God.

The letter continues in this tone, largely about various trivialities that the adolescent future poet is already adept at discussing with great charm. Austin Gill, who cites this letter in his book about Mallarmé's early years, takes a dimmer view of Mallarmé's youthful piety. He thinks the letter is largely a joke on the kind of sentiments normally inspired in a Catholic culture by as important an event as a child's first communion. "The mimicry involved in these pious sentiments and their expression is patent," he says, "whether it is of standard practice or family usage." He mentions that Mallarmé sent his sister a "flurry of letters" in honor of her first communion. In Gill's opinion this "underlines" his mimicry.[3]

What Gill says may be true. Does it settle the question of Mallarmé's belief or nonbelief? Not convincingly. Another commentator, L.-J. Austin, in an article that presents a kind of spiritual biography of Mallarmé, says that Mallarmé was quite traditionally and sincerely religious as a child. He cites as evidence several of Mallarmé's juvenile creations in which the word *Dieu* is used.[4] Some undoubtedly see raillery where Austin sees piety and would conclude from this and other material that Mallarmé was a skeptic from an early age. I am not persuaded that the matter is so simple. To attribute great religious devotion or great skepticism to a teenager strikes me as placing undue importance on thoughts that have not yet matured. As it happens, most biographers and commentators do not see things Gill's way and insist that Mallarmé was unquestioningly religious as a boy, just because he was raised to be that way.[5]

Some of the best evidence on the question of Mallarmé's religious attitude comes later. Every artist needs to have a metaphysical crisis at some point, and Mallarmé had his when he was in his early twenties. He made three related discoveries at that time: Nothingness, Hegel, and the idea for his future creation called the Book. His correspondence charts the progress of this strange episode. The central experience seems to have been an encounter with Nothingness (*le Néant*), followed by a revelation about Beauty and the Absolute. "I will tell you that for the past month I have been in the pure glaciers of Aesthetics—that after finding Nothingness, I have found Beauty," he writes to his friend, the minor poet Henri Cazalis.[6] "I have died and been reborn," he exclaims in another letter.[7] Over and over again we find the word *Néant* in Mallarmé's letters of this period.

We also find a kind of popularized Hegelian vocabulary. There are in the correspondence references to the Idea and the Absolute. There are passages describing thought as it thinks itself out, suggesting vaguely the development that Hegel describes in *The Phenomenology of Spirit*. And we read of "Pure Conception," of a "supreme synthesis," of a "Spiritual Universe" as it "sees itself and develops." Mallarmé, it seems, had recently become acquainted secondhand with Hegel's aesthetics and had appropriated some of the terms and concepts as he had understood them.

Once the crisis was over, Mallarmé wrote to Cazalis what was to become one of his most frequently cited letters. This letter is particularly valuable because in it, in addition to describing once again the crisis that he had been talking about for more than a year, in addition to revealing the resolution to that crisis more completely than he had done before, in addition to flaunting his Hegelian vocabulary, Mallarmé puts the whole experience in a religious perspective. The confrontation with Nothingness had apparently been accompanied by a confrontation with God, and in the end both had to be replaced.

> I have just had a terrifying year: my Thought has thought itself out and has arrived at a pure Conception. Everything my entire being suffered as an aftereffect during this long agony is indescribable, but fortunately I died completely, and the most impure region where my Spirit may venture is Eternity,

my Spirit, that habitual hermit of its own Purity that even the reflection of Time no longer darkens.

Unfortunately, I got there by means of a horrible sensitivity, and it is now time for me to envelop that sensitivity with an external indifference, which will replace for me my lost strength. I am now at the point, after a supreme synthesis, of slowly gaining strength—incapable, as you see, of distracting myself. But how much more so I was a few months ago, first of all in my terrible struggle with that old and wicked plumage, now crushed, fortunately, God.[8]

Mallarmé goes on to talk about what has replaced God. He uses the word *Synthesis* (this time with a capital *S*) again, saying that he has "marked out the opus [*oeuvre*] that will be the image of this development." That opus will be a collection of poems, including "four prose poems on the spiritual conception of Nothingness." A little bit farther on he says, "I have made a rather long descent into Nothingness so that I can speak with certainty. Beauty is all there is—and beauty has only one perfect expression, Poetry."[9]

I mentioned earlier that Sartre saw the death of family members as having a profound impact on Mallarmé's spiritual outlook. He talked about the death of Mallarmé's mother and sister and the way it contributed to the poet's religion of absence and Nothingness. In 1879, more than a decade after his metaphysical crisis, another death intervened that once again forced Mallarmé into an evaluation of his spiritual "situation," to use the Sartrean term. Once again Mallarmé reacts in a way that shows the basic structure of religious thought, and once again a conscious effort is made to replace God with something else. This time it was Mallarmé's eight-year-old son, Anatole, who died. The father's memorial to his son was to be a work (*oeuvre*) of some sort, a *tombeau* like the one he had written to Edgar Allan Poe in 1876. The *tombeau* for Anatole never got written, and all that remains is a project for the text in the form of manuscript notes, which Jean-Pierre Richard published in 1961 under the title *Pour un tombeau d'Anatole*.[10]

It's hard to make sense of these notes. Richard, in his excellent introduction, gives what interpretive insights he can on a collection of pages whose very status is ambiguous (are they plans for a poem, are they fragments of that poem, or are they something else altogether?). One thing is clear both from the notes themselves and from Richard's commentary, and that is Mallarmé's continuing flirtation with religion—not just any religion but specifically Catholicism, the faith in which he was raised. Referring, for instance, to the various objects associated with the dead boy in the notes, Richard says that they are "reinterpreted by an entirely metaphysical imagination." The ritual gestures expressing mourning "find their complete meaning only as they are situated in a perspective of religious faith and transcendental salvation" (p. 51). All the traditional gestures, Richard says, maintain for Mallarmé their usual prestige in spite of the poet's rejection of God in 1866. Richard thinks all this represents an effort on Mallarmé's part to establish a "natural foundation" and a "human origin" for religious objects and practices, just as Mallarmé will later find a way of laicizing Catholic ritual by likening it to an ordinary Sunday concert. But the fact is that the impulse to respond religiously remains intact.

And so the death of Anatole is seen as a sort of theophany, Richard says, because it "humanly places in evidence the transcendence, present in him [the boy], of death" (p. 63). Mallarmé speaks continually in the manuscript notes of the survival of his son after death, but without ever using a word for "soul." As Richard points out, however, even though Mallarmé had for some time separated himself from the church and its beliefs, "all the images or expressions he uses to evoke the survival after death of Anatole represent little more than hesitating approximations of this word [that is, soul]." Richard sees other evidence of a Christian doctrine of resurrection in Mallarmé's notes, which show a faith in the process by which "bodily decomposition prepares the release of the spirit" (p. 72).

Mallarmé begins to look a bit more like a Dostoevsky character torn between the temptation to believe and the temptation to renounce. The solution he finds to his dilemma, however, is the same one he had found to his actual crisis of 1866. It is a solution that will allow him to live the resurrection myth, but without giving up the religious skepticism and doubt he had embraced twelve or thirteen years earlier. The only trouble is that the secular solution he envisioned was not realizable. In the crisis letter of 1867 Mallarmé had talked about a work of some sort that would reflect the new supreme synthesis he had arrived at. The solution to the new dilemma in 1879 will be the work I mentioned, a book that will allow the "spiritual essence of his son," as Richard calls it, to endure (p. 84). There is not much in the manuscript notes to specify what sort of oeuvre Mallarmé had in mind this time. As we'll see, though, the whole project of a work or a book for Mallarmé was always conceived from the outset as something that could not be actualized. All that we have of whatever Mallarmé thought he was going to create in memory of his son is the two-hundred-odd sheets of virtually incoherent scribblings Richard has published. The same is true of another, much larger project for a book, which resulted in a similar pile of strange-looking notes. But we'll get to that shortly.

ICONOLOGY-IRONOLOGY

Mallarmé's characteristic procedure thus seems to be to move from religious crisis—brought on by the contemplation of death or Nothingness—to a religious structure in which the divinity has been replaced by an aesthetic quality or object. It may be a Hegelian term like Beauty or the Idea, or it may be a mysterious object like the "work" or "Book" that Mallarmé so often talks about. It thus makes sense to speak of a religion of aesthetics or an aesthetics of religion, as many Mallarmé scholars have done.

This brings us to a curious series of prose pieces that Mallarmé published between 1892 and 1895 and then grouped under the title "Offices"(Religious services). There are three of them: "Plaisir sacré" (Sacred pleasure), "Catholicisme" (Catholicism), and "De même" (The same [that is, the same subject as in the previous essay]). The theme throughout is Catholic rites, the liturgy specifically, treated in a mock-serious way. Mallarmé's conceit is that the liturgy resembles drama or any kind of performance, even a Sunday symphony concert. What is especially valuable about these pieces is that, better than almost any of his other writings, they show Mallarmé straddling the neighboring territories of religion and art. And his rhetorical device for doing so is the use of religious terms in a dual, religious-secular sense.

The cynical premise of "Offices" may be found in the piece called "Catholicism." Mallarmé says this:

> A race, ours, to which has fallen that honor of lending the very womb to the fear that a metaphysical and claustral eternity, otherwise than as human consciousness, has of itself, and of expiring the abyss in some firm yelp into the ages, would be . . . ordinary, unharmed, vague; because not a trace remains, at a moment of posterity—when even life reconquered and born does not blossom.
>
> (OC, p. 391)

What this appears to mean is that religion is born from the fear of eternity once that eternity begins to be perceived as something other than human consciousness contemplating itself (a very Hegelian idea).

Consciousness lends permanence to this fear by expiring (that is, breathing out) the abyss (eternity in its most fearsome aspect as Nothingness) into future ages. This process permits a race, like the French, to endure. Such a race would be ordinary and vague unless life, reconquered (as it is in the Resurrection), is allowed to blossom.

And so church ritual becomes mere show—or mere show becomes church ritual. Religion becomes aestheticized, and art becomes divinized. Religious words become secular, and secular words become religious. "Our communion or share of one to all and of all to one, thus, removed from the barbarous food that the sacrament designates—in the consecration of the host, nonetheless, the Mass, prototype of ceremonials, in spite of the difference with a tradition of art, asserts itself" (OC, p. 394). In the rest of the paragraph where this statement comes from, Mallarmé sets up a confusion between Catholic mass and tragedy. Liturgy fades into drama, participants become actors, and the presence of Christ becomes the presence of the pagan god. " 'Real presence': or that the god should be there, long-winded, complete, mimed from afar by the unobtrusive actor" (OC, p. 394), the poet says in a mocking reference to belief in the actual presence of Christ in the consecrated host.

What goes on in a church is described repeatedly in these writings as a mystery, and here, too, Mallarmé is being intentionally ambiguous. Does he mean mystery as divine truth concealed, or as a medieval mystery play, or in the ordinary sense as something obscure? The medieval mystery play had a liturgical structure, placing the actor-hero in the role of priest and the audience in the role of congregation. Mallarmé evokes this setting repeatedly. "Always that, in this place, a mystery is put on: to what degree does one remain a spectator, or does one presume to have a role in it?" (OC, p. 395). "Mystery, other than representative and [other] than, I'll say, Greek, Play, [religious] service" (OC, p. 393). But this "mystery" is clearly not a sacred event since the author continually makes us aware of a decor that is modern and very secular. We keep seeing the elegant finery of feminine *toilette*, and we keep being reminded that all we're really doing is going to a Sunday concert: "Performance with concert," announces the author in one paragraph, indulging his taste for desecrating art by imitating the style of an advertising poster (OC, p. 393).

"Let's penetrate into the church, with art," says Mallarmé (OC, p. 395). And to show just how much we are penetrating into the church "with art," he describes its interior, during mass, in a passage that cleverly blurs the boundary between art and religion:

The nave with a crowd I won't say of onlookers, but of elite: whoever can
from the most humble source of his gullet hurl out into the vaults the response
in misunderstood but exultant Latin partakes, between everyone and himself,
of sublimity meandering out towards the chorus: for this is the miracle of
singing, one projects oneself as high as the shriek goes. Say whether it is
artifice, prepared better and for many, egalitarian, this communion, aesthetic
at first, in the hero of the divine Drama. Even though the priest of this church
is not qualified as an actor, but officiates—designates and repels the mythic
presence with which one has just merged"

(OC, p. 396).

Read in one way, this passage is quite cynical. The "real presence" of
Catholic doctrine is reduced here to "mythic presence," the priest becomes an actor, and the liturgy becomes a "divine Drama." That's if we
read it as a comment on Catholicism. Read in another way, however,
the passage has the effect of exalting drama (or whatever sort of performance Mallarmé is talking about). This is the source of Mallarmé's
irony. Irony, after all, involves the clash of two meanings or systems of
meaning in a single utterance, frequently where one meaning is serious
and the other is not. I would be reluctant to say that anything here is
entirely serious, but it's likely that Mallarmé is more serious in his comment on art (drama is like a religious ceremony) than he is in his comment on Catholicism (religion is like a Sunday stage performance).

But maybe it doesn't matter whether Mallarmé thought his reflections
in "Offices" were a joke. The fact is that he exerts a great deal of effort
in surrounding the ceremonies of art with the rituals of religion, so that
the first resemble the second as much as possible. In "L'art pour tous"
(Art for everybody) the young Mallarmé had likened art to religion and
had sought to establish a sacred status for art objects (see above, p. 64).
As in "Offices," Mallarmé had focused on the quality of mystery, although in the earlier essay he was a little less mysterious about what *he*
meant by mystery. The tone there was almost as skeptical as in "Offices": "Every sacred thing that wishes to remain sacred envelops itself
in mystery," the poet had said in a passage strongly suggesting that
religions intentionally cloak themselves in mystery just so as to project
a quality of sanctity. But if the young Mallarmé was skeptical about
religion, he appeared to be quite serious about art, for instance, in his
admonition to the artist to "remain an aristocrat" (OC, p. 259).

Guy Delfel, in his book on Mallarmé's aesthetics, talks at length of
Mallarmé's "aesthetic religion."[11] "Aesthetic religion" is exactly the way
Delfel wants to put it, not "religious aesthetics," because for him Mal-

larmé's aesthetics is a kind of religion. But *what* kind of religion needs
to be clarified. As Delfel says, Christianity has accustomed us to the
idea that the existence of God and the immortality of the soul are necessary components of any religion. That is not true, he says; Mallarmé
is a perfect example of a religious man who believed in neither.[12] And
he *did* believe in neither, Delfel insists. Mallarmé remained a man of
faith ("You can't do without Eden"); it's just that faith was a part of a
religion that did not include God or personal salvation.[13]

What did it include? Delfel agrees with a great many other commentators on Mallarmé that one important ingredient was the notion of
essences. He speaks of Mallarmé's tendency to renounce sensible matter
in favor of the "transcendence of aesthetic essences."[14] In *L'univers imaginaire de Mallarmé* (Mallarmé's imaginary universe) Jean-Pierre Richard speaks of Mallarmé's belief in the possibility of discovering, by
means of some sensible form of language, an "idea" inside an object.
Richard renames that idea "concrete essence."[15] As he shows with many
examples, Mallarmé frequently expressed a belief in essences, notions,
and ideas. In a passage I quoted before, Mallarmé describes the process
by which a "fact of nature" is "transposed" (through poetry) into its
"vibratory almost-disappearance," with the result that the "pure notion" emanates from it (*OC*, p. 368).[16] The whole concept of poetic
language that I described, with its strong endorsement of virtuality and
vagueness, rests on the conviction that there is an essence to be discovered, through language, in things. Perhaps that is Mallarmé's Eden. A
sentence like the following (which I cite out of context) could have been
written only by a hardened essentialist: "The moment of the Notion of
an object is thus the moment of the reflection of its pure present in itself,
or its present purity" (*OC*, p. 853). Never mind what this statement
means in its widest applications. What we need to keep in mind is the
urge—call it Platonist, call it Hegelian—to see essences or absolutes in
things and in language. It is yet another example of the mystification
with which Mallarmé surrounds both art and the vocation of being an
artist. Is the old joker fooling us again? What difference does it make?
His successors seem to have taken him quite seriously, and that's all that
matters for us.

The question remains what Mallarmé's mysticism has to do with literary works. What would a literary work—an actual book or poem—
be like if art really were invested with the kind of religious essence that
Mallarmé suggests? Mallarmé certainly *wrote* plenty of literary works,
but they are no help at all. What we are interested in is his thinking

about what literary works are. The good thing is that Mallarmé wrote so much about this object called the work (*l'oeuvre*) or the Book (*le Livre*). The bad thing is that what he wrote is often indecipherable, and what isn't indecipherable leaves more questions than answers about what Mallarmé is saying. On that less-than-hopeful note, let's turn to the Book.

... AND IN THE END IS THE BOOK

"Everything, in the world, exists to end up in a book," Mallarmé wrote in a piece published in 1895 (*OC*, p. 378). Fine. But what is a book (or Book)? This question is one of the trickiest in Mallarmé scholarship because Mallarmé used the terms *livre* (book), *Livre* (Book), *oeuvre* (work), and *Oeuvre* (Work) in different senses at different times and in ways that indicate that he meant different things by them. His musings about this elusive something began in the context of his crisis of 1866, and they can be organized into about four stages. I already quoted the passage from Mallarmé's letter to Henri Cazalis in which he mentions the work (*oeuvre*) he is contemplating and says that this work will contain certain of his poems. Toward the end of the same letter Mallarmé speaks of the heartache he would experience if he were to "enter the supreme Disappearance" without having finished his work, "which is *The Work*, the Great Work, as the alchemists, our ancestors, used to say."[17] The last phrase contains an example of an additional interpretive problem, one that does not come through in English translation. The passage in French reads, "ce ne serait pas sans un serrement de coeur réel que j'entrerais dans la Disparition suprême, si je n'avais pas fini mon oeuvre, qui est *L'Oeuvre*, le Grand'Oeuvre, comme disaient les alchimistes, nos ancêtres." The word *oeuvre* in French is normally feminine. Mallarmé uses it here in the masculine, which is reserved for two senses: the complete opus of an artist and, in the phrase *grand oeuvre,* the philosopher's stone of the alchemists (the stone that transforms base metals into gold).

In 1885, almost twenty years after his crisis, Mallarmé wrote a letter to the symbolist poet Paul Verlaine in response to a request for biographical information. The letter has come to be called the "Autobiography," and it, too, has a reference to the Work, or Book:

> I have always dreamed of and sought something else, with the patience of an alchemist, ready to sacrifice for it every vanity and every satisfaction, just as

in the old days one used to burn one's furniture and the ceiling beams in order to stoke the furnace of the philosopher's stone [*Grand Oeuvre*]. What? it's difficult to say: a book, quite simply, in several volumes, a book that will be a book, architectural and premeditated, and not a collection of chance inspirations no matter how marvelous they might be . . . I will go so far as to say: the Book, persuaded that, in the end, there is only one [. . .] The Orphic explanation of the Earth, which is the sole duty of the poet and the literary game *par excellence*.

(OC, pp. 662–63)

Whatever it is that Mallarmé has in mind in this letter, there's no doubt that it's something different from just a collection of poems.

A decade after the "Autobiography" Mallarmé published a series of four essays under the title "Quant au Livre" (Concerning the Book). Once again, it is not entirely clear what Mallarmé means by "Book." In the first essay, "L'action restreinte" (The restricted action), he explores the mysterious nature of the act of writing. In the second, "Étalages" (Displays), he speaks of the commercial aspects of the Book. The third, "Le Livre, instrument spirituel" (The Book, spiritual instrument), examines the dialectic between the physical book and its spiritual dimension. The fourth is a meditation on language and reading (and other things).

By far the most interesting document is Le *"Livre" de Mallarmé: Premières recherches sur des documents inédits* (Mallarmé's "Book": Preliminary research on some unpublished documents), edited by Jacques Scherer.[18] This book itself requires some description. Almost half of it is a scholarly study, by the editor, of the other half. That other half is a printed version of some manuscript notes Mallarmé had made. Scherer thinks Mallarmé wrote the notes in the last few years of his life, although he may have begun them earlier. They certainly respond to ideas he had had since as far back as 1866.[19] Mallarmé had left instructions to have these notes and other loose papers burned after his death. Perhaps we would all have been better off if those instructions had been followed, but thanks to Mallarmé's disciple, Paul Valéry, who intervened after Mallarmé's death to preserve the notes, we now have at our disposal Scherer's pile of 202 sheets of . . . well, it's hard to say what they're *of*. Some pages do not even contain words but are filled instead with geometric designs and patterns. One page has simply a set of lines, points, and arrows arranged in an almost, but not quite, symmetrical fashion (74 [B]; see illustration). Others have elaborate mathematical calculations. Many pages contain writing, diagrams, and numbers. Much of

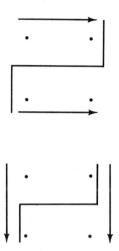

From Jacques Scherer, Le *"Livre" de Mallarmé: Premières recherches sur des documents inédits* (Paris: Gallimard, 1957), p. 74(B).

the writing looks like instructions for a performance of some sort, while some of it consists of abstract terms and abbreviations arranged in complicated patterns. And some of it is just downright incomprehensible.

There has been considerable controversy over what this material means. Scherer is convinced that the sheets he has selected contain plans for the Book that Mallarmé had envisioned in his other writings. Other scholars are not so sure, some because they don't see the same themes that Scherer sees in these notes, others because they don't think there was ever any such thing as a Book that Mallarmé projected but never created.[20] But it's not absolutely necessary to settle the controversy over whether Scherer's notes have to do with the same thing that Mallarmé refers to in other writings when he uses the words *book* and *work* (or whether he always means the same thing in those writings). The notes are a fascinating document that shows, at some indefinable and pre-publishable stage, Mallarmé's musings on some sort of book or work. There is much to be said about these musings, and I'm afraid I will have to say it piecemeal since the Book is central not only to religion, but also to the remaining two parts of *this* book. For now, let's talk about religion.

In the other writings about the Book there is not much to suggest that the concept was fundamentally religious. Certainly the idea of a Book with the kind of mystical significance Mallarmé associates with it conjures up, without much effort, the idea of the Scriptures. The title "Le

Livre, instrument spirituel" has a mystical, religious ring to it. At one moment in the essay of that title Mallarmé says that the crease in the page of a book (any book) is "almost religious" (*OC*, p. 379). The Book as the "Orphic explanation of the earth" is clearly a religious, if not a Christian, concept. The essays in "Quant au Livre" betray the same taste for humorous profanation as the essays in "Offices" (which, curiously, are placed directly after "Quant au Livre" in the *Oeuvres complètes*). But the thing being profaned in "Quant au Livre" is not as clearly religious as in "Offices": in "Quant au Livre" it is more the commonplace idea of the sacredness of literature (which is characteristically profaned by its juxtaposition with the much more commonplace idea of the commerciality of literature).

But Scherer's manuscript notes are another story. I mentioned that many of the pages in that collection contain instructions for a performance of some sort. Mallarmé appears to have in mind an elaborately planned event that by the simplest description will just be a reading of his poems (or the Work, or the Book). The event is to be presided over by an enigmatic personage named the operator. There are repeated references to various elements of the event, including where it is to take place. For instance, we read of a yacht from time to time, and there is even a page that contains the rudiments of a narrative, something like a plot for the event (169 [A]).

In the midst of these stage directions (or whatever they are) are words and phrases that suggest a religious ceremony. The phrase *Messe en Musique* (Mass in Music) occurs at one point (3 [A]), and *passion* occurs a few pages later. What sort of reading is it to be? We find this strange note:

Lect

12 personnes.

Lect. la

messe. La +   (34 [B])

I don't pretend to know exactly what this means, but *Lect.* is clearly an abbreviation for *Lecture* (Reading) or *Lecteur* (Reader). This curious little passage seems to have something to do with a reading of the mass. Among the directions concerning the location we read "cloister" several times. And included in the ceremony are two sacraments, baptism and marriage (168, 169 [A], 182). There is even a reference (crossed out subsequently) to "laicized priests" (7 [A]).

The most compelling evidence of the religious nature of the event is the numerous terms that suggest a mystery play. Over and over again we see the words *hero, drama, mystery, hymn, theatre,* usually abbreviated and arranged in patterns on the page (rarely as part of intelligible sentences). Mystery plays were originally performed with priests and clerics before an altar. They typically represented a biblical story, like the Passion story or some aspect of it, and, as I have said, they frequently had a liturgical structure. In France, during the sixteenth century, popular audiences were fond of seeing scenes with different settings in close succession. Advances in stagecraft made it possible to rearrange the stage quickly and show a variety of scenes in a short time. Mallarmé seems to have something like that in mind in his directions. In addition to the many references to drama, mystery, and hymns, we read of a complicated scheme that will allow the reader or operator of Mallarmé's event to shuffle and redistribute (for example, in little pigeonholes) pages from the Book in the place where the event is staged. He speaks at one point of "mobile pages" (112 [A]), and at another he says that "the volume is mobile" (119 [A]).

One has the impression that the entire set of notes is a plan for a mise-en-scène of the mysteries Mallarmé talked about so much in "Offices." Everything suggests a hieratic stage event, with the same combination of elements as Mallarmé had offered in "Offices": mystery play, mass, passion, tragedy. Even the irony is reproduced here because interspersed in the baffling array of stage directions are equally numerous and equally complicated calculations of the profits the author will realize from the sale of tickets and books. It's really quite astonishing how the sacred impulse was always so reflexively tied to the urge to profane.

Scherer's notes were not available to the public until they were published in 1957. So why talk about them? No one read them for more than a half-century after their author's death, and even then only a handful of Mallarmé specialists have shown much interest in them. The reason is that they show, in a form uninhibited by any concern for the response of a readership or audience, in a form that thus reveals the extremes to which Mallarmé's thinking reached, an impulse that did have a significant impact on succeeding generations. This is the religious impulse I've been talking about.

I've been careful to show all along how the serious and the sacred in Mallarmé are often subverted by the facetious and the profane, and I've said that this creates Mallarmé's special irony. But why pay so much attention to Mallarmé's humor when his legacy is so serious? That is the whole point. In *After the New Criticism* Frank Lentricchia demonstrates how American literary criticism, when it imports theories from France, as it did so avidly in the last few decades, has consistently concentrated on the Platonic elements, ignoring other important aspects of the theories—for instance, their historical aspects.[21] The implication is that the American critical mind would insist on seeing the eternal and the essential even if the eternal and the essential were not there. When French structuralism caught on in the 1960s, Lentricchia thinks, it was "mediated" by American critics in such a way as to preserve one of the most important articles of faith from the era of New Criticism, namely that literary artworks are timeless objects containing eternal and unchanging values. Now I don't believe that structuralism is entirely free of this faith any more than the New Criticism was, but Lentricchia's point is that the Americans largely overlooked those elements of structuralism that were primarily secular, namely those that stressed historical change.

If what Lentricchia says is true—if it is true that the American critical mind tends toward the eternal and essential—then it makes sense that it should invent a Mallarmean legacy that includes only the serious, religious side of his aesthetic and overlooks the threatening, subversive element that always accompanies the religious one. And this invented legacy is entirely consistent with the notion of a flight from Eden. Not only is the religious element there in Mallarmé, but also American criticism has focused on it almost to the exclusion of elements that stand in opposition to it. With such an attitude it makes sense that American criticism continues to be bound by the urge to return to mysticism and essentialism, in short, to Eden.

CHAPTER FIVE

Icon and Logos,
or Why Russian Philosophy
Is Always Theology

Russia does not really have a philosophical tradition in the same sense that other European cultures do. If you were looking into the subject for the first time and went to one of the English-language anthologies of Russian thinkers, you would be amazed to see, first, that almost no one who lived before the late eighteenth century was represented and, second, that most of the writers who were represented were not philosophers at all. If you had ever had a course in Russian literature, you would be surprised to recognize in the anthology the names of a great many writers you had heard of as either novelists—Dostoevsky and Tolstoy have earned the distinction of being considered "thinkers"—or literary critics. There would be political writers and social critics (which in nineteenth-century Russia often mean the same thing as literary critics), and there would be religious thinkers. But almost none could be classified as philosophers in the same way we classify, say, Kant or Hegel as philosophers.

Historians, in their search for themes and patterns, have not yet been able to decide whether the characteristic style of Russian thought is secular, religious, or a maddening, Dostoevskian hesitation between the two. For that matter they have not been able to decide which writers to include in books on the history of Russian thought (or philosophy, when they insist on using the word). The Polish scholar Andrzej Walicki, for example, has written a book titled *A History of Russian Thought from the Enlightenment to Marxism*, which, though it certainly includes sections on the important religious thinkers of the nineteenth and early twentieth centuries, leaves the reader with the impression that the greatest contribution of Russian thought was in the area of social and political criticism.[1] The bulk of his discussion of the twentieth century is devoted to the evolution of political thought that results in Leninism. The reader would have a much different impression from reading another of the standard works on the subject, N. O. Lossky's *History of Russian Philosophy*.[2] Lossky was himself a religious man who emigrated to this country and spent the last years of his scholarly career at the Saint Vladimir Russian Orthodox Seminary of New York. Although he mentions most of the social and political thinkers that Walicki discusses, he devotes more than half his book to mystical and religious thinkers of the early twentieth century. One is likely to come away from Lossky's book with the idea that the religious current in Russian thought is central and the political current an aberration.

Of course, it would be foolish to pretend that either current, the religious or the secular, exists to the exclusion of the other. Russian culture contains a great many dualisms, and this is one of them. But it distorts matters to decide with Walicki that the early twentieth century in Russia is largely the affair of Marxism simply because Marxism triumphed in the end. As it happens, the late nineteenth and early twentieth centuries were an extraordinarily rich period for religious thought in Russia. Naturally, few of the strictly religious ideas of this period caught on or had any obvious lasting effect in postrevolutionary Soviet culture, and many of the most important writers of this era, like Lossky, emigrated to the West shortly after the revolution. Nonetheless, this is precisely the period when a great creative upheaval took place in Russian culture, the brief interlude of freedom that produced many influential works in Russian arts and letters. It is the period of the transformation that Eagleton speaks of, a period that yields an uncanny number of isms in an amazingly short time: symbolism, Acmeism, Futurism, Formalism, and on and on. It is also the period that produced the young Roman Jakobson.

My own view is that the religious current in Russian thought is far more determining than the secular, political current, at least as concerns later developments in literary aesthetics in the West. There is no doubt that Marxism triumphed politically in Russia, even if we countenance the argument that Soviet Marxism is merely another form of religious faith. But the mass emigration of intellectuals who found by the late 1920s or earlier that the new regime had no place for them—and Jakobson was among these—brought to the West the legacy of centuries of religious thought, often in covert form.

ICONS

A critical moment for Russian culture occurred before there was any such thing as Russia and more than two centuries before the country that later became Russia converted to Christianity. It has to do with the church father Saint John of Damascus, who led the theological battle in the eighth century against the forces of iconoclasm in the Byzantine Empire. Images representing religious figures had been in use among Christians for some time before the days of Saint John, but there had been opposition to them among certain believers on the grounds that worshiping them meant worshiping false gods. Iconoclasm gained political force by the eighth century, and in 754 Emperor Constantine V convened a church council in Constantinople at which the veneration of icons was declared both heretical and illegal.

John of Damascus was a theologian who devoted much of his life to defending icons against the iconoclasts. Since he lived first in Syria and then in Palestine, under the protection of a Moslem caliph, he was free to write in defense of icons at a time when Christians elsewhere were having difficulty embracing that position. When the Ecumenical Council of Nicaea was convened in 787 to condemn iconoclasm and reverse the position of the Council of 754, church authorities used many of the arguments that John had presented in his defense of icons.

The case for the defense of icons rests on the analogy between icons and the Incarnation. God is invisible, immaterial, immeasurable. By the Incarnation, however, God became visible in his Son and thereby partook of the flesh and blood of corporeal beings.[3] This meant that through Christ men were able to have a limited understanding of the intangible, since visible things serve as corporeal models of the invisible (*DI*, p. 20). The Son is therefore an image (*eikon* in Greek) of the invisible God, since an image is defined as the result of God's having become visible by partaking of flesh and blood (*DI*, p. 19; *PG*, 94:1240c). Images, or icons, thus stand in the same relation to God as does the Word made flesh, or Christ. "I do not draw an image of the immortal Godhead, but I paint the image of God who became visible in the flesh, for if it is impossible to make a representation of a spirit, how much more impossible is it to depict the God who gives life to the spirit?" (*DI*, p. 16). To refuse to bow before images is the same as refusing to bow before the Son of God (*DI,* p. 28).

John's purpose was specifically to refute the iconoclasts' notion that venerating icons meant venerating false gods. The iconoclasts wanted to prohibit the worship of icons because they regarded such worship as idolatry, and idolatry (*eidololatreia*) implies the adoration (*latreia*, a form of respect due only to God) of idols (*eidola*). Adoring idols thus meant considering them as gods, in the view of the iconoclasts. But venerating icons is different from idolatry, says John. For one thing, the form of respect is not the absolute adoration that should be reserved for God alone; it is, literally, a bowing down before (*proskynesis*), a form of obeisance that one makes to people or things to whom honor is due. But more important is that images are not held to *be* gods. One cannot make an image of the invisible, immeasurable God, says John, and it is therefore absurd to suppose that in bowing down before an image one is bowing down before a god different from the one, immeasurable God.

The consequences of this doctrine are incalculable for Eastern Orthodox theology. The fundamental idea is the act of condescension or humiliation by which God became flesh in his Son. The Greek word for this act is *kenosis*, which means an emptying and refers to the way in which God emptied himself of his divinity to take on the form of man in his Son. The condescension is seen in many different realms of being and is thus essential to the broadness of the doctrine that John outlines. Christ is God made flesh and represents a humiliation of God the Father. Images are visible things, and "visible things are corporeal models which provide a vague understanding of intangible things"; so images, too, are a humiliation (p. 20). In fact, all creation is the result of the same kind of humiliation, and thus, says John, to prohibit the veneration of images is to assume that matter itself is despicable. But matter is not despicable, for it was created by God, as were men and their human practices (pp. 60–61): "You see that the law and everything it commanded and all our own practices are meant to sanctify the work of our hands, leading us through matter to the invisible God" (p. 67).

If the iconoclasts were afraid that Christians were worshiping inanimate objects with pictures drawn on them, John felt he could allay their fears by pointing out one of the most important facts of icon veneration: the honor given the image is transferred to the prototype, to what the image stands for (p. 40). God himself is never represented in icons; icon painters had at their disposal a limited number of subjects, usually Christ, the Mother of God, and a few saints. But by the doctrine of God's condescension an image of any of these subjects is an image of God incarnate, and so the prototype of an icon is ultimately the divinity. The essential thing about icon veneration is that the image is an incarnation and that one venerates the image not as God but as the image of

God incarnate (p. 40). "We see the invisible made visible through the visible representation," in the words of Simeon the Great, as John cites them (p. 104).

This is the doctrine that was adopted in the final definition (*horos*) of the Council of Nicaea in 787, and it is the one that has been in force ever since. That definition begins by recognizing the two natures of Christ—one divine, one earthly. The two natures are united in one person, or hypostasis. We make iconographic representations, the council members said, "for the purpose of ascertaining the incarnation of God the Word."[4] "He who venerates the icon venerates the hypostasis of the person depicted on it."[5]

There is thus an implicit epistemology in this doctrine of icon veneration, if epistemology is the right word. The doctrine of prototypes means that the worshiper has to *see* the icon in a different way from that in which he or she sees other objects. An ordinary act of seeing an object is not accompanied in most people by an idealist sense that the object they are perceiving is not physically real, that it is merely an intuition of an object that can never really be known in itself. But the perception of the icon apparently must be accompanied by such a sense because the physical object, the piece of wood adorned with colors and lacquers forming a picture of the Mother of God, is understood as a mere facade for the grace that stands behind it. One has to look *through* the wood and paint into the invisible and immaterial, into something beyond that cannot be seen. The icon is like Christ: it has two natures united in one object. Christ's two natures meant that through him mere mortals could participate in the grace of God the Father, in a limited way, because they shared with Christ at least his physical nature. The icon performs the same service: it allows the worshiper a limited contact with the immeasurable through the intermediary of sensible matter. So icon veneration has a kind of idealism built into it that operates in the mind of the ordinary worshiper.

Plenty of things happened in the history of Russian Orthodoxy to insure that this doctrine would subsist and that it would be intuitively accepted by as many people as possible. For instance, the Orthodox church required that icon artists work anonymously. The main idea was that they were to work for God's glory, not their own. But the requirement was also founded on the belief that the icon artist contributed nothing of his own to his pictures. Every iconic image was meant to be an imitation of a previous image, which was itself an imitation of a previous image, and so on, back to an image based on an actual physical view of the person represented. Icons were thus never designed to be appreciated for their beauty. The "aesthetic" posture of the viewer was discouraged by the prominent sense that the picture was authorless and not "real": it always pointed back either to a tradition or to an invisible prototype. The principles of icon theology were destined to become widely known as icons themselves became increasingly common. By the sixteenth century they were already frequently displayed in private homes, and thereafter they became a fixture.

LOGOS

In Christian theology the expression *Word of God* refers to the Second Person of the Trinity, or Christ. Christ is the Word (Logos) made Flesh. Icon and Logos are thus closely related concepts, since the nature of the icon derives from the Incarnation of the Word. Logos is a complicated term. In Greek it refers to a whole range of things, from spoken discourse in general, to narrative, to thought, to the New Testament Word of God. In theology the chief ambiguity of the Logos is between its sense as Son of God and the ordinary sense having to do with language. Theology, I said earlier, is God-talk, or God-word. In Russian it is *bogoslovie,* from *bog,* "god," and *slovo,* "word." The very term for the discipline is meaningfully ambiguous.

Because of the intimacy of the concepts *icon* and *logos,* because of the hesitation of logos, or word, between theological and other meanings, philosophy of language in Russia has generally been explicitly or implicitly a kind of theology. The late nineteenth century brought a revival of theological thought in Russia together with a surge in philosophical activity. But philosophy and theology were characteristically not entirely distinct in this period just as in others, and one result of the revival of both disciplines was the appearance in the early twentieth century of an Orthodox philosophy of language.

Naftali Prat, a Russian scholar now living in Israel, has investigated this often-neglected episode in the history of the early modern era in an article titled "Orthodox Philosophy of Language in Russia."[6] Prat identifies several sources of this trend: Platonism as it traditionally dominates Orthodox theology, German idealism, Husserlian phenomenology, and Russian poets. The dominant source, however, is Platonism, and Platonism implies the doctrine of the logos. Prat shows that logos in this tradition has to do with the unity of thought and language and the notion of adequately expressing a thought by means of the word. In the Russian philosophico-theological tradition the message of Plato's *Cratylus* is not the conventionality of language but rather that part of the name that *is* given by nature. Names express the essence of named objects through the *eidos,* or idea, of that object, Prat says (p. 3). In a strictly religious arena, in the early years of the twentieth century, language and the nature of names were the subject of an intense debate. At issue was the doctrine of *imjaslavie,* or glorification of the name, according to which God is immediately present in his name. Prat believes that the dispute over this Christian Platonic doctrine gave the "decisive impulse" to establishing an Orthodox philosophy of language in this century (p. 2).

If the logical origin of icons is in the doctrine of the logos, then it is not surprising that the two concepts should have analogous natures or that the logos should suggest an epistemology similar to the one we saw in the icon. The icon contains its reference to an invisible prototype. The logos contains its invisible essence or idea, whether by "logos" we mean the Second Person of the Trinity or simply a name. Icon and logos require a similar act of seeing, one that goes beyond the physical object toward an immaterial essence, idea, or grace, and thus they come together in the notion of idealism. Neither concept can exist without the ultimately Platonic sense that the physical thing stands for, or points to, something purely ideal.

Early modern literary aesthetics in Russia is completely dominated by this kind of thinking. I have not been able to find any important thinkers of that age that escape it. Even the most "scientific" writers, like Jakobson and his precursors the Formalists, perpetuate the idealist assumptions underlying Orthodox theology and language philosophy. Russian literary aesthetics in this period and the related disciplines that have fostered so much of our subsequent thinking about literary texts in the twentieth century are really an iconology, a logology, an Orthodox Christology, if only in disguise.

But sometimes it is not in disguise at all. We have an entirely false picture of the intellectual climate of turn-of-the-century Russia because all we ever hear about is the ostensibly secular and scientific thinkers that have been adopted by later twentieth-century schools of criticism. There is a whole range of immensely important and influential thinkers who unabashedly used the language of Orthodox theology. Some were genuinely religious; others were not (or were less so). Some continued to write until well after the revolution, although for those who had not

emigrated it became difficult toward the end of the 1920s to write anything that sounded like theology. If we take a look at what some of the
more overtly religious writers were saying about art and language, then
we can see that they did not form an obscure, deviant branch of philosophy in an otherwise secularized age. On the contrary, they are the
ones that set out the terms of the discourse; the "secular" thinkers appropriated those terms. There is a great deal more coherence in this age
than we might think. After all, was it merely an accidental combination
of words that Shklovsky, the great Formalist, hit upon when he titled
one of the central aesthetic proclamations of the day "The Resurrection
of the Word"?

VLADIMIR SOLOV'EV

It makes sense that the best (some might say the first, or even the only)
Russian philosopher of the nineteenth century should be as deeply a
religious man as Vladimir Sergeevich Solov'ev (1853–1900). Like so
many other Russian thinkers, Solov'ev was not only religious but fundamentally ambivalent about Russian Christianity, flirting at various
stages of his life with Orthodoxy's two greatest temptations, atheism
and Catholicism. He was staggeringly precocious, beginning his mature
writing career when he was in his twenties. He was astonishingly ver-
satile, writing philosophy, poetry, and humorous theatre. And he was
enormously influential: the whole symbolist movement in Russian letters
finds the source for much of its essential thinking in him.

The root of Solov'ev's thought is the same as for John of Damascus
and the same as for the entire Russian kenotic tradition. It all goes back
to Christ, the Word incarnate: two natures, one person. Solov'ev's *Lectures on Godmanhood,* which he began writing at the age of twenty-
four and which contain many of the principles he was to write about
for the rest of his career, take their point of departure in the notion of
Christ's—and consequently man's—dual nature.[7] Duality underlies
everything for Solov'ev, who is an idealist in virtually every sense of the
term. There is God and his creation; God and man; Christ's divinity
and Christ's humanity; the world of ideas and the world of matter; the
absolute, permanent, objective idea in the individual and the purely subjective, personal idea; and on and on.

History is the dynamic process of the unfolding of the world spirit,
which Solov'ev defines as the "tendency toward the incarnation of the

Godhead in the world" (SS, 3:145). The Incarnation of the Word is the last link in a long chain of physical and historical incarnations. It is the crowning event in history because through it Christ abdicates his divine glory, thus simultaneously divinizing his humanity and humanizing his divinity. With the Incarnation it is no longer a question of simply a transcendent God: we now have the God-Logos, the personal incarnation of God. The Incarnation points up the duality of man's own nature and makes possible Solov'ev's dream of Godmanhood, by which he means an assertion of the divine and absolute that inheres in each of us (as it did in Christ through the miracle of the Incarnation). Solov'ev's dualism is thus not the dualism of radically separate entities; the whole point of *Lectures on Godmanhood* and the underlying doctrine of the Incarnation is to show the original unity and the continuity of God and nature. God inheres in nature; the ideal inheres in the material.

This is how we get to Solov'ev's doctrine of beauty and art. Beauty in nature and beauty in art are not different in kind for Solov'ev. Art is not an imitation of nature or even a mere duplication of nature's work; it is rather a continuation of what is begun by nature. What is begun by nature is the same kind of incarnation we found in the Godman. Beauty in nature is "the transformation of matter through the incarnation in it of another, supramaterial principle," Solov'ev says in an essay called "Beauty in Nature."[8] Thus beauty in nature is ultimately the expression of a purely ideal content. It is the "incarnation of an idea" (SS, 6:43) or, as Solov'ev puts it later on in the essay, the "sensible incarnation of a certain absolutely objective, completely single idea" (SS, 6:73). A diamond, for example, is an object of beauty because it represents an almost perfect embodiment (incarnation) of an idea, namely the idea of illuminated stone. The beauty of a diamond resides neither exclusively in its substance (coal) nor exclusively in the light it reflects and refracts, but in both. The substance provides a means for embodying the supramaterial, ideal agent of light, and this very embodiment embodies the idea of illuminated stone.

In an essay titled "The General Meaning of Art" Solov'ev shows where nature leaves off and art picks up.[9] "The beauty of nature," he says, "is merely a veil cast over evil life and not a transfiguration of that life. Man, therefore, with his rational consciousness, must be not only the end of the process of nature but also the means by which an ideal principle can exert an inverse, deeper, and fuller influence on nature" (SS, 6:78). Man enhances and furthers the work of the ideal in nature by creating artworks, and this act of creation consists precisely in the type of incarnation whose result we see in diamonds and other objects of natural beauty. Beauty always represents the incarnation of an idea. The artistic activity of man incarnates an idea by uniting "a spiritual content and a sensible expression"; thus, through the "mutual penetration" of this content and this idea, "a material phenomenon that has truly become beautiful, that is, that has truly incarnated in itself an idea, must become just as enduring and immortal as the idea itself" (SS, p. 82).

The repeated use of the word *incarnate* and its various related forms in this essay is sufficient to show the theological character of Solov'ev's thought. The root notion is always condescension or kenosis, which translates, in aesthetics, as any process by which something that is not physical gets expressed in something that is. The triple task of art, says Solov'ev, consists in "(1) the direct objectification of those deepest internal determinations and qualities of the living idea that cannot be expressed by nature, (2) the animation of natural beauty and, through this, (3) the immortalization of the individual phenomena of that beauty" (SS, 6:84). It is almost senseless to speak of an iconology in Solov'ev, if by iconology we refer to a separate science of icons. Everything is iconic for him. All creation is pervaded with the ideal, and almost everything would seem to invite the kind of perceptual act I just described. But artworks are even more iconic than other things because in them the work of the ideal has been enhanced by man. More than other things, presumably, artworks highlight their own iconicity.

ANDREI BELY

Bely's most ambitious essay from his symbolist period is "The Emblematics of Meaning."[10] It is terribly long, maddeningly digressive, and absurdly disorganized. There is little likelihood that many of Bely's contemporaries (or successors, for that matter) bothered to read through and understand the whole thing, and so it is equally unlikely that one can speak of any direct impact the essay had on subsequent thought. And yet the essay contains perhaps the essence of Bely's whole doctrine. That essence is hinted at in the way the fields of language theory and theology usually overlap in Bely's thought. In "The Emblematics of Meaning," however, Bely has stepped back from language theory to confront a more general area, one that subsumes language theory. His concern in this essay is meaning, understood in its broadest sense. Meaning is involved in virtually every realm of human endeavor, so Bely's essay of logical necessity takes account of not only language, art, and artistic language but also many other fields. His approach to meaning amounts to a kind of formalistic, secularized, twentieth-century version of Orthodox iconology.

There are two broad categories of meaning, as Bely sees it: symbolic meaning and emblematic meaning. Symbolic meaning is meaning presented in images; emblematic meaning is meaning presented in concepts. Symbolic meaning corresponds to creation, emblematic meaning to cognition. But the formal process by which both types of meaning are apprehended is identical, and since Bely could find no generic term to cover the two species *symbolic* and *emblematic,* he simply used the word *emblematics* in his title. "The Emblematics of Meaning" means that meaning *is* emblematic, which means that it comes into being by the formal process Bely defines in his essay.

Bely calls that formal process symbolization, by which he means something very similar to incarnation. Symbolization starts with an ideal quality and embodies (incarnates) that quality in some intelligible medium (an image or a concept). The result is a symbol or emblem. Bely was so pleased with his description of the logical origins of all meaning that he made a diagram of the various fields of human endeavor to show how they stack up in relation to one another. The diagram is a large triangle subdivided into many small triangles, each standing for a field of human knowledge (*S*, p. 639; *SE*, p. 145). The schema is hierarchical: the closer a field is to the ideal, which appears at the summit of the triangle, the farther up on the triangle it is located. The farther it is from the ideal, the lower down it appears. "Higher" fields are thus characterized by meanings with a greater ideal component, lower ones by meanings with a lower ideal component, which is to say that their meanings are more concrete. Any field on the triangle is in a sense derived from the one immediately above it by the same process of symbolization that yields all objects of meaning, and thus it stands in relation to that superior field as an object of meaning stands in relation to its ideal content. The higher field supplies the ideal for the lower field, and the lower field then "symbolizes" that ideal.

What is peculiar about Bely's system is how he appropriates the fundamental terms of Russian Orthodox iconology and logology but corrupts them by integrating into his system a set of godless philosophical concepts taken from some of the neo-Kantian thinkers then in vogue in Russia. I said earlier that the honor given to an icon is transferred to its prototype, which must ultimately be understood as the divinity. What is the prototype for Bely? We can find it by looking at the summit of his triangle since the summit shows what is symbolized by everything beneath it. The highest small triangle on Bely's diagram bears the inscription *Value*. At the summit of this triangle, which is also the summit of the entire diagram, are the words *Symbol Embodied* (or *Symbol Incarnate*—there is no distinction in Russian).

The term *value* comes from the epistemological system of Heinrich Rickert. Rickert had reformed the Kantian theory of knowledge by asserting that values are the true objects of ordinary acts of cognition (see above, p. 51). Values are apprehended by an act of the will because for Rickert ordinary cognition has come to be based on a kind of ethical affirmation of truth. In connecting the ethical element with the will, Rickert was simply following Kant, for whom the will is the faculty that comes into play in our decisions of right and wrong. But for Kant the will connects us with the realm of freedom, and freedom is a transcendental idea (like the idea of God or the idea of immortality), something we cannot "know," something metaphysical that is not accessible to ordinary knowledge. Oddly enough, however, Rickert was antimetaphysical and saw his theory of knowledge as entirely scientific. His whole system was meant to reject the Kantian notion that there is a suprasensible world existing beyond the world of appearances. In fact, the modern notion of value philosophy, something that had just come into fashion at the end of the nineteenth century, represented an effort to provide secular and relativistic answers to traditional ethical questions. So when Bely jumps on the value bandwagon, he is for all intents and purposes committing himself to an antireligious philosophy.

But the structure of Bely's system is the structure of Orthodox iconology, and Bely is not in the least troubled by the easy mingling of religious and nonreligious terms that characterizes his essay. The summit of the value triangle, I said, is labeled *Symbol Embodied*. Bely often refers to this supreme term simply as the Symbol (with a capital *S* to distinguish it from ordinary symbols). What he appears to mean by it is the prototype of all symbol-forming activity, together with the reminder that such activity is a type of incarnation (embodiment). The ultimate, prototypical principle of value, and thus of everything meaningful, is the Symbol. How does the Symbol come to be expressed? Bely uses the example of the three triangles situated immediately under the value triangle: metaphysics, theosophy, and theurgy. "The Symbol is expressed in symbolizations," he says, "and, in the present case, metaphysics, theosophy, and theurgy are such symbolizations" (*S*, p. 101; *SE*, p. 160). What is symbolization? "The Symbol cannot be given without symbolization. This is why we embody it in an image. The image embodying the Symbol is called a symbol only in a more general sense of the word. God, for example, is such a symbol, when seen as an existing something" (*S*, p. 105; *SE*, p. 164).

Here we can see how closely bound Bely is to his theological tradition. Remember that "embody" translates the Russian word that is used for the theological sense of "incarnate." Symbolization is the same sort of thing as incarnation. The last sentence of the passage I just quoted should leave no doubt about the analogy. How does God come to be "seen as an existing something"? Through his creation, or through his Word—that is, through the condescension that occurs in the act of Incarnation. A few sentences after this one Bely says, "The reality created by God is a symbolic reality" (*S*, p. 106; *SE*, p. 164). Thus symbolization is like God's creation, which is like the Incarnation of the Word.

This brings us back to the epistemology of icon worship. Bely chooses to call his objects symbols instead of icons, but the posture of the perceiver is the same in both instances. Like the Christian worshiper venerating icons, the perceiver of symbols is always looking through a level of concretion to something invisible beyond, and Bely has seen fit to call that something value (or the Symbol Embodied). Symbols can be all sorts of things, associated with all sorts of fields of endeavor. If they are associated with art, then we have a theory of aesthetics that is clearly traced on the original of Orthodox iconology. Has Bely theologized aesthetics or aestheticized theology? It doesn't make much difference. Even if the result of his efforts is an entirely faithless and formalistic system—in the sense that Bely isn't claiming a personal belief in God or literally suggesting the presence of God as a prototype behind all objects of meaning—the structure of his thought is clearly theological. And when we apply it to aesthetics, the possibility for confusing aesthetic reception with faithful adoration is very great indeed.

SERGEI BULGAKOV

The twentieth-century thinker who most successfully blurred the boundary between language philosophy and theology was probably Sergei Nikolaevich Bulgakov (1871–1944). Bulgakov's impact on later generations in his own country is difficult to assess exactly, but it is certainly not great. His most important work on language, *Philosophy of the Name,* was written in 1919 but not published until 1953, after his death.[11] Bulgakov was forced to emigrate in 1922 since his religious views were clearly out of step with the views of the new Soviet state. A chapter of *Philosophy of the Name* was published in German translation in 1930, but it could not have been widely available in the Soviet Union.[12] Bulgakov's importance lies not so much in the degree to which he may have influenced other thinkers, Russian or not, as in the way he exemplifies overtly a tendency that is often only covert in his contemporaries, namely the tendency to approach language philosophy as Orthodox logology.

Bulgakov is a Platonist in the grand tradition of Orthodox theology. "What is the Word?" is the title of the first chapter of *Philosophy of the Name,* and the answer has to do with essence. The essence of a word is its *eidos,* says Bulgakov. As usual, Bulgakov gives an Orthodox coloring to a Platonic notion. The idea or *eidos* of a word is the same as the "inner word," the "sense" of the word (*FI,* p. 21), and this gives rise to a peculiar property of words. "Logos," says Bulgakov, switching freely into the Platonic-theological idiom (and using the actual Greek letters, too), "has a double nature: in it the Word and the thought, the body and the sense, are inseparably and unamalgamatedly fused" (*FI,* p. 19). If we didn't know this was a book about words we might simply think Bulgakov was explaining the Orthodox doctrine of the Logos. The Logos is Christ, and Christ has two natures in one person. In Christ the fleshly and the divine are inseparably united, just as body and sense (which is the same as the inner essence or Platonic idea) are united in Bulgakov's word. Christ is the Word incarnate, and Bulgakov naturally resorts to the Orthodox concept of the Incarnation to describe things that initially appear to have to do only with language. Meanings, he says, are ideas that become incarnate by means of words (*FI,* p. 21).

Bulgakov's subject is ambiguous from the outset. By calling his book *Philosophy of the Name,* instead of, say, *Philosophy of Language* or even *Philosophy of the Word,* Bulgakov is placing himself squarely in the same theological tradition that generated so much speculation about God's presence in his name. When Bulgakov comes to talk about language in an apparently grammatical context, he plays on the possible confusion between linguistics and theology by using the Russian word for "name" as the central term in his discussion. He can do so because several of the Russian words for parts of speech contain the word "name" (*imja*), instead of the word "word" (*slovo*). The expression for "noun" in Russian, for instance, means something like "essential name" or "being-name" (*imja suščestvitel'noe*).

The transition from word to Word and from word to name is thus an easy one for Bulgakov. So, for that matter, is the transition from word to icon. Bulgakov is one of the few thinkers of the era to give explicit formulation to the analogy of word and icon and to locate the source of the analogy in the doctrine of kenosis. "Every icon is a name that has taken root and sprouted," he says (*FI*, p. 182). God's name is a "verbal icon of the Godhead" (*FI*, p. 184). The name of God "reveals itself in the word, our human word made up of sound," and this human word, declares Bulgakov, is an icon (*FI*, p. 190). God comes to be present in his name and in the names of human language through precisely the same kenosis as allowed for the Incarnation of the Word of God in God's Son. There is an implicit hierarchy in Bulgakov's conception, not unlike the one we find in Bely. At the top is God, in the sense of the *idea* of God, who is present in his own name. Next there is Christ, the humiliated divinity. The name of Jesus reflects this status, Bulgakov says; it *is* the name of God, but with a human element. At the next level down we have the words of human language. God's name reveals itself in these words, as I said a moment ago. Each new type of name, from the name of God down to the names, or words, of human language, represents an additional stage of concretion, of condescension, just as it had in Bely's pyramid. All names or words ultimately have a prototype, as they do for Bely. For Bulgakov this prototype is God, not value, but that does not alter the basic model. The same epistemology is implicit in Bulgakov's scheme. In Bulgakov, as in Bely, the act of apprehending an object of meaning is the same as the act of worshiping an icon: it means looking through and beyond to something that cannot be apprehended by fleshly beings.

Earlier I said that iconic thinking was so pervasive in Russia that even the apparently scientific thinkers like Jakobson did not escape its clutches. Jakobson will have to be considered as part of the same tradition as the more overtly theological thinkers I have just been talking about. The most curious thing about Bulgakov in this regard is that he is part of the same European *linguistic* tradition as Jakobson and all other early twentieth-century linguists. In the notes and appendixes to *Philosophy of the Name* we find references to Humboldt, Max Müller, Heymann Steinthal, Michel Bréal, and a host of other nineteenth-century philologists and linguists. So it is not true that Bulgakov was a theologian and nothing more, approaching the study of language from the perspective of a tradition buried in the recesses of Orthodox church history. On the contrary, he was quite a modern man, almost as much of one, in fact, as Roman Jakobson. Nor is it true that Bulgakov took his modern linguistic heritage and gave it a surprising and ungainly twist to make it fit his theology. Bulgakov's view of language is not substantially different from the prevailing Russian view of language. The theology that appears to the Western mind to be artificially superimposed on modern linguistics fits in a way that is completely natural for the Russian tradition of language philosophy. The proof is that we find the theology in Jakobson, too.

PAVEL FLORENSKY

The last figure I will talk about in this context is undoubtedly one of the most amazing intellectuals ever to have lived. It's worth saying again how tragic it is that history in the twentieth century intervened to eclipse the careers and reputations of so many Russians who would otherwise have been celebrated for astonishing achievements even beyond what they were able to accomplish before being condemned to oblivion—or death. Pavel Florensky (1882–1937) was so many things that it would be hard to decide which to list as his principal occupation: theologian, priest, mathematician, scientist, inventor, or philosopher. He wrote on art, language, organic chemistry, mysticism, Kant, sculpture, Dostoevsky, Flaubert, Aegean culture, arithmetic, idealism, iconography, electromagnetism, microscopy, carbolic acid, asbestos, Pythagorean numbers, Aleksandr Blok, ecclesiology, and an absurd variety of other topics. After the revolution he was one of the few intellectuals with conservative views to be permitted to remain professionally active in the country, at least for a time. His training in science made him useful in the early years of the Soviet Union, when he applied his expertise as an electrical engineer to various public-works projects. It is a testimony to the enforced, selective blindness of Soviet history that until recently the achievement for which Florensky was perhaps best remembered officially in his own country was his invention in 1927 of a noncoagulating machine oil.

Before the revolution, in a climate that was more receptive to the full range of Florensky's interests, he was not obliged to concern himself with asbestos and machine oil. His most important writing is a monstrously large book called *The Pillar and Ground of the Truth,* an attempt to elaborate an entire Orthodox metaphysics based on the ideas of love and friendship.[13] Florensky was also a leading figure in the cult of Divine Wisdom, or Sophia, a movement initiated by Solov'ev. Sophia was seen as various things: a kind of supreme prototype in the universe, a fourth member of the Trinity, the church, God's love, and another expression for the Mother of God.

The point of departure for Florensky's thinking shows what a Platonist and essentialist he was. The basic truth for Florensky is the existence of two worlds, a visible one and an invisible one. The first chapter, or "letter," of *The Pillar and Ground* is called "Two Worlds," and Florensky's long essay on icons, "Iconostasis," begins with reflections on the division of the world into visible and invisible. I have referred repeatedly to kenosis, the condescension of God in the Incarnation. Florensky describes kenosis as the entering of God into flesh, of one "I" into another "I" (*SU*, p. 92). This then serves as an analogy for a number of fundamentally related concepts: love, too, is the entering of an "I" into another "I." The condescension of God into human flesh thus becomes an act of love linking the invisible with the visible. Human cognition bears a significant analogy to love and kenosis because it consists in "the real going-out of the cognizing [subject] from himself or—what is the same—the real entering of the cognizing [subject] into the cognized [object]—the real union of cognizing [subject] and cognized [object]" (*SU*, p. 73). This means that cognition has to do with truth, which is the subject of Florensky's big book. "The essential cognition of Truth," he says, "that is, a communion with Truth itself, is, consequently, a real entering into the depths of the Divine Triunity. . . . Therefore, true cognition—the cognition of Truth—is possible only through the transubstantiation of man, through his deification, through the acquisition of love as Divine essence. . . . In love and only in love is the actual cognition of Truth thinkable" (*SU*, p. 74). Love, truth, cognition, kenosis, and, by implication, the Incarnation are thus all profoundly linked together. All either actually or by analogy bridge the gap between the visible and the invisible worlds.

Florensky came to the attention of literary scholars in recent years because of his writing on language and art. Members of the Tartu school of structuralism and semiotics, a group of Soviet scholars working at the University of Tartu in Estonia, rediscovered Florensky's writings some twenty years ago and, in the early 1970s, published several of them with footnotes and commentary. One of these is titled "Iconostasis."[14] The iconostasis is a screen in Orthodox churches that separates the sanctuary from the nave and is covered with icons arranged in prescribed, complicated patterns. The essay is about icons, and it gives one of the most extended and complete philosophical treatments of the subject in the history of Russian iconology. It was written in 1922 but never published until 1972.

Much of what Florensky says about icons fits the standard formulations. In some cases, however, he has come up with novel ways of thinking about icons and novel terms in which to conceptualize them. He starts out by pointing to the truth underlying the existence of icons, namely the existence of a visible and an invisible world. Florensky says that the iconostasis represents the border between these two worlds. Icons are not art, they do not represent things, and icon painters do not create anything. Instead, icons are the means by which the prototype "witnesses" itself. Florensky says that when he sees an icon of the Mother of God, "in my consciousness there is no representation: there is a board with paints on it, and there is the Mother of our Lord Herself" (SS, 1:226). The prototypes that icons give us (or whose "self-witnessing" they give us) are suprasensible ideas, *eide* (the plural of *eidos*) (SS, 1:225). The true icon artist seeks "the artistically embodied truth of things" (SS, 1:236). This is natural since for Florensky the apprehension of truth already has to do with the notion of embodiment or incarnation. It makes sense that the icon should be the artistic incarnation of truth because the icon is by nature a kenotic object, standing on the border between the visible and the invisible, and its apprehension, to follow what Florensky had said in *The Pillar and Ground,* is an act similar to love or to the apprehension of truth. Icon painting is thus a metaphysics of being (SS, 1:296).

This analysis is not significantly different from what we see in other writings in the Orthodox theology of icons, except perhaps for Florensky's emphasis on the concrete reality of the prototype that we experience in an icon. Florensky shows the same Platonic essentialism as others who had written in this field before him. In fact, at one point in the essay, he even mentions the closeness of Platonic ontology to iconography (SS, 1:290).

When he turns to language the Platonic essentialism and a Humboldtian myth of origins persist in Florensky's conception, but with a twist that is entirely new. There are two important places where we can learn Florensky's thoughts on language. There is *The Pillar and Ground of the Truth,* which contains numerous etymological excursuses on various concepts. And there is a short article titled "The Construction of the

Word," which Florensky wrote sometime before 1922, but which was not published during his lifetime.[15]

In *The Pillar and Ground* Florensky shows a fondness for philological speculation that anticipates Heidegger. We find the same simple faith in the myth of original purity, the same sense that a primitive, essential core dwells in a word over the centuries and continues to have signifying force for the speakers of a particular nation. In his chapter on truth, for instance, Florensky examines the words for "truth" in a number of different languages and includes an analysis of the Greek word *aletheia* similar to Heidegger's celebrated treatment in his 1943 essay "Aletheia." We find, too, the same willingness to cross the boundary between sober scholarly accuracy and pure fancy in his etymological work. In fact, Florensky openly acknowledges and even justifies his transgressions in a footnote to one of his etymological analyses in *The Pillar and Ground*: "Philosophy *creates* language, not studies it." He then strangely cites as his authority Humboldt and the theory that language is a dynamic process (*SU*, p. 786).

"The Structure of the Word" contains a theory of language that is extraordinary for the way it combines the traditional romantic myth of origins with a more "modern," contextual theory. Florensky's point of departure is the observation that a basic antinomy underlies language. Every word, he says, derives at once from a set of primary elements common to all speakers and from the mind and thoughts of the individual speaker. The word is thus both public and private. It contains elements that must not change from utterance to utterance in order for a community of speakers to have a fixed means of communication. At the same time, since the word is used in actual utterances, it contains elements that are peculiar to those utterances and to the speakers making them.

Florensky then builds on this antinomy a theory of inner and outer form clearly derived from Potebnia, except that he performs a fascinating reversal of Potebnia's terms. Outer form, according to Florensky, is what he calls the body of the word. It is the word's unchanging composition, which serves common reason. Inner form, by contrast, is the very soul of the word. It is constantly changing, always being born anew, and it serves individual reason. Potebnia, remember, had equated the inner form of the word with its closest etymological meaning. Florensky retains both the idea of inner form and the idea of a closest etymological meaning, but he changes things around and associates the closest etymological meaning, what he calls the *etymon*, with outer form. That's because the *etymon,* which is the true flesh of the word, provides the constant element in a word, the element that does not appreciably change from one utterance to the next. Florensky uses the same terms as Potebnia to describe this changeless element in a word. It is the old etymological myth of origins. The *etymon* for Florensky is the word's "original [*pervonačal'noe*] or truthful [*istinnoe*] meaning."[16] Florensky gives an example of a word with its etymological derivation to illustrate what "primeval [*pervobytnyj*] man" thought about the object designated by that word.[17] But Florensky's conclusion is entirely different from Potebnia's. For Florensky, the *etymon* is merely part of the outer form of the word, that is, the form that serves the needs of the community of speakers. It is not the soul of the word.

The soul of the word is its inner form. Florensky also calls this the "sememe." The sememe is what belongs to the particular speaker on the particular occasion of a particular utterance. "The sememe of a word constantly wavers," says Florensky, "it breathes, it is iridescent and has no independent meaning that exists separately from *this* speech of mine, spoken right *here* and *now,* in the whole context of lived experience and also in the *present* place of this speech."[18] The notion that speech is, at least on one level, linked with inner, private experience leads Florensky to the following bold observation: "Words are unrepeatable; in every instance they are spoken anew, that is, with a new sememe, and in the best case this will be a variation on an earlier theme. . . . Only the *outer* form of a word can be objectively one and the same thing in a conversation, but never the inner form."[19]

What do we make of an assertion like this? There is no doubt that the Platonist and essentialist impulse is there. The whole doctrine of inner form as it was modified by Potebnia was Platonic because it linked the essence of the word with something basically ahistorical. Florensky may have seen himself as returning to Humboldt's notion of inner form, which had to do with the dynamic nature of language and not with frozen, ahistorical meanings. But there is an important difference here, too. For Humboldt, the dynamic, generative nature of language had to do with a concept of nationhood. It was the *Volk* with all its generative cultural energy that was responsible for the constant process of renewal that languages undergo. With Florensky, however, the emphasis is on the individual utterance, on the implicit isolation and uniqueness of any act of speech. His use of the word *context,* the idea that speech can be understood only in relation to a total "lived" set of circumstances, is particularly striking since it anticipates all those lonely twentieth-century postmodern theories of language, which see language as ultimately unstable because it is always "implicated" in a ceaselessly changing historical context. This contextuality is what Florensky appears to regard as essential in language. But the most Platonic and essentialist concept in Florensky's theory of language is associated for him with the aspect of language that is least essential, namely its outer form.

Earlier I said that Bulgakov was an important figure not because of any impact his writings had on his contemporaries or on future generations but because his thinking arises from the same tradition as the thinking of figures that did have an enormous impact on future generations in the West. This is true of Florensky, too. But with Florensky we can speak of a few actual points of contact with his contemporaries. Aage A. Hansen-Löve, for instance, in his huge book on the Formalist movement, asserts that an essay by Florensky on perspective in art was known to the Formalists, although he doesn't say to which Formalists it was known or what sort of response it drew from any of them.[20] Another scholar mentions Florensky as part of a history of Soviet semiotics, saying that Florensky and a few better-known writers contributed to the study of the relation between signs and extralinguistic reality.[21]

Most important of all, however, is the connection with Mikhail Bakhtin. In Bakhtin's theory of discourse all speech is part of a dialogue. The word never exists in isolation but gets its meaning from the context in which it is uttered. Thus for Bakhtin, too, words are unrepeatable, since contexts are unrepeatable. Bakhtin spent most of his life in obscurity or in internal exile in the Soviet Union, and his writings were not widely known even abroad until the 1970s. But he has since become popular in the academic literary establishment. As it happens, Florensky and Bakhtin were part of the same intellectual circle in the 1920s, and there are affinities between their ways of thinking that can perhaps be explained by the circumstance that Bakhtin was, to a surprising extent, a religious man in the Orthodox tradition. Katerina Clark and Michael Holquist, who have written the standard biography of Bakhtin, show the religious bases of his theory of language. There are two concepts, both deriving from the familiar doctrine of kenoticism. The first is something called *sobornost'*, which Clark and Holquist translate as "communality."[22] It refers to the brotherhood on earth of Christian worshipers, and it derives from the idea of the shared experience with Christ that was made possible by the kenosis. As Clark and Holquist explain, this idea serves as a foundation for Bakhtin's notion of the dialogic. Dialogic communication rests on the fundamental act by which one consciousness recognizes another. All human interaction is an example of this kind of self-other relation. In his earliest work Bakhtin explicitly makes the connection between this model of human interaction and the idea of Christian community.

The second concept, Clark and Holquist say, is "a profound respect for the material realities of everyday experience."[23] Since the kenotic tradition emphasizes the Incarnation so strongly, it has always insisted on the miracle of creation itself as another instance of incarnation and thus has always revered the material world. This was the injunction of John of Damascus, who cautioned men not to despise matter. Bakhtin, as Clark and Holquist explain, was fascinated with the material dimension of language for precisely this reason. But he also reverted to the standard terms of Orthodox logology to describe the word, referring to the two-sided nature of the word and implicitly confusing "word" (a unit of human language) and "Word" (the Word of God that was made flesh).

It's easy to see the resemblance between this idea and the doctrine that Florensky has briefly elaborated in "The Construction of the Word." Bakhtin's communal conception of language would later develop into a full-fledged theory of linguistic contextuality, and that is exactly what Florensky proposes in his essay. And Bakhtin's point of departure is the recognition of the fundamental duality of language, a recognition that comes from the way the kenotic tradition views the relation between the visible and the invisible. That was Florensky's point of departure, too.

CHAPTER SIX

Roman Jakobson, or How Logology and Mythology Were Exported

It's certainly fair to say that Roman Jakobson is the biggest name in modern linguistics. No other figure dominates the field quite the way he did. This is only partly because of his uncanny productivity. It is also because he was around for so long and in so many places. Since he spent the last forty-one years of his life, from 1941 to 1982, in the United States, he is regarded as almost an American academic fixture. But before he came here, he had spent a couple of years in Norway and Sweden and almost twenty years in Czechoslovakia. He spent the first twenty-four years of his life in Russia, where he was born in 1896.

This geographically and chronologically wide-ranging career allowed Jakobson to have an extraordinary international impact on both linguistics and literary theory. In his early days he was closely associated with the Formalists and Futurists in his native country. After he went to Czechoslovakia in 1920, he founded the Prague Linguistic Circle, which is mentioned in every account of the history of structuralism. And in the United States his long career in the academic establishment made him a continuing presence in various schools of literary theory.

No one doubts the importance of Jakobson in the history of structuralism. The facts can be stated briefly: Jakobson received his copy of Saussure's *Cours de linguistique générale* in 1920, although he had been familiar with Saussurian doctrine since 1917. He was troubled by certain aspects of Saussure's system, above all its inability to accommodate the notion of ongoing change in language, so he elaborated a new view of language that would take account of this temporal factor. The document in which this view appears is "Problems in the Study of Literature and Language," which Jakobson coauthored with Formalist critic Yury Tynianov and published in 1928. This programmatic list of principles and recommendations introduced the notion that language is a "system" that "necessarily exists as an evolution." But it also contained a proclamation that was to play a significant role in the development of structuralist thought: "An analysis of the structural laws of language and literature and their evolution inevitably leads to the establishment of a limited series of actually existing structural types (types of structural evolution)."[1] The following year, at the First Congress of Slavists in Prague, Jakobson proposed new modes of poetic analysis and, as he tells the story later, "christened" them the "structural method."[2] Thus, by Jakobson's account, the foundation was laid for the elaboration of structural principles into a broad methodology.

Jakobson was interested not only in linguistics but in poetics as well. In fact, many people today feel that his work in poetics is superior to his work in linguistics. Some of his most obvious contributions to modern structuralism were in this field. For instance, the famous study of Baudelaire's "Les Chats" that he coauthored with Claude Lévi-Strauss in 1962 reads almost like a parody of the structuralist method. It combines semantic, grammatical, syntactical, phonetic, and prosodic methods of analysis to provide a ridiculously complicated set of organizational schemas—all for the purpose, the authors say, of giving the poem "the character of an absolute object."[3] The article has its own involved history in the annals of modern criticism, a history that has secured it a place in virtually every account of the rise of structuralism. But then Jakobson's entire association with Lévi-Strauss, which had begun in the first years Jakobson spent in the United States, was a formative influence in that movement.

Another thing for which Jakobson is particularly well remembered in literary circles and in the history of structuralist method is his distinction between the two "poles" of language: the metaphoric and the metonymic. The idea is that all language production occurs on two "axes": the vertical axis of selection and the horizontal axis of combination. In other words, as we speak we perform two different operations: we select units as if from a vertical column of choices and then we string them together as if on a horizontal track. When we select, we act on the basis of a principle of similarity (because the different choices in the vertical column will necessarily bear some resemblance to one another), and when we combine, we act on the basis of a principle of contiguity (because, in the simplest sense, the units we combine go next to each other). These two operations have to do with two basic figures of speech: metaphor and metonymy. When we use a metaphor, what we are really doing is substituting one thing for another, which is to say that we are performing a "vertical" operation of selection. Thus when I refer to someone as a weasel, I am selecting from a whole column of terms that suggest furtiveness or some other quality belonging to both weasels and the person I am comparing them with. When we use a metonymy, what we are really doing is finding something that is associated and "contiguous" with the first term. When I refer to the food I eat as my board, it is not because food and board are similar, but because the idea of food calls to mind something contiguous with it, namely the table, or "board," on which it is served. *Contiguity* here, of course, has a slightly different sense from the one it has when we talk about the horizontal axis of selection.

In an article on two types of aphasia, Jakobson actually used neurological research to support his findings. He found that one type of aphasic disturbance consists in a similarity disorder, that is, where the metaphoric pole of language has been disturbed and the subject has trouble choosing individual words, whereas the other type consists in a contiguity disorder, that is, where the metonymic pole has been disturbed and the subject has trouble stringing words together. These findings confirmed for him that the two axes of language actually represent two basic mental operations involved in speech formation.[4]

What is important in Jakobson's observations on metaphor and metonymy is the conclusion that he draws from them. If there are two basic figures of speech, two principles of language production, it is because there are two basic types of language: our old friends, poetry and prose. Poetic language, since it is rich in metaphor, relies more on the axis of selection. This makes sense because poetry is less a temporal and sequential form of language than is prose. Prosaic language, by contrast, is sequential and linear and thus relies more on the axis of combination. In fact, the principle of similarity, or equivalence, is so dominant in poetic language that it fairly overwhelms any instances of combination that we might find in language of this sort. Thus we arrive at Jakobson's celebrated statement, set in italics in his article "Linguistics and Poetics": "*The poetic function projects the principle of equivalence from the axis of selection into the axis of combination*" (*SW*, 3:27). What this means is that in poetry even the combination, the linear sequence of words, is dominated by principles of similarity.

But here, too, the main thing is how poetic language calls attention to itself "as such." In "Linguistics and Poetics" Jakobson gives his well-known schema of the six "functions" of language. Among the functions he lists are the poetic function and the "referential" function. The referential function is also called the "denotative" and the "cognitive" function, and it has to do with what we normally think of as the transmission of information in simple communication. Each function is distinguished by its orientation toward one of six corresponding factors. Referential language is oriented toward the *context*. Poetic language is oriented toward the "*message* as such, . . . the message for its own sake" (*SW*, 3:25). Once again, the idea is that poetic language is different from ordinary language because it calls attention to itself.

What is a man of science like Jakobson doing concerning himself with the difference between poetic and prosaic language? Hasn't this problem been strangely resistant to any kind of scientific solution? Isn't it more and more tempting to conclude, in the face of so many failed attempts to solve it, that there *is* no such scientifically describable difference? As it happens, Jakobson from the very beginning was wrestling with all the old myths, and his later attempts to come up with a scientific formulation for some of them make a lot more sense if we look at what he was doing early in his career.

Jakobson's own account of his linguistic genealogy is puzzling. In the "Retrospect" to the first volume of his *Selected Writings* he mentions a few linguists that helped inspire him to take a new direction in language studies. But he also says that the strongest impulse came from the "great men of art born in the 1880s," and he lists Picasso, Joyce, Braque, Stravinsky, Khlebnikov, and Le Corbusier (*SW*, 1:631–32). He goes on to say that his first topic for the analysis of language "in its means and functions" was the poetry of Khlebnikov (*SW*, 1:633). In the "Retrospect" to another volume he credits Bely with inspiring him to take on the analytic study of verse (*SW*, 5:569). I mentioned earlier that Jakobson was closely associated with Formalists and Futurists. What he says about himself and much of the evidence about his early career suggests that the fundamental aspects of his thinking about language came not from professional linguists but from other sources—chiefly poets, artists, and literary critics.

One of Jakobson's earliest published writings is a long essay on Khlebnikov called "Modern Russian Poetry."[5] If ever there was evidence that Jakobson was a man of his age and a product of indigenous tradition, this is it. The only thing that distinguishes it from the work of, say,

Shklovsky is that Jakobson pays slightly more attention to the grammatical aspects of his subject. Otherwise the essay is pure Formalism, complete with all the mythical and Platonic baggage we saw in Shklovsky's work.

The effort is always to locate the essence of poetic language, to find the quality in poetry that makes it different from ordinary discourse. When Jakobson proposes solutions to the poetry-prose puzzle, we find the same phrases and concepts turning up as we had seen in the writings of Futurist poets like Khlebnikov and Kruchenykh and Formalist critics like Shklovsky. Poetic language is different from ordinary language because in it "linguistic representations (both phonetic and semantic) focus more attention on themselves" (SW, 5:304). He quotes Khlebnikov approvingly and says that "poetry is the formation of a self-valued, 'self-spun' word" (SW, 5:305). In passages reminiscent of Shklovsky he describes how words undergo a gradual process of petrification until they cease to be felt as words. When words reach this point, we read, a poet needs to come along and revive them so they can be felt as such. Or better yet, a poet can come along, as Khlebnikov has done, and invent whole new words, which can't avoid being felt as new because they are. "The form of words in practical language easily ceases to be consciously felt, it dies away, becomes petrified, whereas the perception of the form of a poetic neologism, a form given in statu nascendi, is absolutely compulsory" (SW, 5:333). Khlebnikov seems to have accomplished the resurrection of the word that Shklovsky had called for five years earlier. When the poet exploits consonant similarities in adjacent words, Jakobson says, "the word acquires a sort of new sound characteristic, the meaning bestirs itself, the word is perceived like a friend with a suddenly unfamiliar face, or like a person we don't know, but in whom something familiar can be divined" (SW, 5:342).

When Jakobson had spoken of the self-valued word and the tendency of poetic language to call attention to itself, he was really just answering the question of what poetic language *does*, not what it *is*. But he returns again and again to the question of what there is about poetic or literary language that *makes* it poetic or literary. "Poetry is language in its aesthetic function" (SW, 5:305). What quality is there that makes poetic language have this aesthetic function? Jakobson started out by considering literary language in general, without for the moment distinguishing literary from poetic language. He came up with a name for the distinctive quality in literary language: *literaturnost'*, or "literarity." In a famous sentence that gave the term currency in the Formalist movement, he says that "the object of a science of literature is not literature, but literarity, that is, what makes a given work a literary work" (*SW*, 5:305).

Naturally, neither Jakobson nor any other Formalist thinker ever came up with a truly satisfying definition of *literaturnost'*. This ultimate object of the "science of literature" always seemed to be on the other side of the horizon. But that makes perfect sense, because *literaturnost'* is intrinsically an ideal, essentialist concept; and if it is ideal, then it is not accessible to the kind of knowledge implicitly understood in the phrase *science of literature*. No, unfortunately, Formalism was no science at all. It was founded in mystical and mythical notions. Now it appears that it was an essentialist and idealist doctrine as well, and Jakobson's quest for that pure aesthetic quality of literary language is a perfect example.

In the first part of this book I talked about inner form and showed that it was one of the most pervasive concepts in Russian language theory. It was also one of the most unscientific concepts in theories that masqueraded as scientific. Not surprisingly, the term springs up in Jakobson just as naturally as it had in Potebnia, Bely, and Shklovsky. At one point Jakobson discusses Khlebnikov's word inventions, saying that words of the sort that he creates "seem almost to be seeking out a meaning for themselves. In this case," he continues, "one cannot, say, speak of the absence of semantics. These are, to be more precise, words with negative inner form" (*SW*, 5:353). A few paragraphs later he says that the word in Khlebnikov's poetry "loses its object-quality [*predmetnost'*], then its inner and finally even its outer form" (*SW*, 5:354). It's hard to extract from these statements a precise sense of inner form as Jakobson understands it. Still, the mere fact that he doesn't pause to explain the term suggests that he is using it in what at least he regards as its customary sense. Inner form seems to have to do with the word's meaning and, more than this, with the mysterious way in which the word means that meaning. Thus a word with "negative inner form" is one that appears to retain the connectedness with its meaning even though the meaning—in the sense of a true, "objective" meaning—is lacking.

But isn't inner form just another essentialist doctrine when it comes right down to it? Doesn't it make perfect sense that the Russians should have seized hold of this concept from a romantic thinker like Humboldt, then redefined it in such a way that it would now satisfy their indigenous, age-old religious need for essences, ideals, *eide*, iconic prototypes, and such Platonic otherworldly notions? Potebnia had taken what for

Humboldt had been a dynamic concept and, in characteristic Russian fashion, replaced it with something static, fixed, and eternal.

This search for essences is utterly typical of Jakobson's thought. A curious chapter in the Jakobson story that is seldom mentioned helps account for Jakobson's essentialism (or his essentialism helps account for *it*). It is his association with phenomenology. Anyone familiar with this movement in early twentieth-century philosophy knows how difficult it is to define phenomenology, above all since Edmund Husserl seemed to want to redefine it every time he wrote a new book about it. But one can say at least that, in the eyes of Husserl's contemporaries, it was a philosophy of pure thought. The phenomenologist sought, through the "phenomenological reduction," to abstract or "bracket" from thought all prior experience, all presuppositions about the world, in order to isolate "thought" itself. At another stage, the phenomenologist, through the application of "eidetic intuition" and "eidetic reduction," brackets away the qualities in a phenomenon (that is, anything that appears to consciousness) that are peculiar to that phenomenon in order to arrive at the essence or *eidos* common to all similar phenomena. Phenomenology is thus, among other things, a science of essences. This is undoubtedly what made it appealing to the Russian mind in the early twentieth century. A number of Russian intellectuals came to champion Husserl's cause in their own country, largely at the instigation of one Gustav Shpet, who studied with Husserl. Interestingly enough, Shpet was later to write an entire book with the Humboldtian-Potebnian title *The Inner Form of the Word*.[6]

Elmar Holenstein has investigated the Jakobson-Husserl connection and shown the degree to which Jakobson's thought was formed by his exposure to phenomenology. He feels so strongly about the impact of phenomenology on Jakobson, in fact, that the subtitle to his book on Jakobson's theory of language describes that entire theory as "phenomenological structuralism."[7] One fundamental feature that phenomenology and Jakobsonian linguistics have in common is precisely the notion of essences, Holenstein thinks. In an article devoted exclusively to Jakobson and Husserl, he shows how the notion makes its appearance in both fields. Holenstein describes the search for essences in phenomenology as "the search for invariants in all the variations, for the general in everything particular."[8] This is because in phenomenology essences have to do with those qualities in a thing that remain unchanged despite variations in the way the thing is perceived. For example, the quality of extension is invariant because an object cannot exist without it. The two chief concepts in Jakobson that Holenstein sees as analogous are literarity (Holenstein translates it as "literaricity") and poeticity (*poètičnost'*), a term that Potebnia had used and that Jakobson reintroduced about a decade after the Khlebnikov article to describe the quality that makes a specifically poetic work poetic.[9] Holenstein then draws an important conclusion from his observation. "Jakobson," he says, "knows just as well as Husserl that in the search for the essentialities success is not to be had with induction and statistics, but only with phenomenological analysis and insight into the object of investigation itself."[10] The standard tools of empirical science thus have no place in this central task of linguistics. In other words, to the extent that it seeks essences in the objects of its own investigation, Jakobsonian linguistics, that important precursor to the scientific methods of structuralism, is not a science in the sense many of us understand when we speak of a science of language.

I don't know whether phenomenology was the reason for the essentialist impulse in Jakobson, or if the essentialist impulse was already there and was the reason for Jakobson's interest in phenomenology. The second hypothesis makes more sense, for essentialism was a native organism of long standing in Jakobson's mother country. But it doesn't really matter much in the end. The fact is that Jakobson's thought is fundamentally essentialist and that if phenomenology either fed or caused his essentialism, if it played a role in the development of his thought as he himself acknowledges, then the essentialist impulse is a strong one in the formation of structuralism. Holenstein is not the only person to have asserted that phenomenology in some sense leads to structuralism.[11]

Jakobson's essentialism was not merely a feature of the youthful thinking associated with his early Formalist-Futurist period; it was to remain with him for his entire career. For instance, the concept of poeticity that Holenstein mentions comes from an article that Jakobson published (in Czech) in 1933 and 1934 called "What Is Poetry?"[12] Even at that date, well after the heyday of Russian Formalism and presumably well after the era of romantic and mystical language philosophy, Jakobson is trotting out the same old notions about the specificity of poetic language. "Poeticity," he says, "is present when the word is felt as a word and not a mere representation of the object being named or an outburst of emotion, when words and their composition, their meaning, their external and inner form acquire a weight and value of their own instead of referring indifferently to reality" (*SW*, 3:750).

Even better evidence of the tenacity of Jakobson's essentialism is his 1965 article titled "Quest for the Essence of Language" (*SW*, 2:345–59). Early in this article Jakobson refers to Saussure's idea of *l'arbitraire du signe* (pointing out, by the way, that the idea is twenty-two hundred years old) and then embarks on his own quest for instances where the *signe* is not so *arbitraire*. In some cases, he says, borrowing terms from Charles Sanders Peirce, there is a "diagrammatic resemblance" between the sign and the signified. For example, the phrase *veni, vidi, vici* bears a diagrammatic resemblance to the signified because the order of the words is the same as the order of the actions they designate. Another place where the diagrammatic resemblance shows through is in the length of words. With few exceptions the length of words corresponds to the notions of degree and number (superlatives are almost always longer than positives; plurals are almost always longer than singulars).

So strong was Jakobson's faith in the "essence" in language that he was led to adopt some strangely paradoxical positions later in his career. In his 1965 article "On Linguistic Aspects of Translation" Jakobson introduces another one of his favorite ideas, namely the interdependence of *signatum* and *signum*. "There is no *signatum* without a *signum*," he says (*SW*, 2:260). This is a striking sentence, because it means there is no signified thing (*signatum*) that exists independently of the sign (*signum*) standing for it. The signified exists only when and because there is a sign for it. In other words, language is a kind of enclosed universe unto itself that is ultimately indifferent to the existence or nonexistence of a "real" world without. This sounds much like the lonely, postmodern language philosophies of the 1970s, when it was fashionable to see language as a big subterfuge, forever undermining itself and always refusing to point to any kind of concrete reality. I don't mean to suggest that Jakobson is taking such an extreme position, but what he's saying certainly seems out of step with any theory that cherishes the idea of an essence in language. In the interdependence theory the relation between sign and signified, like the relation between sign and outside world, is bound to be arbitrary: sign and signified depend on each other; the signified exists as a function of the sign. But the signified cannot be said to *necessitate* the sign, and if the converse is true, namely that the sign necessitates the signified (which exists, remember, only as a function of the sign), then it will have to do so by means that are mysterious indeed. Essentialist theories, by contrast, always want to see a necessary connection between sign and signified, sign and thing, or sign and concept.

Naturally, poetic language was always there to restore Jakobson's faith. In 1965, only seven years after writing "On Linguistic Aspects of Translation," Jakobson writes about poetic language, saying that in it there is "an essential change in the relation between the signifier and the signified, just as there is between the sign and the concept."[13] In other words, you may speak all you like about the interdependence of sign and signified, provided that you're speaking only of everyday language. When it comes to poetry, however, there is an "essential change." Jakobson doesn't say here just what this change is, but it's easy enough to fill in his meaning. In "Quest for the Essence of Language," written in the same year, he borrows a term from Peirce and refers to certain "iconic" properties of language, by which he means properties that show a factual similarity between signifier and signified. One highly significant iconic property in language may be found in the selection of phonemes. That is, certain sounds in language bear a factual similarity to the things they signify. Jakobson even cites Mallarmé's "Crise de vers" and the paradoxical example of *jour,* a dark-sounding signifier with a light signified, and *nuit,* a light-sounding signifier with a dark signified. Amazingly, Jakobson's point is not, as it was for Mallarmé, that this example proves the arbitrary nature of the sign-signified connection but instead that Mallarmé was "deceived" (Jakobson's translation of Mallarmé's *deçu,* "disappointed") by the perversity of this one case. Jakobson has been busy showing how the connection is nonarbitrary when it comes to the phonemic qualities in words, and he now goes on to say that the connection is particularly nonarbitrary in poetic language. The trouble with this view is that it brings all kinds of factors from the external world into the picture and thus wrecks the serene isolation of the interdependence model. Sign and signified are no longer purely interdependent; now they depend on something outside, like the lightness of the day or the darkness of the night.

Essentialism was similarly at the root of Jakobson's theories of poetic language. In Jakobson's immediate cultural context the idea of the "word itself," poetic language that calls attention to itself, goes back to the *zaum'* theorists, who believed that poetic language should be ideally signifying. Poetic language that created its own signified world signified that world through an ideal and necessary connection between sign and signified. Poetic language that did not create its own world simply signified through an ideal, direct connection. In both cases the word had to exist "as such" and call attention to itself, because, owing to its ideal signifying powers, by calling attention to itself it was also calling attention to its signified.

When Jakobson refers to the iconic properties of language, he is using *iconic* in a sense borrowed from Peirce. And yet isn't his whole notion of poetic language iconic in the Orthodox sense, too? All Jakobson's essentialist notions—literarity, poeticity, inner form—point to the presence of an immaterial, invisible core in words, a core that is ultimately neither accessible to ordinary perception nor susceptible of scientific description; it is incarnate, like the prototype in an icon, like the Word in the Son of God, like God in creation. What this means is that despite his efforts to make the study of language a respectable, scientific discipline, Jakobson is really proposing the same Orthodox model of the aesthetic epistemological attitude as we have found in Bely and in the overtly religious thinkers I have spoken of. The way Jakobson sees things, the reader of poetic works of art performs the same operation as the worshiper of icons. Reading means reaching beyond the material dimension of language back to that irretrievable essence, whose existence is known only by faith, just as the existence of the prototype of the icon is known only by faith.

Jakobson was no stranger to religious doctrine. This dimension of his work is often overlooked. Though he was Jewish by birth, he converted to Orthodox Christianity in the late 1930s, and though he was not an overtly religious man, he devoted a considerable amount of scholarship directly or indirectly to religious matters. Over a period of at least sixty years he produced a staggering amount of scholarship on early Slavic texts, almost all of them religious. During his years in Czechoslovakia he devoted a tremendous amount of time to the study of early Czech writing, most of it religious. One of his chief scholarly interests for many years was Saint Cyril, the ninth-century Macedonian missionary who, together with his brother, Methodius, is credited with inventing a Slavic alphabet and is responsible for spreading the use of the Slavic vernacular in the liturgy. Jakobson's interest in these subjects is generally linguistic and historicolinguistic, but a glance at his writings shows that he was intimately familiar with Christian theological doctrine in the Czech and the Russian traditions. Any linguist studying liturgical texts is certain to run up against the theological notion of the Word and is thus likely to raise many of the same issues I have been discussing. This is true for Jakobson.[14]

The volume of Jakobson's *Selected Writings* in which the early Slavic material is collected was published only in 1985, and this may partly explain why the standard books on Jakobson contain almost no mention of it. A more reasonable explanation, however, is that the commentators on Jakobson have not quite known what to make of it. They like to think that the Jakobsonian canon is restricted to the basic set of principles usually associated with him and officially sanctioned by American literary academia. But this view is just as narrow as the view that accepts Jakobson's more widely known theories as scientific.

One could describe even the method of poetic analysis that Jakobson uses in one of his most scientific, analytic texts, his article on Baudelaire's "Les Chats," as iconic. The effort there is to pierce through the material veil of word-sounds so as to discover underneath an invisible abstraction of grammatical relations. This method, of course, has a more familiar name: structuralism. But it is clearly iconic in its conception. This means that the iconic principle is likely at the heart of Jakobson's contribution to the entire structuralist enterprise. What does one find once one has pierced the material veil? What is the hidden god? A prototype. Or an abstract structure of relations. And this, conveniently enough, is the subject of the next part of this book, where Jakobson will play a significant role once again.

PART III

Relationalism

CHAPTER SEVEN

Numbers, Systems, Functions—and Essences

Sometime in the nineteenth century, mathematics underwent a profound change that was to have lasting effects in a variety of fields.[1] Ernst Cassirer described the change in the last volume of *The Philosophy of Symbolic Forms*.[2] There were two major trends in modern mathematical thinking, Cassirer says. One is associated with Leibniz, the other with Kant. The trend associated with Leibniz is formalistic, whereas the trend associated with Kant is intuitionistic. A formalistic mathematics is one that emphasizes functions and ordering operations over the empirical reality of the elements that are ordered. What the elements are is not important—they can be numbers, symbols, apples, almost anything. An intuitionistic mathematics recognizes ordering operations and may even regard them as existing a priori, that is, as existing in the mind prior to experience, but it emphasizes the agreement between these ordering operations and the elements that they order. It regards these elements either as being empirical facts or as referring to empirical facts. "Thoughts without content are empty, intuitions without concepts are blind," said Kant in what has become probably the most famous single sentence of the *Critique of Pure Reason*.[3] For Kant, all experience is ultimately grounded in sense intuition (the process by which we receive, or "intuit," sense data), and this means that the concepts we use to order the elements of our experience, even if those concepts logically precede experience, must always be inseparably *tied* to experience.

Modern mathematics, Cassirer says, has followed Leibniz rather than Kant. The elements that mathematical propositions deal with are now seen as purely ideal, that is, as having no necessary grounding in any sensuous, empirical reality; and no matter what these elements are, the emphasis is not on them but on the structure of relations between them. Developments in nineteenth-century mathematics illustrate this fact. Non-Euclidean geometry, for example, helped turn mathematics "more and more into a hypothetical-deductive system, whose truth value is grounded purely in its inner logical coherence and consistency, and not in any material, intuitive statements" (3:364). Modern symbolic logic, developed by the English mathematician George Boole in the mid-nineteenth century, shows how "the validity of analytical processes is dependent not on the interpretation of the symbols that occur in them but on the laws of their combination" (3:364). In other words, it is not important to know what the symbols are or what real things they stand for; it is important only to know how they are related to each other. By the end of the nineteenth century, Cassirer says, the whole notion of truth and validity in mathematics has been reformed. It is no longer necessary to seek the truth value of a mathematical proposition in the contents of its elements since these elements are seen as purely ideal. Now, instead, we have to look for that truth value in a "complex of relations." The meaning of the purely ideal elements of mathematical propositions, Cassirer says, "can never be disclosed in particular representations directed toward a concrete, intuitively tangible object, but only in a complex network of judgments" (3:400).

This is a startling development. Before the period Cassirer talks about, mathematics was thought of as always ultimately making claims about a sensuous reality. The symbols of mathematics were just that—symbols *of* something. This something might not be specific and might not be named, but the idea was that something concrete could always be filled in for the symbols. Now, though, it is not the symbols that are important; it is the *relations* between them. Hence the most important concept of the entire era, namely the concept that we can call generically the system. Cassirer uses the expressions *systematic context, complex of relations,* and *complex network of judgments.* By the early twentieth century everyone is using this terminology: there is talk of systems, networks, sets, structures, fields, anything that sounds like a collection of elements in which the way the elements are related to each other is more important than what the elements are.

And there will be talk of *groups.* The mathematical group is the system concept par excellence, the great testimony of the nineteenth century to the new worship of pure abstraction. Group theory even has a romantic history to it, a history that, thanks to the efforts of a spoil-sport historian, has been shown to be false but that survived for a century and a half unmolested.[4] The theory was discovered by a Frenchman, Evariste Galois, and legend had it that he made the entire thing up in 1829, when he was twenty, on the night before a duel in which he knew he might perish (and in which, of course, he did). The real story is actually almost as exciting as the legend. Galois did discover group theory by the time he was twenty. He did die in a duel, and he did spend his last night feverishly working on the theory. It's just that he had discovered it and written about it earlier and was now, the night before his death, merely revising a manuscript for publication.

The precise definition of a group is technical, and its finer details are not worth going into here. Simply put, it goes something like this: A group is a collection of elements that are subject to a combinatory operation. It doesn't matter what the combinatory operation is; it can be an arithmetic operation like addition or multiplication, or it can be an entirely different sort of operation, like a rule for arranging cake crumbs in the squares of a checked tablecloth. There are two requirements that must be met for a collection of elements with its combinatory operation to be a group. The result of combining any two elements (the sum if the operation is addition, the product if it's multiplication, and so on) must always be a member of the original collection of elements, and certain algebraic properties must hold. These requirements give the group what is called *closure*, which means that the group is always self-contained because it can never generate anything but its own elements.

An example of a group is the set of all integers with multiplication assigned as the combinatory operation. The set is infinite, but that doesn't matter because the product of any two integers is always another integer, and the algebraic properties all hold. Even though it contains an infinite number of elements, this group still has closure because only integers are admitted, and only integers can be generated by the combinatory operation. Another example is the toy known as Rubik's cube, which was popular in the early 1980s. The cube consists of a number of smaller cubes of various colors that can be twisted and rearranged relative to one another. The stated goal is to arrange the small cubes so that the colors on each face of the large cube will be the same. How is Rubik's cube a group? The elements here are the small cubes, or to be more precise, the positions of the small cubes. The combinatory operation is the twistings—determined by the physical properties of the toy—that rearrange the small cubes. The same physical properties that define the combinatory operation give the group its closure: no twisting of the toy (that is, no twisting that doesn't break it) will render anything but a new set of positions (these are the elements of the group), and the various algebraic properties are all observed.

Group theory is a perfect illustration of Cassirer's remarks about nineteenth-century mathematics. The very definition of a group places the emphasis not on the elements of the group, that is, not on what these elements are, but instead on the relations between them—their configuration, their structure, the principles by which they are ordered. Cassirer shows in other writings how extensively the concept was ramified and how influential it had become by the end of the nineteenth century. One ramification was responsible for introducing group theory into the logic of a great many fields in the natural, social, and human sciences. Developments in geometry led mathematicians to ponder the behavior of what they called *transformations*. A transformation is any operation that takes the members of one group of elements and generates from them a new group of elements. The field known as projective geometry is especially concerned with transformations. Projective geometry studies, for example, what happens to geometric figures when they are "projected," as if by a light source behind them, from their original space onto a new space. The transformation thus takes the arrangement of the points of the original figure (the elements of the first group) and "transforms" it into the arrangement of the points of the new figure (the elements of the second, "transformed" group).

What especially interested mathematicians about transformations was those instances where certain elements were left unchanged by the transformation. These elements were called *invariants*. Let's take as an example a standard Cartesian coordinate system (that is, a graph with an x-axis and a y-axis). The transformation will be defined as any rotation of this graph around the point where the axes intersect. Any such rotation will clearly produce a change in the graph relative to a fixed observer. But certain things will remain unchanged. For example, no matter how much we spin the graph on its central point, the distance between any two points on the graph will remain the same. The distance function, that is, the mathematical expression of the distance between any two points on the graph, is thus said to be invariant.

Group theory was taken to a higher level of abstraction as transformations of the sort I have described were themselves treated as elements of groups. Like the elements of a group, transformations can be anything at all, and that is why the theory had such wide applications. For instance, by the early twentieth century the concepts of groups, transformations, and invariants were pervasive in perceptual psychology. Cassirer studied this subject in a number of articles that he wrote in the last years of his life.[5] The central problem was how human subjects order the flood of sense impressions they receive so as to retain a sense of constancy in the objects before them. When we look at an object and then change our position, the sense data we receive from it in our second position are quite different from those we received in our initial position. If we imagine the retina as a film that simply records light impressions two-dimensionally without interpreting them three-dimensionally, then we realize that what we actually see when we look at, say, a cube is a quadrilateral—formed by light reflected off the cube—whose shape differs depending on the position of the cube relative to the retina. If we look at the cube from two different positions, the film impression we get is of two different quadrilaterals. If we look at a sphere of uniform red color, the film impression will show not uniform redness but an infinite range of shades of red. If we change our position, then the distribution of shades changes. And yet in both cases we remain convinced that we are dealing with an object whose actual shape or color is unchanged. In both cases we act *against* the sense data to remain convinced that what we see from several angles in the first instance is a cube, not a variety of quadrilaterals, and what we see in the second is a uniformly red sphere, not a collection of circles each with various shadings of red.

Cassirer shows how the theory of groups and transformations allowed perceptual psychologists to construct a conceptual model for this phenomenon. The idea is that as human subjects we automatically perform mental transformations of the type I described in projective geometry, and these transformations allow us to orient ourselves in space. (I am simplifying and shortening Cassirer's argument.) The transformations can be thought of as imaginary geometric reorderings of the visual field that are accomplished instantaneously and involuntarily; that is, they are part of the very process of object perception. In the theories of some late nineteenth- and early twentieth-century scientists these transformations exist as groups and follow the mathematical logic of groups. The principle of invariance is what permits us to establish a sense of constancy in the otherwise chaotic mass of sense impressions we receive. Thus the act of perceiving a red sphere involves both a complicated group of transformations, which are made to counteract the direct film impression of the sphere, and a principle of invariance, which leaves the red color fixed in the course of the transformations. Henri Poincaré, the French mathematician and philosopher, went so far as to assert that the group concept is a priori, that is, that it actually preexists in our minds and allows us to understand geometry, which he defines as the study of groups of transformations.[6]

Perceptual psychology was not the only field outside of mathematics where groups, transformations, and invariants put in an appearance. If we can believe Roman Jakobson, the concept of the invariant turned out to be the vital principle not only in mathematics but also in linguistics. He wrote on this subject a number of times. For example, in an article for a special issue of *Scientific American* in 1972, he talks about the important era of discovery for modern mathematics and linguistics and locates that era in the 1870s. He mentions the German mathematician Felix Klein, who in the 1870s proposed a new geometry based on the notion of invariant properties in transformations. Jakobson then demonstrates how similar principles arose in linguistics around the same time, and he cites the work of the most prominent linguists of the age, including Jan Baudouin de Courtenay and Ferdinand de Saussure. The link that Jakobson sees between mathematics and linguistics in that fruitful era is the shared concern for "the conjugate notions of invariance and variation" and for how these notions "brought forth the corollary task of eliciting relational invariants from a flux of variables."[7]

How does the shared concern in linguistics and mathematics show up in linguistics? The idea in the late nineteenth century and early twentieth century was to overthrow the prevailing approach to linguistics, that of the so-called Neogrammarians. This group of linguists viewed language primarily in a temporal sequence—in other words, historically, in its gradual and ceaseless unfolding from one stage to the next. The new, "avant-garde" linguists, as Jakobson calls them, were more interested in language as a relational system *now*, in the present. Relationalism and relativity were key concepts for this crowd, and Jakobson documents the parallels between the early school career of Albert Einstein and the developing ideas of the Swiss-German linguist Jost Winteler, with whom Einstein roomed as an adolescent when he was at school near Zurich. Winteler had always believed in something he called configurational relativity, and Jakobson intimates that this theory might well have played a role in the development of Einstein's own theory of relativity.

That suggestion might sound a bit extravagant, especially to those who accept the standard mythical view of Einstein as the half-mad scientist who knew no peers and whose ideas sprang to life spontaneously and unbeckoned in his disheveled head. There is no doubt that Jakobson is attempting to establish the respectable standing of twentieth-century linguistics by placing it on a level with the science that gave us the nuclear age. But he is also saying something serious about linguistics, namely that relationalism (of a sort that possibly bears analogy with relativity in physics) became dominant in it starting late in the nineteenth century. I mentioned in chapter 2 that even Potebnia's theory of language is relational.

What does relationalism look like in linguistics? Consider two prominent ideas in modern linguistics, ideas that, by chance, are among those that Jakobson himself championed during a good part of his career. The first is what Jakobson calls the markedness-unmarkedness distinction. In any linguistic system (in the relational era one speaks of "linguistic systems," not languages) features are distinguished by being marked (present and noticeable) or unmarked (absent and not noticeable, neutral). For example, in some linguistic systems masculine gender in a noun referring to a living creature does not necessarily indicate masculinity in that creature, whereas feminine gender does indicate femininity. In this instance, grammatical masculine gender is "unmarked," that is, it is neutral and carries no positive information about biological gender. Grammatical feminine gender, by contrast, is "marked," that is, it is nonneutral and carries positive information about biological gender.

The other prominent idea is "the continual, all-embracing, purposeful interplay of invariants and variations."[8] Jakobson had contemplated the tremendous variety of sounds in the languages of the world and had attempted to come up with properties that were common to all sound systems. He found the solution to his problem in the theory that there are certain invariant structures in the production of vowels and consonants, like the oppositions between "compact" and "diffuse" (qualities of the resonance chamber in the mouth), "grave" and "acute" (terms describing the kind and degree of occlusion of air as sounds are produced), and "voiced" and "unvoiced." These oppositions are what Jakobson calls distinctive features.[9] Let's say we were comparing the sound systems of French and English. Under the old way of thinking we would have tried to liken similar sounds, and we would have discovered that, for instance, an English *b* is different from a French *b* and that an English *p* is different from a French *p*. In both instances the French consonant would be far more tense and explosive than its English counterpart. The English and French equivalents are far from identical, and this sort of comparison would soon show that the two sound systems had relatively little in common. If, however, we examine the *relation* between b and p in each language, then we discover something that really is identical (invariant) in both, because both languages contain an opposition between a voiced consonant (b) and an unvoiced consonant (p) that are formed in roughly the same way (namely by the lips). What is invariant is not the individual sound p, treated in isolation, but the opposition in French and in English between p and its voiced counterpart, b. Thus no matter how widely the actual sounds of different languages may vary, there will always be a meaningful opposition between factors like the ones Jakobson mentions.

What distinguishes this approach from former approaches is precisely that it is relational. In both the marked-unmarked distinction and the interplay of invariants and variations truth is defined relatively. The isolated sign has no meaning by itself. The marked feature signifies what it signifies only because there is an unmarked feature that stands next to it, and the unmarked feature signifies what it signifies only because there is a marked feature that stands next to *it*. There is no universal trait in the languages of the world that signifies gender. Similarly, there is no way of reducing all the sound systems of the world's languages to a limited set of sharply defined, individual features. Consonants that we classify as guttural in one language are likely to sound completely different from those that we classify as guttural in another. A classification that is based on isolated qualities like guttural, palatal, and labial is doomed to be only approximate and therefore unsatisfactory. But we can safely talk about the universality of *oppositions* because when we do this, we are saying nothing about the absolute qualities of the individual sounds that are being opposed to one another. Each sound signifies what it signifies only because its opposite stands next to it, and this opposition has meaning only in the context of the entire language viewed as a system. Meaning is relational.

Jakobson wrote about this creed in many places. In Part II of this book I mentioned the "Retrospect" in which Jakobson describes his own intellectual genealogy by referring to various turn-of-the-century artists. In that essay he twice mentions the relational view of meaning. Here, too, he sees parallels between diverse fields. "Those of us who were concerned with language," he says, referring to the early years of his career, "learned to apply the principle of relativity in linguistic operations; we were consistently drawn in this direction by the spectacular development of modern physics and by the pictorial theory and practice of cubism, where everything 'is based on relationship' and interaction between parts and wholes, between color and shape, between the representation and the represented" (*SW*, 1:632). He approvingly quotes Georges Braque's phrase, which is similar to many others of the age: "I do not believe in things, I believe only in their relationship" (*SW*, 1: 632). Later on, he describes what he calls the topological approach to linguistics, one in which definitions are "purely relative and oppositive." This time he invokes the Scottish-American mathematician E. T. Bell, who said essentially the same thing as Braque: "It is not things that matter, but the relations between them" (*SW*, 1:637). In a lengthy article that Jakobson wrote in 1967, "Linguistics in Relation to Other Sciences," he talks about the interaction between linguistics and a number of sciences, including mathematics. Again Jakobson focuses on the branches of mathematics most concerned with relationalism and the system concept—set theory, Boolean algebra, topology, statistics, calculus of probability, theory of games, and information theory, which, he says, "find a fruitful application to a reinterpretative inquiry into the structure of human languages in their variables as well as their universal invariants. All these mathematical facts offer an appropriate multiform metalanguage into which linguistic data may be efficiently translated" (*SW*, 2:661).

Some of Jakobson's most extensive comments on the historical connection between mathematics and the rise of modern linguistics can be found in his article "The Kazan' School of Polish Linguistics." The article is largely about the Polish linguists Jan Baudouin de Courtenay and Mikołaj Kruszewski, whom Jakobson always considered to be trailblazers in modern linguistics. Jakobson says here, as in the other essays, that the crucial era was the 1870s, since that is when the concept of invariance "became the dominant principle in mathematics" and when "the first glimmerings of the theory of linguistic invariants also showed up" (*SW*, 2:412). It is the time when Baudouin made his "first attempts at uncovering the phonemic invariants lying beneath the fluctuating surface of speech, which is filled with countless combinatory and optional phonetic variations" (*SW*, 2:413). Jakobson places Baudouin in the illustrious company of two of the greatest mathematicians of the nineteenth century, Nikolai Lobachevsky and Carl Gauss—Lobachevsky because, like Baudouin, he had published bold new ideas in the bulletins of the backwater Kazan University, and Gauss because all three men had been subjected to intimidation from contemporary critics. As in other passages, Jakobson appears to be craftily suggesting connections that probably aren't there. Let's be honest: in the history of Western thought, no matter how great his contribution to modern liguistics may have been, Baudouin de Courtenay is simply not in the same class as Lobachevsky and Gauss. Who besides linguists and some literary critics has ever heard of him? Nor does Jakobson demonstrate any kind of connection between Lobachevsky and Baudouin. Lobachevsky proposed a non-Euclidean geometry, a theory that has enormous importance for the trend in mathematics I've been talking about, so it would be nice to show a connection between the two men. But Baudouin doesn't appear to have taken his idea of invariance from Lobachevsky.

Still, the important thing is that the idea of relationalism is present in Baudouin and that it coincides historically with similar ideas in mathematics. There's no doubt that Jakobson is right. In the same article he mentions Jost Winteler and shows how the notion of invariants appears in his work in the 1870s. Moreover, as in the later "Retrospect," he draws the parallel between linguistics and physics, using E. T. Bell as his authority to say that the concept of invariance was not fully understood until it was supported by the theory of general relativity (SW, 2:427).

Jakobsonian linguistics played an important role in twentieth-century criticism, particularly in the rise of structuralism, as I explained in chapter 6. Many others besides Jakobson have recounted the rise of structuralism in general and structural linguistics in particular, and a number of writers have pointed to the role of mathematics and relationalism in this story. Once again Ernst Cassirer comes to mind. In 1945, a few months before his death, he delivered a lecture titled "Structuralism in Modern Linguistics," which was subsequently published in the journal *Word*.[10] Cassirer returns here to a theme that had become familiar in his writings: the change in the logic of sciences that took place in the late nineteenth century. The change could be described as the rejection of the old mechanistic models of physical phenomena in favor of systems models. The best example is the quest for a model that would explain electromagnetic waves. Traditional mechanical models, which attempted to provide a purely material explanation of electromagnetic phenomena, did not succeed because they became too intricate, says Cassirer. The solution was the concept of the electromagnetic field, in which individual parts have no independent meaning but exist only functionally, in relation to the entire system. Thus in this model an electron "is embedded in the field and exists only under the general structural conditions of the field" (p. 101). Cassirer speaks of similar developments in other fields and shows how linguistics developed along similar lines. The emphasis is always on the system concept, which Cassirer illustrates with examples from the Danish linguist Viggo Bröndal and Jakobson. The passage excerpted from Bröndal reads like a definition of the system concept: it's all about "system" and "structure," "coherent sets" and the "interdependence of elements" (p. 104).

The most unequivocal statement I know of the mathematical origins of structuralism was made by Jean Piaget, the Swiss psychologist. In his book on structuralism he devoted an entire chapter to the concept of structure in mathematics. He asserts in that chapter that although we cannot tie someone like Lévi-Strauss directly to mathematics, structuralist thinking is nonetheless directly adapted from algebra. Piaget launches into an extensive (at least for the general reader) mathematical discussion of groups and transformations as a basis for an understanding of modern structural thinking.[11]

No one can beat Michel Serres, however, for the elegance of his description of the modern structural theory of meaning and its origins in mathematics. It is the subject of a number of essays in *Hermès ou la communication,* which Serres wrote during the 1960s and published in 1968, at the height of the structuralist fever in France.[12] Mind you, Serres does not claim to be writing about the structuralist movement as such. He's not interested in the specific expressions of the type of thinking he analyzes, so he doesn't spend his time talking about Lévi-Strauss, Roland Barthes, A. J. Greimas, Tzvetan Todorov, and others associated with that movement. Rather, he is interested in communication, as the title of his book suggests, and communication has to do with meaning. It's not always clear exactly what Serres has in mind historically when he refers to things that are modern. Sometimes he appears to be talking about his own age; at other times he appears to be talking about the twentieth century and its intellectual origins in the middle and late nineteenth century.

In any case, his argument, simplified, runs something like this: The traditional view of meaning, until modern times, has been a linear one. That is, meaning was thought of as tied, in a direct, "linear" fashion, to things. Serres uses the term *symbolism* in a rather uncommon sense to designate this notion of meaning. In symbolism objects of meaning "stand for" things, and things directly give meaning. A symbol is always linked in a linear way with its sense. The modern age changed the old way of thinking, Serres says. Instead of a linear view, in the modern age we have a "tabular" view of meaning. That is, we have replaced the "symbolist" view with a view that places the emphasis not on things themselves but on the relations between them. Meaning in the modern age is an affair that can be visualized as a chart or table (hence "tabularity"), a chessboard, on which only relative positions are important. We have accomplished this change precisely by importing the idea of structure from mathematics, and thus we have benefited from the same revolution in mathematics that Cassirer describes, namely the revolution that changed mathematics (to use Serres's terminology now) from a "symbolic" science (in other words, Cassirer's intuitionistic mathematics, where symbols always stand ultimately for sensuous objects) to a formal science. Tabularity has resulted in the notion of structure, which Serres defines thus (putting the whole passage in italics): "A structure is an operational group with indefinite meaning . . . that groups elements, which exist in any number and whose content is unspecified, and relations, which exist in finite numbers and whose nature is unspecified" (p. 32).

The idea of structure has thus given us a whole new method for classifying things. Previously things were grouped, according to principles of similarity, around a single archetype. In the modern age, instead of families of things grouped around an archetype we have families of *models,* and instead of an archetype we have what Serres calls a "structural analogon of form," which he identifies as the "operational invariant that organizes [the families of models], all content having been abstracted away." The true triumph of the modern age consists in our ability "to construct a cultural entity by taking a form and filling it with meaning." Structural analysis "dominates, constructs, gives" meaning, where in the past we were always at the mercy of preestablished meanings (p. 33). This is the glory of the modern age of abstraction.

It's not important to pause and define all the terms that Serres uses. He writes in a dense style that makes it difficult to excerpt from him without losing a meaning that comes with the context (in this sense he is an illustration of his own subject). But he really has said all that can be said about relationalism and its logical origins in mathematics. Serres is fond of mathematics and sees mathematical ideas at the origin of lots of different things. In his discussion of modern structural thinking there is no doubt that he is right, provided we don't assign too strict a historical sense to what he says. Structural thinkers didn't go to mathematicians, learn about group theory, and then come up with interpretations of novels. But the logical origin is certainly in mathematics, and it is not purely a matter of coincidence that relationalism showed up in so many different fields at around the same time. This is an age when Braque's phrase, "It is not things that matter, but the relations between them," is echoed by many different writers. Everybody is suddenly interested in sets and groups, systems of relations, invariants, models, complexes, fields, gestalts, combinatory operations, and similar concepts expressed with various other phrases. In literary theory it is the age of impersonality, where the essence of a literary work of art is not the author, not even some kind of eternal truth; now the essence is a complex of relations, exactly as it will be when the structuralist critics come along to give their stamp of approval to ideas that had been around for a century. Many of the same writers who, in a backward turn to a theological era, spoke of essences and treated literary texts as religious objects seem at the same time to have come up with a paradoxically secular answer to the question of what those essences are. No one is comfortable any more with the idea of being overtly religious and theological. The religious and the theological survive in the form of myths of essence, and now, as if to disavow any sort of metaphysical status to that essence, modern thinkers make it an abstraction, a relational structure ostensibly emptied of all symbolic (in Serres's sense) meaning.

CHAPTER EIGHT

Descartes in Relational Garb

"Why do we eat?" begins the popular French cookbook *Je sais cuisiner* (I know how to cook), by Ginette Mathiot. "Everyone has a pretty good idea. 'We need to eat in order to live.' " The question is how to do it. "In the present era, when the scientific spirit is increasingly asserting itself, nutrition often continues to be the victim of custom and prejudice and is governed by chance or caprice. But knowing how to nourish oneself is a science that one cannot scorn without detriment to one's health and to the family budget." Mme. Mathiot then goes on to explain that food responds to two "essential needs of our organism": the need for matter and the need for energy. Foods can thus be divided into two categories, depending on whether they provide energy or matter.[1] A few dozen pages later the reader has all the necessary information, together with the fundamental principles, to prepare a nutritious, economical, and tasty meal for any occasion that may arise.

A little less than three hundred years before the publication of *Je sais cuisiner*, René Descartes published his renowned *Discourse on Method*. In that work Descartes proposed a new "method" of thinking or problem solving. His method consisted of four rules, which Descartes writes in the informal, first-person style of the entire *Discourse*: (1) "to accept nothing as true that I did not know to be evidently so," (2) "to divide each of the difficulties I was examining into as many particles as I could," (3) "to conduct my thoughts in order, beginning with the simplest objects and those that are easiest to understand, and progressing, as if by degrees, to the understanding of the most compound," and (4) "always to carry out enumerations so complete and reviews so general, that I would be certain of having omitted nothing."[2]

Let's see how Descartes's method applies to a given problem—eating. Why do I eat? That's easy: I need to eat in order to live ("to accept nothing as true that I did not know to be evidently so"). How do I determine what to eat? Subdivide: there are two different categories of food, and each of these may be divided into various actual species of edible things ("to divide each of the difficulties I was examining into as many particles as I could"). What to do with all these edible things to make them nutritious, economical, and tasty? Start with the basic principles of nutrition, move to the basic principles of cooking, and continue building from there ("to conduct my thoughts in order, beginning with the simplest objects and those that are easiest to understand, and progressing, as if by degrees, to the understanding of the most compound"). What do I do, now that I'm ready to head for the kitchen and prepare something to eat? Stock my kitchen with all the utensils necessary for successful cooking (Mathiot lists them on pages 51–52) and consult a list of thousands of recipes ("to carry out enumerations so complete and reviews so general, that I would be certain of having omitted nothing").

I don't know anything about Ginette Mathiot's upbringing and can't say whether or not she was a scholar of Descartes. But the method is unquestionably in her cookbook. How many American authors of cookbooks start out with the basic question and the most clearly evident truth about their subject and then reason in so systematic a fashion to the real substance of their books, namely the recipes?[3] The Cartesian method is pervasive in French thought. One sees again and again in writing of all sorts this urge always to start back at the beginning of a thing and then carry it through its steps to the general and abstract conclusions that follow from it. All American students of French know this style of thinking, just as French schoolchildren do, because when they learn to write those infuriating and tedious exercises in literary analysis called *explications de texte*, they are taught always to start with the facts, to reason from the concrete to the abstract, from the simple to the complex, from the specific to the general.

In his late work *The Crisis of European Sciences and Transcendental Phenomenology* Husserl made the claim that Descartes is the "original founding genius of all modern philosophy."[4] Descartes's contribution to the modern spirit was to expand Galileo's "mathematization of nature" into a global notion of philosophy as a "universal mathematics" (*Universalmathematik*).[5] Descartes's entire method was based on mathe-

matical principles and designed to bring thought itself into accord with
these principles. In the posthumously published "Rules for the Direction
of the Mind" Descartes had written, several years before the *Discourse*,
that to eliminate any obstacles in our efforts to discern the true from the
false, we must follow an orderly method, like the one we see in the
mathematical sciences. "Those who seek the straight path of truth must
not concern themselves with any object about which they do not have
certainty equal to [that afforded by] Arithmetic and Geometry."[6] In the
Discourse and elsewhere Descartes talks repeatedly of the "certainty"
and the "evidence" (that is, the state of being evident) of mathematical
reasoning. I can't say for sure whether or not Descartes was the "original
founding genius of all modern philosophy," but there is no mistaking
the traces of his method in French thought.

MALLARMÉ AND THE LIGHT
OF RECIPROCAL REFLECTIONS

In the first part of this book I suggested that Mallarmé was satirizing
the Cartesian method in his introduction to *English Words*. If that is
true, then it is no surprise to see the young Mallarmé in 1869 dreaming
up a project for a book in which all the factors I've been talking about
come together. It seems that in the late 1860s Mallarmé was considering
taking a degree in linguistics, and in a fragmentary note somehow related
to this plan he writes:

> A strange little book, very mysterious, a bit in the manner of the Fathers,
> very distilled and concise—this in places that could give rise to enthusiasm
> (study Montesquieu).
>   In others, the great and long period of Descartes.
>   Then, in general, some La Bruyère and some Fénelon with a hint of Bau-
> delaire.
>   Finally, some me [*du moi*]—and some mathematical language.
>   (*OC*, p. 851)

A paragraph or two farther on, he mentions the *Discourse* (misquoting
the title) and then says, "We have not understood Descartes, foreigners
have taken possession of him: but he did arouse French mathematicians"
(*OC*, p. 851). Mallarmé never explains the intriguing little phrase about
mathematical language. If by chance he meant something like the rigorous, methodical mode of exposition that Descartes's principles suggested, then we know that the closest he ever came to adopting the
Cartesian method in his own writing was to parody it. And perhaps the

effort to parody that method was made only as the result of Mallarmé's having first internalized it.

The mathematical imagination had clearly seized hold of Mallarmé. But it is the "modern" kind of mathematics, the relational kind, that shows up time and again in his writings. Earlier I said that the theory Mallarmé appears to be proposing in "Crisis in Verse" led to a relational notion of language. In fact, if we look at that essay again, we can see that Mallarmé, without knowing it, is essentially giving us an illustration of Serres's argument about linear and tabular meanings. The "unique-stamp" view of meaning, where words turn out to be "materially truth itself," is really the linear view, or the symbolist view (in Serres's sense of symbolism). In this view one can draw a straight line from the signifying object to the thing it signifies. But in Mallarmé's enlightened view of language, meaning comes from the "reciprocal reflections" of words, and this sounds like Serres's notion of tabular meaning.

The idea of a group of relations appears several times in Mallarmé in one form or another. Later in "Crisis in Verse" he refers to music as "the set [*ensemble*] of relations existing in everything" (*OC*, p. 368). Virtually the same phrase occurs in "The Book, Spiritual Instrument." Just after Mallarmé says, "Everything, in the world, exists to end up in a book," he lists the qualities that will be required in his book: "hymn, harmony and joy, like the pure set, grouped in some fulgurating circumstance, of relations between everything" (*OC*, p. 378). These phrases were composed later in Mallarmé's life. But even as early as 1866 he had adopted a relational view of poetic language. In a letter to François Coppée he says, "What we need to aim for above all in the poem is for words . . . to *reflect on one another to the point where they appear no longer to have their own color but to be only the modulations of a scale.*"[7] In a curious passage in a letter to another friend that same year, Mallarmé uses an image that suggests the same model. The young poet writes that he has just cast the plan for his entire oeuvre, after having discovered his own "center," "the center of myself, where I sit like a sacred spider, on the principal threads that have already come out of my mind and with whose help I will weave *at the points of contact* marvelous lacework."[8]

The place where we see Mallarmé's mathematical imagination at its best is his writings about the Book. In chapter 4 I described the manuscript notes that have been published under the title *Le "Livre" de Mallarmé*. It is full of numbers, calculations, and geometric designs. Some of the calculations appear to have to do with the number of spectators at a performance of this mysterious work. Others have to do with the arrangement of pages in the work. Still others are about as apparently mundane a question as the amount of money the author will be able to collect from ticket sales at the performance. Sometimes all three appear together (see illustration).[9]

But even though it's hard to say what these manuscript notes are, we can see that the numbers are an essential part of the work that Mallarmé was contemplating. This is not just scratch paper on which the author figured his monthly budget. The recurrence of certain significant numbers, usually multiples of four, shows that all these details were integral to the work. Whatever this "work" was supposed to be, we can say with some confidence that its numerical properties were not going to be left to chance. In fact, one has the impression that the "content" could never be more precisely spelled out than it was because the essential nature of the work was not the content but exactly these numerical properties. Consider again the drawing on page 95. What is it? Not just doodling, because there are other designs in the manuscript that look similar and are accompanied by various terms that have occurred in lots of other places in the manuscript notes. It appears thus to have something important to do with what the work is. It's as if Mallarmé had set out to determine a set of geometric coordinates for his work and once that was done had decided nothing more was necessary.

How can a work have geometric coordinates? For one thing, it can be a performance in which the disposition of seats, spectators, and performers (the "operator") is an integral part of the work. In that case the work has coordinates in the literal sense, coordinates that belong to actual points in the space in which the performance takes place. Or it can be the sort of thing where there are mystical numerical correspondences between numbers of spectators and the amount of cash they pay for admission. Then the coordinates cannot be assigned to actual physical locations but exist instead as abstractions, and these abstractions are diagrammed in the manuscript notes. Or it can be a book whose pages may be shuffled and reshuffled in any number of combinations to generate as many different "works." In this "mobile-pages" conception the pages of the book are distributed in various determined locations of the space where the book is performed. In any of these cases the essential point about the work is that it is a relational structure.

One of the strangest things Mallarmé wrote is the text called *Un coup de dés* (A throw of the dice), published in 1897. There's no exact word for what this work is. In fact it's not even clear that *Un coup de dés* is

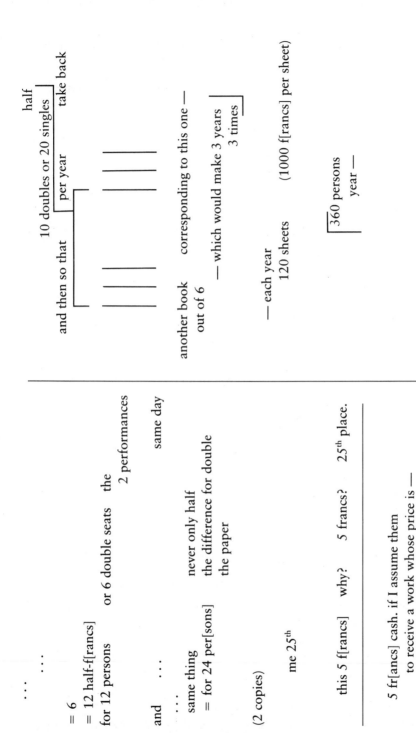

From Jacques Scherer, *Le "Livre" de Mallarmé: Premières recherches sur des documents inédits* (Paris: Gallimard, 1957), pp. 37(A)-38(A).

the title. The text, twenty-one pages long, contains the sentence "Un coup de dés jamais n'abolira le hasard" ("A throw of the dice will never abolish chance") spread out in four pieces over seventeen pages ("Un coup de dés / jamais / n'abolira / le hasard"). This central sentence is printed in oversize type. In between its fragments are numerous phrases and sentences written in a variety of smaller types. The "poem," if that's what it is, is of course tricky to read. The main sentence gives it a kind of syntactic completeness and serves as a unifying device. The problem is what to do with all the other words. It is tempting to read them as a highly complex network of parenthetical and dependent clauses, where the clauses printed in smaller type depend on the ones printed in larger type. But even if you try to read it in this way, you get hopelessly bogged down in twenty-one pages of interlocking grammatical dependence and soon give up. Paul Valéry, who claims to be the first human being (other than the author) ever to see this work, says that Mallarmé first read it to him "in a low, even voice, without the slightest 'effect,' almost to himself."[10] The text actually may be read in many different ways: you may read one type size at a time, you may read through the text in the order in which the words are printed, or you may simply read in any order you choose. Once again we have a shuffling game, a relational scheme whose most prominent feature is precisely its refusal of linearity. This refusal is both syntactic and semantic—syntactic because a linear reading of the text is almost impossible, and semantic because this is one place where even the most old-fashioned thinker will see that meaning does not arise word by word in a linear fashion.

There is also no linear connection between the text and the person who wrote it. How do you establish an authorial voice for a thing that can't really be read in any of the traditional senses? No, there can be no sign of the author's presence, and strikingly enough, the disappearance of the author (a much-touted idea in Mallarmé's age) seems to be explained by the relational quality of the text. Think back to the passage in "Crisis in Verse" in which the notion of reciprocal reflections is introduced: "The pure work implies the elocutionary disappearance of the poet, who instead yields the initiative to words, mobilized by the clash of their inequality; they light up from their reciprocal reflections, like a trail of fire on gems, taking the place of that palpable breath in the lyric inspiration of yore or the enthusiastic personal direction of speech" (OC, 366). Once words start reflecting off each other, they can no longer reflect back to the author, or so the author appears to be suggesting. Right before the passage where Mallarmé talks about the "pure set . . .

of relations between everything" he says that the volume should "require no signatory" (*OC*, p. 378). In his autobiographical letter he speaks of a "text speaking of itself and without an author's voice" (*OC*, p. 663). And in Scherer's manuscript notes we read on the next-to-last page about a volume "for whose sense I am not responsible—not signed as such," this in the midst of a flurry of calculations determining the order and placement of pages (201 [A]).

"Things exist, we don't have to create them; all we have to do is grasp the relations between them; it is the threads of these relations that form verses and orchestras" (*OC*, p. 871). A sentence like this looks very structuralist *avant la lettre*. In fact, this and other passages convinced James Boon to write *From Symbolism to Structuralism,* in which he points out the affinities between the thought and poetics of French symbolist poets (Baudelaire, Mallarmé, Rimbaud, Verlaine, and, oddly, Rousseau and Proust) and the ethnology of structural anthropologist Claude Lévi-Strauss. For Boon, the passage I just quoted is emblematic of the whole worldview he sees in Mallarmé. Everything in Mallarmé's universe is relation, analogy, connection, and structure, just as it is in Lévi-Strauss. The emphasis in both writers is always decisively shifted away from content. The one thing Boon doesn't discuss is the mathematical foundations of this type of thinking, but we know it's there for Mallarmé as it is for the entire structuralist movement.[11]

VALÉRY AND THE DISCOURSE ON *HIS* METHOD

Paul Valéry lived his life as though he had been put on earth to provide the rest of us with a caricature of the French mind. "Ce qui n'est pas clair n'est pas français," goes the timeworn eighteenth-century expression that our French teachers taught us in high school. But *clair* in French means both "clear" in the sense of comprehensible and "light" in the sense of bright, and Valéry's poetry is filled with radiant Mediterranean sunshine. The mind strives for the clear and comprehensible because what is comprehensible is radiant. Valéry worshipped the human mind, especially his own. The "hero" of his prose work *Monsieur Teste* (Mister Head) says something that perfectly describes the author and his characteristic pose: "Je suis étant, et me voyant; me voyant me voir, et ainsi de suite . . . " ("I am [in the process of] being, and seeing myself; seeing myself see myself, and so on . . . ").[12]

Valéry loved admiring the workings of his own mind. Wrapped up with this fascination for the mind was a fascination for mathematics that went far beyond the numerical fantasies of Mallarmé. Unlike Mallarmé, Valéry actually fancied himself a mathematician, and he devoted an astounding amount of time and energy to studying contemporary mathematical theory and then trying to find applications for it in the most extraordinary fields. His friend Pierre Féline introduced him to a number of areas of mathematical study, among them group theory and transformation group theory. Valéry was apparently fond of using his knowledge of mathematics to dazzle his other friends, people like André Gide, who knew very little about such things.[13] The twenty-nine-volume set of Valéry's notebooks is a startling record of a mind obsessed with numbers, with itself, with its obsession with itself, with a mathematical expression of its own workings, and so on—a kind of monument to neo-Cartesian narcissism.[14]

Valéry's notebooks show a curious attitude toward "the original founding genius of all modern philosophy." To begin with, even though he devoted a substantial number of pages to ruminations on philosophers, Valéry was fond of playing the part of someone who is foreign to hard-core philosophy and doesn't quite understand it all. So when it comes to Descartes, he likes to talk about things that fussy, scholarly people would consider trivial. In one fairly long notebook entry he mentions the qualities that have struck him personally in various philosophers—this after saying that philosophers are boring to read and that their language is antipathetic to him. Of Descartes, Valéry can say only that it is the "individual" that "appears" to him, meaning, I assume, that he is attracted by the personal style of Descartes's writing.[15] He returns over and over again to the subject of Cartesian doubt and the most famous phrase from the Discourse on Method, "I think, therefore I am." And he speaks of the "insignificance" of the principles in the Discourse, saying that the charm of the work is "above its substance" (C, 16:728 [1:673]).

Like Descartes, Valéry sought clarity, certainty, evidence (again in the sense of "state of being evident"), and he sought it in mathematics. "Descartes. No occult qualities—made the greatest effort for Clarity," Valéry muses at one moment in his notebooks (C, 10:103 [1:595]). "On Descartes: Clear and distinct ideas," he writes a number of years later (C, 20:508 [1:700]). But the model he used was always the structural one, the one that placed the emphasis on the relation between elements rather than on the elements in and for themselves. Valéry saw the mind as essentially a relational system whose operation he attempted to describe in the language of group mathematics. "Every act of understanding is based on a group," he says (C, 1:331). "My specialty—reducing everything to the study of a system closed on itself and finite" (C, 19:645). The transformation model came into play, too. At each moment of mental life the mind is like a group, or relational system, but since mental life is continuous over time, one "group" undergoes a "transformation" and becomes a different group in the next moment. If the mind is constantly being transformed, how do we account for the continuity of the self? Simple: by invoking the notion of the invariant. And so we find passages like this one: "The S[elf] is invariant, origin, locus or field, it's a functional property of consciousness" (C, 15:170 [2:315]). Just as in transformational geometry, something remains fixed in all the projective transformations of the mind's momentary systems, and that something is the Self (le Moi, or just M, as Valéry notates it so that it will look like an algebraic variable). Transformation theory is all over the place. "Mathematical science . . . reduced to algebra, that is, to the analysis of the transformations of a purely differential being made up of homogeneous elements, is the most faithful document of the properties of grouping, disjunction, and variation in the mind" (O, 1:36). "Psychology is a theory of transformations, we just need to isolate the invariants and the groups" (C, 1:915). "Man is a system that transforms itself" (C, 2:896).

The Notebooks are not the only place where Valéry indulges in this kind of speculation. His mathematical theories turn up in his published writings, too. In an article in Mercure de France in 1899 he wrote about what he called the reversibility of states of consciousness. "The transformations that any given system undergoes are reversible when the system is able to return from a certain state to an earlier state, passing through the same states during the return as it had on its way here, only in reverse order. This definition, though its origin is in physics, is sufficiently general that one can attempt to apply it to the mind and view the mind as a system of transformations" (O, 2:1459). In a piece called "A Few Words about Myself," published in 1944, Valéry describes how he discovered at the age of twenty "that man is a closed system with respect to his cognition and his acts" (O, 2:1518). Later in the same essay he describes the entire credo of his youth:

> There was a time when I saw.
> I saw or wanted to see the figures of relations between things and not the things.

Things made me smile from pity. Those who paused to consider them
were to me sheer idolaters. I *knew* that the essential thing was *figure*.

(O, 2:1532)

The term *system* has at least two important senses for Valéry, and several
of his notebook entries show that the elaboration of the idea of systems
was associated with Descartes. I mentioned earlier that Mallarmé had
a metaphysical crisis in his twenties, which led him to some important
philosophical discoveries that were to occupy his mind for the remainder
of his life. In 1892 Valéry, who had just met Mallarmé the year before,
had a "crisis" of his own. On the face of it, it was a rather trivial matter—a case of unrequited love. It did, however, lead him to a major
turning point: he renounced the emotional life in favor of something
that he would call the System (with a capital *S*). The System was an ideal
program of intellectual contemplation whose chief purpose was to sub-
mit all important phenomena of mental life to rigorous, dispassionate
analysis, the sort of thing we see piecemeal in Valéry's notebooks, which
in a significant sense *are* the result of this program.[16] But system (with
a lowercase *s*) also means relational system in the sense I've been using.
When Valéry talks about the System he often feels the need to mention
systems and to bring up Descartes:

> Grosso modo the System has been the quest for a language or a notation
> that would make it possible to treat de omni re just as analyt[ic] geo[metry]
> allowed Des Cartes [*sic*] to treat all figures.
> The human body (viewed as a syst[em] of variables) must be able to reveal
> this secret.
>
> (C, 9:82 [1:812])

In another long entry, written about fifteen years after this one, Valéry's
subject is once again the System: "It used to be, would have been, is,
was, and would be a kind of method à la Descartes—I mean Geometry—
because it would have to do with a sort of systematic translation of the
diversity of objects and the transformations of consciousness or the mind
into elements and modes of *functioning* (observable or probable) of this
mind." And a little later in the same entry he brings up once again the
notion of system: "In short, it seemed ever more strongly to me that
what appears almost always and necessarily, like *things,* world, ideas,
cognition, was *somewhere else,* the product of a functioning—that is, a
bounded, closed system, forced to return to itself" (C, 20:290–292
[1:846]).

Perhaps the most intriguing of the notebook statements on the System and its Cartesian analogy is the one in which Valéry writes in adjacent columns about Descartes and himself. On the left side of the page are four brief phrases having to do with Descartes: "Discours de ma méthode" (instead of "Discours de la méthode"), "Story 1892" (the year of his crisis), "The finite—reduction to my system," and, in a reference to the Latin version of Descartes's famous sentence, "Instead of Cogito and Sum, my formula." On the right side of the page he writes this: "The System—is not a 'philosophical system'— —instead, it's the *system of me*—my *potential*—my coming and going—my way of seeing and returning" (*C*, 18:55 [1:841]). As this entry and many others show, Valéry regarded Descartes's method not precisely as being similar to his own but as being a kind of analogical model, much as Kant invoked the name of Copernicus to call attention not to the content of his own new philosophy but to its revolutionary character.

The last entry I quoted is especially valuable because it hints at the reason for the difference between Descartes and Valéry. Descartes, too, founded a "system." In fact, his philosophy is often referred to as systemlike because of the coherence of its parts and its "closed" nature. But for Valéry, it is still just a philosophical system, that is, a corpus of writings on "philosophical" subjects. Valéry's System is different because its very logic is different. In Valéry we see the logic of relational systems, the "system of me." And what could be more systematic than a system of thought whose primary characteristic is that it is systemlike?

Valéry was consistent, and we find the system concept everywhere. In a world where the mind is a system, it is natural that the things the mind makes should look like systems, too. "I have eternally sought to define or construct a system of variables (that is, a syst[em] of notations)—and of the relations of the conditions among them that would make it possible to represent tangible life," reads an entry in the *Notebooks* (*C*, 18:608). One important category of things the mind makes is of course artworks, and not surprisingly, these behave like the systems (the minds) that created them. There's a reason for this, but it has to do with the subject of Part IV of this book, so I will put off talking about it until then. For now, let's just observe how the system concept works in Valéry's vision of artworks.

To a certain extent Valéry's remarks on artworks are historical. That is, he sees the relational quality of art partly as a phenomenon peculiar to the modern age. In an early article called "On Literary Technique" Valéry writes about the modern conception of the poet: "He's no longer the disheveled, delirious man, someone who writes an entire poem in a night of fever; now he's a cold scientist [*savant*], almost an algebraist, in the service of a refined dreamer" (*O*, 1:1809). Mallarmé is partly to be credited with the modern spirit in poetry, as Valéry says in another place: he was "the first writer who dared to envisage the literary problem in its full universality. . . . He conceived as algebra what all the others have thought about only in the particularity of arithmetic."[17] But certain types of artwork for Valéry are intrinsically structural, regardless of the historical period during which they were created. Valéry was a firm believer in the poetry-prose distinction. In "Poetry and Abstract Thought" the emphasis is on the difference between poetic language and the language of prose. Valéry felt that the distinction extended to the entire work of art, which is to say that a poem as a whole is different from, say, a novel as a whole. The distinguishing factor is the relational quality of poems, as he explains in his "Homage to Marcel Proust": "And while the world of the poem is essentially closed and complete unto itself, being the pure system of the ornaments and possibilities [*chances*] of language, the universe of the novel, even of the fantasy novel, is connected with the real world." (*O*, 1:770). One of Valéry's favorite art forms was dance, because it so clearly embodied the relational principles he wanted to see in everything. In an essay originally given as a lecture in 1936, "Philosophy of the Dance," he says: "No exteriority! The dancer has no outside. . . . Nothing exists beyond the system that she forms through her acts" (*O*, 1:1398). And a paragraph later he describes dance as "a group of sensations that makes an abode for itself, . . . that emits from the depths of itself this beautiful series of transformations in space" (*O*, 1:1398). Valéry's personal dream was to create the perfect, mathematically determined work of art, something he mused about in his notebook the year before he died:

> To arrive at the completion of a work by means of formal conditions accumulated like functional equations— —
>
> in such a way that the possible contents are more and more *circumscribed*—
>
> Subject, characters, situations result from a structure of abstract restrictions—
>
> (*C*, 28:468 [1:314–15])

If ever there was a prestructuralist thinker, it was Valéry. I say *prestructuralist* not only because Valéry's thought looks like structuralism even before there was any such field as structural linguistics, anthropology, or criticism but also because it shows the logical foundations of structuralism in all their naked, unabashed glory. Few structuralists later in the twentieth century felt the need to expose the mathematical foundations of their thought or repeat the by then timeworn credo about how the importance is in the relations and not in the elements themselves. They had gone beyond this credo, had taken it all for granted as something that didn't need to be said in their elaborate discussions of structures and systems. But Valéry did feel the need to say it—over and over and over again. For him, the real truth—the real essence, to be more accurate—always had to be anchored firmly in the neo-Cartesian logic of relationalism. And the credo was always worth repeating, as if that would keep the relational essence from suddenly slipping away, leaving behind the most dreaded monster of all: *things themselves.*

CHAPTER NINE

How Numbers Ran Amok
in Russia

For the French, mathematics is always tied up with the Cartesian ideal of intellectual clarity and rigor, even if that ideal is there for no other reason than to be ridiculed. But leave it to the Russians to turn mathematics into a forum for impassioned political and theological debate. I gave a simple definition of group theory in chapter 7, and most people would be hard put to figure out how that theory could have anything to do with politics or religion. Alexander Vucinich, who wrote a two-volume history of the role of science in Russian culture, tells the fascinating story of how group theory caught on in Russia at the end of the nineteenth century, after first having been introduced there in the 1860s, and how it came to represent one camp in a struggle among mathematicians for the soul of the motherland.[1] The passion in this struggle appears to have been concentrated lopsidedly in the opposing camp. Classical mathematics, meaning differential and integral calculus in particular and algebraic calculations in general, promoted a mechanistic view of the universe, one in which causality reigned supreme and in which there was no room for "noncontinuous," free phenomena. In other words, classical mathematics is essentially materialistic, or so the argument ran in this camp. Ever since the 1860s, when the philosophy of nihilism came to dominate the political left in Russia—the philosophy, that is, whose basic premises were the material character of all natural phenomena, the nonexistence of free will, and the continuity of the animal and the human kingdoms—a pitched battle had raged between secular materialists on the left and conservatives on the right.

Since the right supported the autocracy, and since conservative nationalist sentiment in Russia was always bound up with Russian Orthodox Christianity, the opponents of secular materialism championed the cause of philosophical idealism, if not outright religious fundamentalism. And so by a leap of logic that will seem astonishing today, the antialgebraists embraced such fields of mathematics as (they felt) supported idealism and freedom of will, two things that the obstreperous materialists on the left had no patience for. "Arithmology," or the theory of discontinuous functions (that is, functions not susceptible of causal explanation, thus "free"), became the favored field, and to free Russia from the scourge of materialism and make the world safe for imperial autocracy, these brave mathematicians set about to arithmetize mathematics.

How, you might ask, could anyone take this program seriously? It's hard enough to understand what idealism and materialism have to do with arithmology and algebra. It's even harder to understand how anyone can translate the study of fields as removed from the physical universe as these into the realm of nationalist politics. The trouble is that the antialgebraists were led by one of the foremost academic mathematicians of the day in Russia, none other than Nikolai Vasil'evich Bugaev, dean of the natural-science faculty at Moscow University and well known in intellectual circles. He was also Andrei Bely's father. Bugaev, as it happened, did not even believe in God. Bely always portrayed him as a severe, contemptuous, and demanding skeptic. He was an odd figure to be supporting ultranationalist causes in a country where ultranationalism was so tied up with the church. But apparently for him, idealism even without religion was close enough to the essential spirit of Russian autocracy, and so he embraced his cause with extraordinary fervor.

Most historians agree that the truly important developments in nineteenth-century mathematics were in precisely the areas that Bugaev and his supporters opposed, those areas, incidentally, that Jakobson considered so fruitful for the development of modern linguistics and that Cassirer considered so fruitful for twentieth-century thought in general. The division between the opposing camps in Russia quickly became blurred in the first decades of the twentieth century, when followers of Bugaev contributed to discoveries in such areas as quantum mechanics and drew on set theory—an algebraic field if ever there was one—for their work.[2] In any case, it would have been hard for nonmathematicians to take sides in a struggle like the one between Bugaev and the algebraists since most people would have trouble understanding the philosophical and political implications of mathematical theory. But that did not stop a great many artists and literary figures from becoming consumed by an overpowering interest in mathematics, and Bely was among them. Few of them could be described as really familiar with current mathematical theory of the sort that Bugaev and his friends were arguing about, but the number mania that took hold in the literary and visual arts (which were often hard to distinguish from each other) in the first three decades of the twentieth century ended up producing the same cult of relationalism in the arts as we find in human sciences like linguistics. And relationalism invariably meant a form of essentialism.

BELY'S BASKETS, ROOFS, AND RHOMBUSES

Nikolai Vasil'evich Bugaev was a respected mathematician, and he and others like him drew all kinds of extravagant inferences about the connection between mathematics and politics. In such a climate perhaps some of the ideas his son came up with aren't so odd. Bely was a student of the natural sciences for a brief period, and at one time he contemplated the possibility of constructing an exact science of aesthetics. In an essay called "The Principle of Form in Aesthetics" he proposed one approach to the problem.[3] The notion was that the various art forms (music, poetry, painting, sculpture, and architecture) are distinct expressions of something single and universal (which we may call art, for the sake of simplicity). Bely wondered if a set of a priori principles could be discovered that would show why art in a certain instance can manifest itself, say, *only* as music or *only* as painting. An exact science of aesthetics would demonstrate that the various art forms are actually subject to a kind of logical necessity, not only in the sense that each art form exists as an art form by logical necessity (before the world existed, one could have predicted that there would be music, poetry, and so on) but also in the sense that any work of art comes by logical necessity to be expressed in the form in which it is expressed.

There's nothing amazing about that idea, and Bely is certainly not the first person to have thought of it. But next he takes it into his head to find a model for his theory in thermodynamics, and he spends the rest of the essay working out the details. If there is a principle of conservation of energy in physics, Bely thinks, then there must be a principle of conservation of creative energy in art. Using terms like *quantity, tension,* and *kinetic creative energy,* Bely bombards his reader with equations and calculations that make what he writes look like a chemistry textbook. The difference between what Bely writes and a chemistry book, though, is in the words between the equations. For example, at one point Bely says:

> While composing large-scale artworks, Ibsen, for instance, attempted at first to expend a certain quantity of energy
>
> $$\left[\frac{a}{b} + \frac{a}{b} + \frac{a}{b} + \frac{a}{b} = \frac{4a}{b} \right],$$
>
> but then, through corrections in his manuscript, heightened the *tension* of the expended effort:
>
> $$\left[\frac{4a}{b}, \frac{4a + a_1}{b}, \frac{4a + a_1 + a_2}{b}, \frac{4a + a_1 + a_2 + a_3}{b}, \ldots \right].$$
>
> This is how Goethe wrote *Faust*.

(S, p. 189; SE, p. 217)

Of course I've quoted this passage out of context, and some of the terms have been used earlier in the essay. But this is not just a cheap trick to make Bely look like a lunatic. The leap from physics to Ibsen and then to that extraordinary final comment on Goethe, which concludes a whole section of the essay and is never developed further, is every bit as wild when it's read in context.

"The Principle of Form in Aesthetics" was a youthful attempt at something Bely did not pursue in later years. Three years after he wrote it, however, he hit on another angle of the scientific aesthetic, one that was to prove much more fruitful. In 1909 he wrote four studies on poetic meter and rhythm in which he set out a method of verse analysis that combined elementary arithmetic and geometry. The result was a highly relational conception of the poetic work of art. What distinguished his approach in these studies from the one he proposed in "The Principle of Form in Aesthetics" was the role of the researcher. In the earlier study the researcher's task was to find, by purely logical deduction, the principles that precede the existence of any actual works of art. In the verse studies, however, the researcher's task is empirical and descriptive, and the conclusions are based on data taken from real works of art. In the earlier essay the method was deductive; in the verse studies it is inductive.

The first of the studies on meter and rhythm is titled "Lyric Poetry and Experiment" ("Lirika i èksperiment") (S, pp. 231–85; SE, pp. 222–73). Almost half of the essay is given over to a discussion of the empirical, descriptive method and its importance for establishing an exact science of aesthetics. The remainder is devoted to the elaboration of the specific method of verse analysis Bely will use in all four essays. Russian, like English, has a syllabotonic versification system; a line of Russian verse consists of a fixed number of syllables with a regular distribution of accented syllables. Because the distribution of accented syllables is regular, Russian verse can be divided into metrical feet. Russian verse accommodates a greater variety of feet than English, and all the basic combinations can be easily found: iambic, trochaic, anapestic, dactyllic, even amphibrachic.

By far the most common of Russian meters is iambic tetrameter, and it is the one Bely concentrates on. Bely was struck by something that no one had paid much attention to before, although it was perfectly obvious. Russian words generally contain only one accent each, and many of them are quite long. In fact, the average proportion of accented to total syllables in Russian prose, it was later shown, is 1 to 2.8.[4] This means that it is impossible to write truly iambic verse in a sustained way without resorting exclusively to the use of short words. What actually happens in Russian verse, of course, is that a great many positions that should be occupied by an accented syllable are not; so when we describe a particular set of verses as being written in iambic pentameter, we are not speaking with strict accuracy. In a given line of iambic pentameter there are likely to be one or more pyrrhic feet (both syllables unaccented). This tendency leads to the capital distinction Bely makes between meter and rhythm. Meter is the regular pattern a poem is *meant* to conform to, and terms like *iambic pentameter* describe it. Rhythm, by contrast, is the *actual* pattern we find in a poem. Since poems don't conform to the ideal pattern of a meter, their rhythm is really a pattern of violations. Bely called these violations either *half-accents,* because we tend to give a slight accent to a position in a verse that should be accented even when no accented syllable occurs on it, or *accelerations,* because in these half-accented positions the lack of a full accent has the effect of speeding up our reading.

The interesting part of Bely's analysis comes next. He decides that a good way to characterize the rhythm (not meter) of a poem is to draw a graph showing all the lines of verse and the four feet in each line. He places a dot in every position where there is a violation (an acceleration) and then forms designs by connecting dots that occur either in the same line or in consecutive lines. Any poem has numerous lines that are metrically regular, and dots are not connected over these, so the figures formed by this connect-the-dots game are usually small. Bely, carried away with enthusiasm by his pictures, then names them. If one line of verse contains a single acceleration and the following line contains two, we get an upright triangle. If the first line contains two and the next line one, we get an upside-down triangle. There are crosses, roofs, rhombuses, baskets, M's, Z's, and many other patterns.

Of course, a descriptive system like this must rest on the assumption that the geometric figures correspond to something perceptible to a listener or reader. An upright triangle, for instance, must come across as a rhythmic pattern of gradual acceleration, since it consists of a line with only one acceleration followed by a line with two. And when we say that baskets and rhombuses are particularly frequent in the verse of a certain poet and so are characteristic of that poet's rhythm, we must be using the words *baskets* and *rhombus* only as a kind of shorthand for something we can hear when we listen to the verse of the poet in question.

But after a short while Bely seems not to care much about whether his system corresponds to anything the listener hears, and his account of rhythm and versification is given over to charts and pictures. One has to ask at this point what the object of Bely's study really is. Toward the end of "Lyric Poetry and Experiment" Bely uses his geometric figures to make a distinction between "rich" rhythm and "poor" rhythm. Rich rhythm is characterized by a relatively large number and variety of geometric figures; poor rhythm is characterized by a relatively small number and variety of them. At one point, having charted the rhythmic patterns of selections from several poets, he says: "Comparing the examples of rich rhythms with the examples of poor rhythms, we see that the rhythmic figures for the rich rhythms are distinguished by greater complexity. The lines here are broken rather than straight, and simple figures join together here to form a series of complex figures" (*S*, p. 271; *SE*, p. 260). Remember that broken lines and straight lines correspond to something that should ultimately be perceptible when we listen to or read the poetry in question. But Bely largely stops talking about that and focuses instead on the designs themselves, which have now become a measure of the worth of a poet's verse. The second of Bely's four essays, "Toward a Characterization of the Russian Iambic Tetrameter" ("Opyt xarakteristiki russkogo četyrexstopnogo jamba") (*S*, pp. 286–330), consists almost entirely of statistical charts and descriptions of geometric figures. For example, we read this passage: "The *roof* is one of the most typical rhythmic devices. Pushkin uses it less often in his Lyceum poems than subsequently. Thus in 596 lines of verse from the years 1814 and 1815 only two roof figures occur. In a corresponding number of lines

of verse from the years 1828 and 1829 we encounter the device in question 8 times. Could this be accidental? When I take another 596 lines
of iambic tetrameter from the poems of 1824–1827, I find the corresponding device 6 times. I conclude from this that the more frequent use
of this figure by Pushkin corresponds to a strengthening of his rhythm"
(S, p. 309). And Bely goes on to provide statistics for the occurrence of
the "roof" in other Russian poets.

This is not at all to say that Bely's system is without value. In fact, he
pulls off a real coup in "Lyric Poetry and Experiment" by showing that
his scientific definition of rich rhythm is borne out by common notions
of the worth of poets. He takes a selection of Russian poets ranging from
great to mediocre and examines 596 lines of verse by each, adding up
for each poet the total number of geometric figures. It turns out that
those with the greatest number are those commonly considered to be
the greatest poets, and those with the lowest number are those most
Russians would agree are second-rate or worse (S, pp. 273–75; SE, pp.
263–65).

Earlier I said that Jakobson gave Bely credit for inspiring him to un-
dertake the analytic study of verse. Jakobson makes his remarks in the
"Retrospect" to the fifth volume of his Selected Writings.[5] It is testimony
to Bely's true importance in our story that Jakobson, writing not too
long ago, begins the "Retrospect" with a discussion of the very essays
I've been talking about. Jakobson disputes Bely's rather exaggerated
view of his own importance in the history of verse studies, but he goes
on to say that "beyond any doubt, Belyj's inquiry was the first to throw
light on the Russian iambic tetrameter, its manifold accentual variations,
and significant modifications which this favorite Russian measure
underwent from the eighteenth to the early twentieth century. He dis-
cerned diverse and formerly unnoticed particulars and posed many questions of wider scope" (SW, 5:569). After this, Jakobson tells of how he
himself attempted to apply Bely's method when he was still a teenager.
He tells of the critique that another Russian symbolist poet, Valerii Briusov, wrote of Bely's verse studies in 1910. Jakobson mentions the work
of the Moscow Rhythmic Circle, which Bely founded and which made
certain advances over Bely's pioneering work. And he describes his own
role in this history, how the Moscow Linguistic Circle, of which he was
a member, systematically revised the work of both Bely and Briusov in
1914 (SW, 5:570).

I can't help thinking, however, that the true legacy of Bely's work is
to be found not in Jakobson's studies on versification, meter, and rhythm

but instead in the study of Baudelaire's "Les Chats" that Jakobson coauthored with Lévi-Strauss. On the surface Jakobson and Lévi-Strauss's study appears to be completely different from Bely's verse studies. Jakobson and Lévi-Strauss are analyzing a poem, to be sure, but the focus is almost exclusively on the grammatical characteristics of Baudelaire's verse rather than on such purely formal aspects as the occurrence and position of accentual irregularities. But if we take a closer look, we see that the method and the results are quite similar. Jakobson and Lévi-Strauss, toward the end of their essay, after having found many different patterns by which the poem may be organized according to grammatical features, say this: "As we now reassemble the pieces of our analysis, let us try to show how the different levels on which we have situated ourselves blend together, complete each other, or combine, thus giving the poem the character of an absolute object."[6] Their idea was to take the poem apart and put it back together again, and the two authors have done so several times over. The result is a whole new object, something different from the poem we started with, something better, something to replace the poem. What we end up with is a wondrous relational web that ties together all the different related points, a kind of transcendent schema that leaves Baudelaire's cats, with the "mystical pupils of their eyes" and their "fecund loins . . . full of magical sparks," in complete obscurity.

This is exactly what Bely had done, too, only he did it in 1909. He was a structuralist long before Jakobson and his friends ever dreamed of the kind of analysis that we see in the Baudelaire study and even before Jakobson began using the concept of structure in his earlier writings. Bely has taken thousands of lines of poetry and replaced them with boxes, rhombuses, baskets, roofs, crosses, and zigzags. He's forgotten what all the poems were about. There's nothing about the poor clerk whose fiancée has drowned in a Petersburg flood, nothing about the cheap pathos of the death of a peasant, nothing about the Georgian beauty singing her sad songs. Just baskets.

When it comes right down to it, Bely is also doing the same thing he did in "The Emblematics of Meaning." He's insisting that all the things around us that signify something are just surfaces hiding an essence. Bely never wants to sound too much like a religious man (how could he, coming from the home he came from?), so he always calls the essence something nonreligious. In "The Emblematics of Meaning" it was "value." In the verse studies it is a geometric system, a relational abstraction, a structure.

I'm not saying that Jakobson learned structuralism from Bely or that we can trace a line directly from "Lyric Poetry and Experiment" to the essay on "Les Chats." What I am saying is that the method was there for Jakobson to see at a time when his ideas were only beginning to take shape, that the method is really the same as the one that Jakobson was to follow later, and that Bely's essays have been largely unknown for decades, whereas Jakobson's writings are known the world over. Would there have been literary structuralism without Bely? Of course. The most ardent Bely enthusiast would never be so audacious or foolish as to claim otherwise. But structuralism might well not have been the same had it not been for him.

A STORY OF SQUARES, RAYS, AND EXHAUSTED TOADS

Mathematicians like Bugaev, no matter how outlandish their ideas about the applications of mathematics, were at least firmly rooted in whatever branch of mathematics they had ideologically committed themselves to. Even Bely, whose geometric figures take on a life of their own, started out with the perfectly respectable goal of using exact methods to analyze certain properties of verse. With the Russian Futurists, however, the connection with any goal as tangible as that becomes increasingly remote, and numbers in all senses—as abstract quantities, as members of relational systems, as printed figures representing quantities—become the object of an almost mystical fascination.

The term *Futurist* is not very precise. It would probably be more accurate to refer to the group of artists I have in mind as members of the Russian avant-garde, where *avant-garde* is used in a broad and unofficial sense. Still, *Futurism* is used loosely to refer to a large group of writers and visual artists who flourished from about 1910 through most of the 1920s. Any standard work on Russian Futurism will explain that the movement (if we can call it that) was divided into several different groups with strange names like Hylaea, Cubo-Futurism, the Mezzanine of Poetry, and Centrifuge, that the groups were usually at odds with each other over issues that would strike anyone from the outside as exceedingly bizarre, and that the members of individual groups were often at odds with each other, with the result that membership in the different groups was highly fluid and unstable.[7]

One writer has observed that the central feature of modernity is how the new comes to be seen in it as an absolute value.[8] This is especially true for the various movements that make up what we call Russian Futurism, which saw the new as a source of human salvation in the twentieth century. The naughty boys of this period were fond of defiling the images of all the classic figures of Russian culture, saying things like, "Throw Pushkin, Dostoevsky, Tolstoy etc. etc. from the Steamship of modernity." They heaped abuse on even contemporary writers they considered old-fashioned (many of them associated with Bely) in manifestos with titles like "A Slap in the Face of Public Taste" and "Go to Hell."[9] Russian Futurism lasted through the revolution, and many figures in the movement embraced the new regime and gave it many of its most lasting images in poetry and in the visual arts. This participation in the new political order is yet another mark of the modernity of Futurism, in several senses. To begin with, art was placed in the service of revolutionary struggle, and what better example could there be of worshiping the new as an absolute value? In addition, a new idea among the Futurists was to tear down the boundaries dividing the different art forms from one another. Bely, in "The Principle of Form in Art," had continued to subscribe to the outmoded idea that some sort of a priori principle obliges us to express ourselves artistically in one of a limited number of mutually discrete media of artistic expression. Many Futurists rejected this notion, seeking forms of art that would combine the traditional media. One of the results is that people in the movement were commonly poets and visual artists at the same time, writing poems, painting pictures, and producing works of art that are located somewhere in between poetry and painting. Vladimir Mayakovsky, undoubtedly the most noticeable member of the whole movement, produced hundreds of propaganda drawings for the revolutionary regime and included on them slogans and bits of verse printed in such a way as to make the words part of the drawings. Anyone who has seen an exhibit of Russian avant-garde art will have noticed how often the paintings include letters and words as prominent parts of their visual fields.

Another new thing was numbers. Maybe the members of the Russian avant-garde considered numbers to be part of a modern trend toward abstraction; or maybe after 1917 they saw them as symbols of the technological and industrial revolution that was to fortify and carry on their recent political revolution. In either case, numbers in this era became the object of a special cult, which expressed itself in some rather peculiar ways. Velimir Khlebnikov, one of the pioneering members of this movement, had studied mathematics at the university and had then developed his fascination for numbers into his own mystical system, which he writes about in many of his short essays and manifestos. For instance, he believed that there were certain key numbers that determined momentous events in human history. The quantities $365 + 48$ and $365 - 48$ were particularly important in this respect, and Khlebnikov fills whole pages of his prose writings with calculations designed to show how units of time based on various multiples of 413 and 317 separate certain key happenings. Of course, anyone who reads this immediately begins to suspect that Khlebnikov came up with his mystical number first and then went looking for facts to support the accuracy of his theory, rather than the other way around. Numbers pervade Khlebnikov's work. If you look through his collected prose writings, you'll see whole sections given over to a veritable riot of numbers and figures that have become, like Bely's shapes, an end in themselves. In fact, the visual impact of Khlebnikov's math mania together with the outlandish ideas he proposes make it difficult to classify his prose writings as essays or theoretical writings in the usual sense. They begin to look like a cross between prose poems and graphic art, the way Mayakovsky's propaganda posters do and the way so much of Futurist visual art does.

But there are a couple of serious messages here, just as there were in Bely. One has to do with the "mode of being" of numbers. The other concerns the relation between numbers and things and has implications for the relational-essentialist view of the literary artwork. Khlebnikov was fond of the fantasy that some sort of universal determinism governed world events and that numbers were its measure. This determinism expressed itself through time (multiples of 413 or 317 years), and so it was accurate to say that "time is the measure of the world," as Khlebnikov titled one of his essays.[10] Khlebnikov loves numbers so much because there is a necessary and determinate relation between them and what they stand for. Hence a comparison suggests itself with language since the necessary and determinate relation that exists between numbers and what they stand for is notoriously lacking between words and what *they* stand for. That was the whole reason behind Khlebnikov's and Kruchenykh's efforts to design a "transrational" language in which this problem would be overcome. Khlebnikov dreamed of the possibility of having numbers replace words as a means for thinking and communicating. In "Time Is the Measure of the World" he says:

> In verbal thinking no basic condition of measurement is present—no constancy in the units of measurement, and the Sophists Protagoras and Gorgias

were the first steadfast helmsmen to point up the dangers of navigation upon the waves of the word. Every name is merely an approximate measurement, a mere comparison of several quantities, of certain equals signs. Leibniz, in his exclamation, "The time will come when people, instead of engaging in abusive disputes, will calculate" (will exclaim: *calculemus*), Novalis, Pythagoras, and Amenophis IV all foresaw the victory of numbers over the word as a method for thinking."[11]

Again and again Khlebnikov came back to this comparison between numbers and words, often in a way reminiscent of Mallarmé. For instance, shortly after the passage I just quoted, Khlebnikov says, "Being an antiquated implement of thought, the word will nonetheless remain for the arts since it is useful for measuring man through the constants of the world. But the major portion of books have been written because people have wanted, by means of the 'word,' to think about things that may be thought about by means of numbers."[12] In another place he suggests that we assign to all the thoughts of the earth a number since there are, after all, so few thoughts around. Then "languages will remain for art and will be freed from an insulting burden."[13] In other places he uses a scheme similar to the one Mallarmé had used in *English Words* and shows that certain initial sounds of words naturally conjure up the idea of certain mathematical operations. But what is most reminiscent of Mallarmé is the suggestion that since words fail in a function in which numbers succeed, namely the function of ideally signifying what they signify, they ought rightly to be left to art. This sounds much like Mallarmé's remark in "Crisis in Verse" that without the imperfections of language "*verse would not exist*: it, philosophically compensates for the shortcoming of languages, superior complement."[14]

Whatever we might call Khlebnikov's prose writings, Khlebnikov himself certainly did not refer to them as poems. There were other poets, however, who did incorporate numerals into their poetry and even provided theoretical reasons for doing so. A relatively minor figure, Ivan Vasil'evich Ignat'ev, wrote experimental poetry in which he used mathematical symbols for their visual impact. David Burliuk (1882–1967), one of the most noticeable members of the movement, though not one of the most talented, used mathematical symbols in his poetry. Burliuk was a painter and a poet, like many others of his generation, and much of what he did was for effect. If he thought it would be visually shocking to use mathematical symbols in poetry, he also must have thought it would be intellectually shocking to call the collection of poems in which

these symbols appeared "The Milker of Exhausted Toads."[15] Nikolai
Burliuk (1890–1920), brother of David, provided the theoretical justi-
fication for the use of mathematical symbols. In an essay called "Poetic
Principles" he talks about the "graphic life of letters":

> How many signs, musical, mathematical, cartographic, and so forth, there
> are in the dust of libraries. I understand the cubists, when they introduce
> numbers into their pictures, but I don't understand poets, who remain foreign
> to the aesthetic life of all these
>
> $$\int \quad \sim \quad + \quad \S \quad \times \quad \male \quad \female \quad \vee \quad = \quad > \quad \triangle \text{ etc. etc.}^{16}$$

The person who can probably be credited with using mathematical
symbols and images to their greatest visual effect was El Lissitzky
(1890–1941). Lissitzky is normally thought of as a visual artist, not a
poet, but his compositions show the same enthusiasm for typography
as we find in many of his contemporaries, and some of his works actually contain narrative elements. Since in this era people in the arts have
to be placed on a gamut that runs from "pure" verbal art at one end to
"pure" visual art at the other, with the entire range of combinations in
between, maybe it would be most accurate to say that Lissitzky belongs
a little closer to the visual end than, say, Khlebnikov (Khlebnikov, as it
happens, produced some fairly good visual art of his own). In 1920
Lissitzky created (how do you say "wrote and drew" in one word?) a
work (a story-drawing) called "Of Two Squares." Actually, the title as
it appears on the cover is not "Of Two Squares," since Lissitzky spells
out only the word translated as "of." "Two" is the numeral 2, and
"squares" is a picture of a red square (only one square because Russian
uses a singular form of the noun with the numbers two, three, and four
and their compounds). On the title page, however, Lissitzky gives the
title in words as "suprematist tale [*skaz*] of two squares in 6 constructions." The constructions are the individual compositions that make up
the work, so "a tale in six constructions" appears to be like "a play in
five acts" or "a novel in six parts." They are geometric drawings in
which the exploits of the heroes of the story, a red and a black square,
are depicted. Accompanying the drawings, in letters that are characteristically arranged so as to be part of the entire visual effect, is the narrative: "They fly to earth from far away," and so on. What kind of work
is this? On the inside of the back cover we are told that it was "con-
structed" (not written or drawn) in 1920, but this doesn't tell us much.[17]
Later, in 1928, Lissitzky made some sketches for a children's book called
"Addition, Subtraction, Multiplication, Division," in which the char-

acters performing the "action" of the four arithmetic operations are numbers and letters drawn to look like various Soviet types: workers, peasants, and Red Army soldiers.[18]

Earlier I mentioned Michel Serres and his analysis of the modern cult of abstraction. In the modern age, Serres says, the emphasis is on structure, models, and relations, not on content. Number mania is just one symptom of the same trend operating in Russian modernism and the Russian avant-garde. Bely's system of verse analysis provided him with the means for abstracting away all content from the literary works he was investigating, for "taking a form and filling it with meaning," as Serres puts it, instead of relying on preestablished meanings.[19] Khlebnikov's funny proposal to number all thoughts and use only the numbers in referring to them is another example of the tendency to abstract away content and leave only a relational structure waiting to be filled with meaning. The same may be said of Lissitzky's typographic experiments, which show a playful approach to the process by which abstraction overtakes traditional content.

Abstraction was the order of the day in Russian art, just as it was in West European art. Cubism developed a real following in Russian art. The Cubo-Futurists are evidence of it, as are the numerous theoretical writings devoted to cubism in that era. The general trend in Russian art from around 1910 through the 1920s is toward increasing abstraction. We can find this trend in pictures that some of the most prominent artists of the period painted between 1909 and 1914. Natal'ia Goncharova (1881–1962) is a good example. After having produced traditional paintings like her iconic "Madonna and Child" in the years around 1905, she adopts a primitivist mode around 1909, devoting her compositions to rustic subjects like *Picking Apples* (1909), *Peasant Picking Apples* (1911), and *Fishing* (1910). These pictures contain recognizable human figures but are composed in "primitive" fashion: the figures are stiff, there is little depth, and the treatment of perspective is noticeably and intentionally childish. Around 1911, however, things begin to change again. Goncharova's major composition of 1911 and 1912 is *Cats*. There are not really any cats in this picture, just the feeling of their scratchiness and the crackling static electricity of their fur, qualities rendered pictorially by patterns of sharply drawn lines, or "rays." Soon Goncharova will be painting pictures with titles like *The Clock* (1911), *The Cyclist* (1912–13), and *Dynamo Machine* (1913), in which elements of the object or objects suggested in the title are arranged on the canvas in new and unrecognizable patterns. Human figures are now separated into fragments of faces and bodies distributed here and there according to rules very different from those followed in classical portraits. The work of another famous Russian painter, Kazimir Malevich (1878–1935), shows the same progression, from Renoir-like treatments of young women in the first years of the twentieth century, to cubist borrowings from Picasso around 1912, to paintings, starting around 1913, consisting of nothing but geometric shapes painted in black or red on a white background.

I'm not pretending that everything happening in the visual arts in Russia at this time was unique. It wasn't. As usual, many Russian artists relied heavily on their contemporaries in Western Europe for inspiration. The first Futurist movement was Italian, not Russian, and even though the Russians hated to admit it and went to great lengths to distort the truth, they borrowed a great many of their themes and ideas from the Italians. One striking feature of the Russian movement, however, was the degree of interpenetration between visual art and literary art. The move toward abstraction in the visual arts is difficult to characterize any more precisely than I've just done if we are limited to an empirical description of pictures. But because so many painters were also poets; because so many poets were also painters; because so many artworks of the era combined elements from both artistic media; and because so many artists wrote theoretical works on their painterly, poetic, and painterly-poetic techniques, we actually can document a move toward the kind of relational abstraction I've been talking about, and we can do so without just describing pictures.

"It has been known for a long time that what is important is not the *what,* but the *how,* i.e., which principles, which objectives, guided the artist's creation of this or that work!" proclaims David Burliuk in 1912 in his essay "Cubism (Surface—Plane)." In the same essay the painter-poet breaks down painting into its "component elements"—line, surface, color, and texture—and claims to have provided, in his epigraph, the "mathematical conception" of surface.[20] Natal'ia Goncharova's cat picture was composed in the "rayonist" manner, and starting in 1913 she and fellow rayonist Mikhail Larionov (1881–1964) published declarations on the principles of their new style. The idea was to get away from concrete forms: "Long live the style of rayonist painting that we created—free from concrete forms, existing and developing according to painterly laws!" How exactly does one go about making a rayonist painting? "The style of rayonist painting that we advance signifies spatial forms arising from the intersection of the reflected rays of various objects, forms chosen by the artist's will." Everything is combination and relation—"the combination of color, its saturation, the relation of colored masses, depth, texture"—and the goal is "a self-sufficient painting."[21]

Another Futurist, Sergei Bobrov, a member of the Centrifuge group, was fond of mathematical terms and concepts. One of his ventures was to continue Bely's statistical work in verse analysis. His theoretical writings are filled with references to various theorems and formulas, references whose application is often difficult to guess. In an essay on poetry called "The Lyric Theme," published in 1913, Bobrov invokes Newton's binomial theorem, the concept of the arithmetic mean, and various principles from geometry. Bobrov's purpose in using these concepts remains obscure, but the main point seems to be the rejection of all the traditional frameworks in which poetry is written and read—especially such content-centered frameworks as metaphysics and religion—in favor of some sort of pure idea of poetry. "The lyric," Bobrov says, "has a direct tie with the idea of the poem. Not, however, with the thought of the poem." Bobrov is after the essential quality of the lyric, which he calls "lyricity" (*liričnost'*) and which appears to be separate from content.[22]

The rejection of content, nature, and objectivity in favor of the pure essence of either painting or poetry became the trademark of much Russian aesthetic theory beginning in the years before the revolution. Kazimir Malevich, who was a prolific writer of manifestos in addition to being a prolific painter, championed the cause of the "nonobjective" in art. In a little book titled *From Cubism and Futurism to Suprematism: The New Painterly Realism* he asserts the importance of keeping painting separate from nature. "The artist can be a creator only when the forms in his picture have nothing in common with nature," he says. Nature must be seen only "as material, as masses from which forms must be made that have nothing in common with nature." The whole purpose was to attain "pure painterly essence" and "nonobjective creation." "Painters should abandon subject matter and objects if they wish to be pure painters," he proclaims. "Our world of art has become new, nonobjective, pure."[23] In the service of this creed Malevich painted many of the canvases that he termed—then or later—"Suprematist": paintings with titles like *Black Square* (consisting of just that, a black square on a white background), *Black Square and Red Square,* and just *Suprematist Composition.*

Benedikt Livshits (1886–1939) was a poet who was interested both in the relational conception of art and in the connections between painting and poetry. In an essay called "In the Citadel of the Revolutionary Word" he discusses poetic language and says "the highest type of structure is for me the one where words are matched according to the laws of inner affinities, freely crystallizing on their own axes, and do not look for an agreement with the phenomena of the external world or of the lyric self."[24] Later on, in a book of memoirs called *The One-and-a-Half-Eyed Archer,* Livshits recalls a time when he was pondering the problem of combining different art forms, above all painting and poetry. He had come to realize a basic truth about this matter, which was that the features one could hope to transfer from one art form to an "adjacent" art form are "relationships and mutual functional dependence of elements."[25] Once again, in the case of poetry, the effort is to remove language from its signifying function as traditionally conceived and to make it part of an abstract relational system.

One of the most fascinating subplots in the drama of Russian modernism and its cult of abstraction involves the mathematics of the "fourth dimension." I won't tell this story in any detail; Linda Dalrymple Henderson, an art historian who specializes in this period, has already done so at great length.[26] The nineteenth century, as Henderson explains, had provided two significant new challenges to traditional, Euclidean geometry. The first, non-Euclidean geometry, would eventually concern itself with the characteristics of shapes and forms in curved, rather than planar, spaces. The second was geometry of n dimensions, a field that got its start early in the nineteenth century. The basic notion was mathematically to characterize "spaces" that contained four or more dimensions. By the end of the century mathematicians were talking about such things as "hyperspaces" and "hypersolids." What are hyperspaces and hypersolids? Well, if we can generate a three-dimensional solid, say a cube, by assembling two-dimensional components (that is, the planes that form the surfaces of the cube), then surely we can generate a four-dimensional hypersolid by assembling three-dimensional components like cubes. Or we can picture a hypersolid as a thing whose surfaces are formed from spheres instead of points. Naturally, a hypersolid will need a space to exist in, and so we arrive at the notion of a hyperspace, one that will accommodate hypersolids and similar objects. The only problem is how to visualize spaces and objects like these. Mathematicians were no help here, so the job had to be done by artists, who set about to solve this problem as the notion of four-dimensional geometry took hold of the popular imagination in the late nineteenth century. To be sure, no one figured out a way to draw a figure whose hyperplane surface was

made up of spheres instead of points, but, as Henderson shows, the idea
of the fourth dimension caught on in Russia as a form of mysticism that
translated itself into literary and visual artwork in a variety of ways.

The history went something like this, in Henderson's account. A minor Russian philosopher, Peter Demianovich Ouspensky (1878–1947),
later known in the West for his role in disseminating the beliefs of the
famous mystic Gurdjieff, wrote of the fourth dimension in a book modestly titled *Tertium Organum: A Key to the Enigmas of the World*
(1911). In this book Ouspensky proposed a Promethean view of man
in the universe, basing his ideas in part on a mystical notion of the fourth
dimension. Next, a painter named Mikhail Matiushin (1861–1934)
adopted certain principles from the French cubists and modified them
in accordance with his understanding of Ouspensky's fourth dimension.
In 1913 Matiushin collaborated on a number of projects with Malevich,
Kruchenykh, and Khlebnikov, to whom he introduced Ouspensky's
ideas. Henderson has shown that the Ouspenskian notion of the fourth
dimension was actually a decisive factor in Kruchenykh's elaboration of
zaum' theory. In the essay "New Ways of the Word" Kruchenykh rhap-
sodizes about transrational language and speaks of a new "fourth unit"
of psychic life, which he calls "higher intuition," citing Ouspensky's
Tertium Organum. Higher intuition was the form of superior mystical
knowledge that Ouspensky associated with the fourth dimension. A couple of pages later, Kruchenykh praises the false perspective found in the
work of contemporary painters, saying that it gives their work a "new,
fourth dimension."[27] References to the fourth dimension then appear in
Larionov's articles on rayonism. The fourth dimension is particularly
important to Malevich, who refers to Ouspensky's ideas in his theoretical writings and applies them to his painting. And in the 1920s El
Lissitzky used his understanding of the fourth dimension, which he eventually came to identify with time (as many others did following a tremendous rise in the popularity of Einstein's theories around 1919), to
develop a coherent theory of painting.

It would be ridiculous to assert that the painters and writers of the
Russian avant-garde were interested in the fourth dimension for the same
reason as mathematicians or that most of them had a truly mathematical
understanding of it. To the artists the fourth dimension meant an escape
from the concrete world and from the obligation of always representing
or signifying it. This is the thought that turns up repeatedly in discussions of the fourth dimension. When it comes right down to it, the fourth
dimension is just another abstraction based in mathematics, like Bely's

baskets, Khlebnikov's numbers, and Jakobson's grammatical structures. Goncharova's painting of cats intentionally overlooks all the physical features we expect in a painting of cats, just as Jakobson and Lévi-Strauss overlook the physical features of cats in Baudelaire's poem about cats. Goncharova wanted the abstract essence of cat in her painting; Jakobson and Lévi-Strauss wanted an abstract essence that had to do with grammar.

Something particularly curious is going on with the Futurists. Their fascination with numbers and mathematical concepts inevitably leads to fundamental questions about the artwork, questions like *what* and *where*. What is an artwork, once it has been reduced to an abstraction? Where does it exist, what sort of space does it or its represented world occupy once that space has been made, by conscious effort, to resemble the familiar space of our world as little as possible? What sort of thing are we dealing with here, anyway? Everything the Futurists did seems designed to raise this question by challenging all our secure notions about art. It's a poem, but then it's like a painting, too. It's a painting, but then it's like a poem, too. It contains recognizable signs, but arranged in unrecognizable ways. The big question is a question of *being*. What is the mode of being of this thing? art of this period continually forces us to ask ourselves. The question seems to have its origin in speculation that is to a significant extent mathematical. At the same time it reflects the essentialist impulse Russian thinkers never seem to escape. Strictly speaking, it is a question of ontology, and that is the subject of the final part of this book.

PART IV

Ontology

CHAPTER TEN

The Being of Artworks

Roman Ingarden, the Polish pupil of Edmund Husserl, starts off his best-known work, *The Literary Work of Art*, begun in 1927 and first published in 1931, with an arresting observation:

> We find ourselves before a strange fact. Almost every day we deal with literary works. We read them, we are moved by them, they charm us or displease us, we evaluate them, we pass various judgments on them, conduct discussions on them, we write articles on individual works, we concern ourselves with their history, they are often almost like an atmosphere in which we live—one would think as a result that we knew the objects of these activities universally and exhaustively. And yet, if someone puts the question to us what a literary work actually is, then we must admit with a certain astonishment that we have no correct and satisfactory answer.[1]

It's true. We read them all the time, these books and parts of books that are offered to us as artworks. We do other things to them, too. We love them, hate them, ban them, abridge them, make them into movies. We study them, analyze them, "deconstruct" them, criticize them, write term papers about them. And yet if we stop for a moment and try to figure out what the *them* in all these phrases is, to what real object in the world the grammatical direct object of all these verbs actually corresponds, we're baffled. Everyone will agree right off that it's not the bound and printed sheets of paper, the "book" in the physical sense. Any book can exist in many different editions, and even two different copies of the same edition may well look like two very different stacks of bound and printed paper, two very different "things."

So what is a literary artwork? The question is more complicated than it might at first appear. When we say that the literary artwork is not the same as the physical book, we are getting at the general problem of writing. What is it we read when we read *anything*? we're asking. Where does the work exist if it's not the sheets of paper with little black markings on them? Is it the little black markings? Is it the understanding (whatever that means) of those markings that we derive when we read them, and if so, does that mean the work ultimately exists in the mind of the reader and nowhere else?

If we ever succeed in answering these general questions about writing, however, we're still left with another set of unavoidable questions. The original question was what a literary *artwork* is. What we want to know is not only what any piece of writing is but also just what it is that distinguishes a piece of writing we consider to be "art" from a piece of writing we don't. What makes *Jane Eyre* different from an insurance policy? As soon as we start to think about it, we realize that we can't very well talk about only literary works of art. We need to ask what makes *any* work of art different from any other thing. What makes the Pietà different from a piece of marble lying undisturbed in a quarry? What makes a famous painting different from the empty stretch of wall right next to where it hangs in a museum? All these questions ultimately concern the *being* of artworks, the peculiar manner of their existence, and so the field of inquiry that they belong to can be described as the *ontology* of artworks.

Ingarden was not the first person to ask these questions about literary artworks, although he was probably the first to give them the kind of detailed attention we find in *The Literary Work of Art*. Credit for the initial discoveries that made possible the modern tradition Ingarden was working in goes to a few thinkers living in the eighteenth century. To start asking pointed questions about the being or essence of artworks, in what space they exist, how they are different from ordinary things that resemble them, it was necessary to assert that artworks do enjoy a different status from that of ordinary objects, and the way to assert this was to insist that the type of perception of which artworks are the object is qualitatively different from the type we use for ordinary objects. The thinker who is responsible for this latter assertion is the same one who is responsible for the eventual application of the word *aesthetic* to the field of artistic beauty: Alexander Gottlieb Baumgarten (1714–1762).

In chapter 8 I mentioned Descartes and his ideal of clarity and mathematical rigor. As it happens, the term *clear* was complemented by another term in Descartes, *distinct*. *Clear* meant simply evident, apparent to the mind; *distinct* meant precise, clear in all possible details. Since something needs to be clear before it can be distinct, distinct is a sub-category of clear. The two terms corresponded for Descartes to two faculties: perception and reason. Something can be clear to sense perception (that is, it can be clearly, vividly perceived) without being distinct. But only reason can grasp what is distinct since distinct ideas tend to be abstract, that is, the sort of thing that mere sense perception cannot apprehend.

Baumgarten followed a similar scheme, dividing knowledge into two "cognitive faculties." The inferior faculty is sensible knowledge, that is, knowledge that derives from the senses. The higher faculty is thought, or knowledge proper, which serves as the basis for scientific understanding. Since the inferior faculty is based on the senses, hence on feeling, Baumgarten used the term *aesthetics* (from a Greek word meaning "to feel") for the discipline that would investigate it. Logic was the field that treated the higher faculty. Baumgarten believed that fine art and poetry were the objects of sensible knowledge, and so they were naturally included under the science of aesthetics.[2]

Art objects were thus set off from at least certain other kinds of objects, in this case because the mode of perception directed toward them is different from that directed toward other objects. This line of thinking found its most thorough and forceful exposition in Kant. Kant had divided knowledge into three areas, which he treated in his three critiques. Ordinary scientific understanding, or theoretical knowledge, the faculty by which we apprehend and structure experience in the natural world, was the subject of Kant's first critique, the *Critique of Pure Reason* (1781, 1787). Then there is the power to know moral laws, the ability to decide that certain things are right and others wrong. It is practical in the sense that it has to do with freedom to act (*praxis* means "action"), and so the critique devoted to this type of knowledge is called the *Critique of Practical Reason* (1788). Finally, there is the faculty that allows us to make judgments of taste, that is, to judge that a thing is beautiful or sublime. It is the subject of Kant's third critique, the *Critique of Judgment* (1790).

Kant's treatises were called critiques because their purpose was to delineate clearly the jurisdiction of each area of knowledge by examining critically the untested assumptions that surround it. The idea was to establish through deductive proof the existence of certain a priori principles, that is, principles that preexist our use of them and that cannot be objects of ordinary knowledge. A priori principles are universal and necessary. How can something as subjective as a judgment of taste possess universality and necessity? The answer, Kant says, is that our faculty of judgment, when it makes judgments of taste, is directed toward the subjective conditions of its own employment. This subjective factor is a priori because it is something that can be presupposed in everyone.

The essential point for our purposes here is that Kant set off something called judgment as a unique faculty with its own set of a priori principles, its own necessity and universality, and its own objects. If one faculty is different in its operation from the other, then the objects of one will certainly differ accordingly from the objects of the other. Thus objects of beauty take on their own mode of being, one that is distinct from the mode of being of ordinary objects.

Still, Kant was hardly elaborating anything we might call an ontology of artworks. The emphasis was in the wrong place for that, as it must be in an idealist philosophy. Kant was interested in delineating the faculty and demonstrating how it determined the object. He was not interested in the object and its ontology; for that we have to wait until the early twentieth century and the advent of Husserlian phenomenology. Husserl did not himself develop an ontology of art. In fact, he had almost nothing to say about art during his entire career. But he did inaugurate a new tradition in aesthetics. Husserl's first major work, the *Logical Investigations,* was published in two volumes in 1900 and 1901, and eight years later the first work in phenomenological aesthetics appeared. It was by one Waldemar Conrad, and it was called "Der ästhetische Gegenstand: Eine phänomenologische Studie" (The aesthetic object: A phenomenological study). Both author and article are now quite forgotten, except by the odd enthusiast of the history of phenomenology.[3]

I don't plan to discuss the *Logical Investigations* in any detail. The essential thing is what Conrad saw in them as preparing the way for his own work. *Presuppositionless* was a catchword of Husserlian phenomenology since Husserl was interested in arriving at the essence of thought by "bracketing" away all the presuppositions that constitute what he called the "natural attitude." By "natural attitude" he meant simply the naive attitude we bring to bear on our everyday encounters with our surroundings. Conrad decided that it might be clever to take the presuppositionless method and apply it to aesthetics. The idea was to describe the work of art presuppositionlessly, that is, in its pure immanence and without any of the naive notions that characterize ordinary perception.

Whether Conrad succeeded in doing this is not important. What is important is his focus on works of art, or aesthetic objects, as different from ordinary objects. They are ideal objects in the Husserlian sense, Conrad says, which we can constitute through fantasy but which have no actual attributes of existence, as objects in nature do.[4] Conrad then goes on to investigate three different types of art: music, verbal art (*Wortkunst*), and spatial art (*Raumkunst*). In each case he makes some preliminary remarks about the art form, gives a general analysis followed by a detailed analysis, and then discusses the difference between art objects of the type in question and objects in nature that are similar.

At the end of his long article he states his conclusions. He talks about the essence (*Wesen*) of aesthetic objects as opposed to two other types of object: objects of nature and geometric objects. The heart of the matter seems to lie in the concept of dependence (*Abhängigkeit*). Objects in nature are composed of a number of properties that exist in a relation of "lawful dependence" on each other. Objects in nature possess the character of "reality." Geometric objects, though not "real" like objects in nature, are similar to objects of nature in that their qualities, too, are dependent on each other. Aesthetic objects, however, are purely ideal objects and possess no character of reality. They have "intentional objectivity," that is, an objectivity that arises as the result of an intention of their creator. Their constituent properties exist in a relation not clearly defined by Conrad but clearly different from the relation of dependence we find among the constituent properties of objects of nature and geometric objects. Aesthetic objects are "realizable." This appears to mean that they have to be realized through an act of mind since they possess no character of reality. They belong not to actual space but to their own space and thus can be called objects without being things.[5]

Conrad's exposition is rudimentary and not very compelling. He never succeeds in giving a particularly sharp definition of aesthetic objects or, for that matter, in providing a truly phenomenological analysis of artworks. But he certainly pointed the discussion in the right direction and cleared the way for more sophisticated phenomenological discussions a few years later. These belong above all to Ingarden, whose formulations in *The Literary Work of Art* and later works show a true debt to the man he credits with being the first to work in the area of phenomenological aesthetics.[6]

Ingarden solved the problem of distinguishing between art objects and real objects partly by relying on Husserl and partly by departing from him. To begin with, Ingarden believed strongly in the objective reality of the world, something that put him in direct opposition to the idealism of Husserlian phenomenology. His longest work, *The Controversy over the Existence of the World* (*Der Streit um die Existenz der Welt*), is devoted to exploring this position. Art objects are what Ingarden calls purely intentional objects. The term is derived in part from Husserl, for whom all acts of consciousness are "intentional," which means that they are directed by the intention of the subject toward some object (whether or not that object is "real"). But Ingarden diverges from Husserl on the issue of intentional objects. For Ingarden, an intentional object is anything (real, imagined, created, ideal, abstract, concrete) that becomes the target of an intentional act of consciousness. Because of his belief in the objective reality of the world, however, he conceives of two types of intentional object. First there are *also intentional objects*. These are objects that are "ontically autonomous" (*seinsautonom,* or autonomous with respect to being), which is another way of saying that they are real, that they exist independently of the perceiving consciousness. They are "also" intentional because they become the object of someone's intentional act of consciousness by chance. Then there are *purely intentional objects*. These are objects that are "ontically heteronomous" (*seinsheteronom*), which means that they depend (heteronomous is the opposite of autonomous and thus means "dependent") for their existence precisely on the intentional act of consciousness whose object they are. Purely intentional objects can be further divided into two types: *originally* purely intentional objects, which exist in consciousness in the pure state in which they are conceived, and *derived* purely intentional objects, which must be constituted through the mediation of "meaning units" (a generic term that comprises words and any other media for the expression of meaning). Literary artworks are thus *derived purely intentional objects.* They are not ontically autonomous, which means that they do not exist apart from the intentional acts of consciousness that create them or those by which a perceiver experiences them, and they exist only by means of the words that make them up.[7]

Ingarden's descriptive analysis makes the literary artwork into a structure consisting of several different strata. There is a stratum of individual words, a stratum of words combined into meaningful units, a stratum of represented objects, and a stratum of something Ingarden calls schematized aspects. The idea is that the reader confronts various levels on which meaning is established, from the level of individual words to the more complicated levels where the reader constitutes and fills in whole states of being as they exist in the world of the literary work. Hence the literary work exists in large part as a function of the reader's ability to make it real, to "concretize" it. A derived purely intentional object does not have independent existence and thus depends on the intentional acts of consciousness that make it real. This notion is what leads Ingarden to his crucial distinction between literary artwork and aesthetic object. The literary artwork is the thing that is constituted by the author. The aesthetic object is a kind of essential core of the literary artwork, and it depends for its existence on the constituting acts of both the author and the perceiver-reader.

I don't mean to insist on the details of Ingarden's aesthetics. I mention as many of them as I do for two reasons. The first is to show how far Ingarden went in probing the question of the existence of artworks and providing a set of terms designed to allow us to distinguish art objects from other kinds of objects. He has not had the last word on these issues, but he must be given credit for focusing serious attention on them. After all, how many writers before Ingarden's time would have thought of *Investigations into the Ontology of Art* as a title for a book?[8] The second reason is that relatively few American students of literature are familiar with Ingarden's books firsthand. *The Literary Work of Art* was not published in English translation until 1973, and before then only shorter writings by Ingarden were available in English. But everybody knows the work of René Wellek, the grandfather of comparative literature in the United States, who taught whole generations of scholars at Yale before Paul de Man and others like him came along to establish the powerful deconstructionist empire that eclipsed Wellek. Wellek, as it happens, is probably more responsible than anyone else for introducing Ingarden to the English-speaking world.

In 1942 Wellek published an article in the *Southern Review* called "The Mode of Existence of a Literary Work of Art," in which he promised to help clarify what a literary work of art is and how it exists. In a footnote to the title of his essay he acknowledged first the Prague Linguistic Circle and then "the logical theories of Edmund Husserl and his Polish pupil Roman Ingarden" as sources for his ideas.[9] The literary work of art in Wellek's view is a "system of norms" (p. 745). A norm, in the sense that Wellek has in mind, is a sort of ideal goal we have an obligation to strive to fulfill. The term has its origin in ethics, although Wellek is careful to point out that his norms are not ethical. His notion is that a work of art implicitly contains a set of goals and that in any experience of the work the perceiver is in a sense obligated to realize these goals. "The structure of a work of art has the character of a 'duty which I have to realize,' " Wellek says (p. 747). In other words, the content of the norms may not be ethical, but our interaction with them is since the nature of that interaction is defined in terms of ethical concepts like duty and obligation.

Wellek doesn't do much to help us conceptualize what the norms in a work are, but that isn't his purpose. His aim is to show that the act of perceiving an artwork is an act of recovery, or attempted recovery, by which we seek to fulfill the norms that inhere in that work. How do those norms exist? To answer that question, Wellek basically adopts the stratum analysis of Ingarden (although he doesn't mention Ingarden by name here), referring to "the sound-structure of a literary work of art," "the units of meaning based on the sentence patterns," and the "world of objects to which the meaning refers" (p. 746). In the next-to-last paragraph of his essay Wellek gives this definition: "The work of art, then, appears as an object of knowledge *sui generis* which has a special ontological status. It is neither real (like a statue) nor mental (like the experience of light or pain) nor ideal (like a triangle). It is a system of norms of ideal concepts which are intersubjective. They must be assumed to exist in collective ideology, changing with it, accessible only through individual mental experiences, based on the sound structure of its sentences" (p. 753).

Not many people would have paid much attention to an article hidden away in a literary journal if Wellek had let the matter rest there. But in 1949 he and Austin Warren published their *Theory of Literature,* a highly influential work that became a fundamental textbook for literary studies in the United States for more than a generation, and they included in it almost word for word Wellek's 1942 article. In the book it forms the bulk of a chapter called "The Analysis of the Literary Work of Art," so the ontological question is not highlighted in this title as it was in that of the journal article. But in one of the few departures from the article, Wellek names Ingarden in the text and devotes a full page to Husserl, phenomenology, and Ingarden's theory of the stratified structure of literary artworks.[10] And so it was that the question of aesthetic ontology passed into the mainstream of literary studies in American universities. I hesitate to say that this is the dominant theme of Wellek and Warren's book, but there is no doubt that it is featured prominently.

A number of professional philosophers on the American scene have written about aesthetic ontology in the twentieth century without necessarily calling it that. Stephen Pepper, in *The Work of Art* (1955), attempts to define what a work of art is and how it is different from an ordinary object. George Dickie, in *Art and the Aesthetic* (1974), gives what he calls an "institutional definition" of artworks, one that locates the peculiar being of artworks in the act by which a certain community (which he calls "the artworld") confers on an object the status of artwork. Nelson Goodman, one of the most distinguished figures in American philosophy, wrote a book called *Ways of Worldmaking* (1978) in which he put a new twist on the standard question of aesthetic ontology by asking "When is art?" instead of "What is art?" And Arthur Danto, in *The Transfiguration of the Commonplace: A Philosophy of Art* (1981), approaches the problem of how to distinguish artworks from other things that represent but that are not artworks.[11]

Ontological questions in aesthetics have apparently been attractive to the "academy," as professional philosophers call it, in America. The line I have just mentioned, however, appears not to have had much impact on specifically literary studies. There is Wellek and his progeny on the one hand, and, on the other, there is a line that has been even more influential in recent years, one that also must claim succession, at least to a certain disputable extent, from Husserl and phenomenology. I'm referring to Heidegger and his various disciples and followers. I have no intention of giving a lengthy summary or analysis of Heidegger and his theories of poetry here. His disciples lovingly say that his theories resist paraphrase and description, anyway, because the master's writing operates on some preconscious realm of experience in the reader. His detractors say that there is nothing so very complicated in his theories and that he was simply a second-rate philosopher who wrote in a "poetic," "difficult" prose. Disciples and detractors can fight this one out for themselves. All I want to do is show something obvious, namely the connection in Heidegger's thought between poetry and being.

The central text by Heidegger on the subject is his essay "The Origin of the Work of Art," first written in 1935.[12] Heidegger's idea about artworks is that art has to do with truth. But Heidegger has redefined truth so that, instead of referring to the agreement between a thing and its concept, it now has to do with a kind of openness, or "unconcealedness of being."[13] Truth is a "mode of being of existence [*Dasein*]," says Heidegger in *Being and Time*.[14] But *Dasein*, which is sometimes translated as "existence" and sometimes left untranslated, is Heidegger's expression for man as a creature that understands Being. Truth, defined as openness, is more a relation between man (*Dasein*) and Being than a metaphysical essence or an epistemological norm of some sort.

This brings us to Heidegger's definition of art. "All art is, as the letting-happen of the advent of the truth of being as such [*des Seienden als eines solchen*], in essence poetry."[15] The uninitiated reader may well not know what this statement means, but that doesn't really matter for my purposes. What matters is the very end of the sentence, where Heidegger uses the word *poetry,* because the simple sentence, without most of what comes between the subject and the predicate, reads, "All art is in essence poetry." What is poetry? First we need to know what language is. Just as he has redefined truth, Heidegger has also redefined language. Language is not simply a means of communication, of transmitting messages. It is something that "brings being as being [*das Seiende als ein Seiendes*—both these *being*s are used as nouns] first of all into the open."[16] Later, in the 1950s, Heidegger devoted much of his writing to language and poetry. At that time he grew fond of calling language the "house of Being" and using all sorts of mystical phrases to describe the way in which language brings about an opening, an unconcealing, an illumination of Being and world.[17]

Art, truth, language, and poetry are all related since all have to do with this notion of unconcealment/opening/lighting-up that Heidegger likes so much. Heidegger explicitly makes this connection in "The Origin of the Work of Art," where he says first that "language is poetry in the essential sense," then that "the essence of art is poetry," and finally that "the essence of poetry is the founding of truth."[18] Poetry is intimately related to truth since both have to do with unconcealment. And when we remember that the unconcealment associated with all these things—art, truth, language, and poetry—is the unconcealment of being and that language is the "house of Being," we can easily see the ontological thrust of Heidegger's theories of art. We can also see their essentialist, theological thrust. Many of Heidegger's commentators have pointed to the underlying theological structure of his thought: recall John Macquarrie's view that Heidegger's system is really just Christian theology dressed up in twentieth-century existentialist garb, with "Being" filling in for "God."

In the first part of this book I briefly mentioned postmodernism, a trend that has shown up in a number of different fields including, in the 1970s and 1980s, literary theory. I said that there is a theory of language associated with postmodernism, which can be found in its most characteristic form in Jacques Derrida's notion of language as a play of "differences," a "tissue" of signs in which any sort of concrete meaning is always around the next corner. For many figures associated with postmodernism, the reason for the instability of meaning in language is that language is "enmeshed" or "entwined" in history. Every individual utterance is determined by the network of its own unique historical context, hence it is improper to speak of fixed, absolute, stable meanings. The context changes at every moment, the reader or listener can never replicate the context of the speaker or writer, and so meaning, bound always to a context that is fleeting and irreproducible, is always elusive. It's a style of thinking that easily moves between postmodern critics of despair like Paul de Man, who focus only on the text in order to pick it apart and show that it never does anything but refer back to itself, and socially progressive critics for whom the idea of the inextricable "entrapment" of the literary text in history fits in well with the idea that everything in the world, especially art, is political (history, of course, is political through and through).

Views like these are generally not ontological per se, and most postmodernist critics and theorists have not treated the subject of the mode of being of texts. But the underlying assumptions of this view really come from a Heideggerian ontology, and that's why Heidegger is often seen as a precursor to theories as apparently diverse as the ones I have mentioned. The whole reason Heidegger abandoned traditional notions of truth and language was that he mistrusted any conception of human existence as something that could be isolated from its "world" (postmodernists would say "context"). Traditional dualistic theories of knowledge envisioned a situation in which there was a conscious subject and a cognized world of things. It was merely a question of using the apparatus of the mind to order the impressions the subject received from the world of things. Heidegger wished to see the subject as inseparable from the world and, consequently, inseparable from the notions of being (or Being) and existence that inevitably become part of human existence. Human existence, or *Dasein,* is thus enmeshed in its "world" and is necessarily ontological (I am using the term *ontological* in a general sense; Heidegger has his own specialized meaning for it).

It would be simplistic to say that all the latest postmodern, deconstructionist, and leftist theories "come from" Heidegger the way Waldemar Conrad's theory "comes from" Husserl. That seems to be what Allan Bloom thinks in his funny but extravagant pronouncement on comparative literature in America, in which he refers to Derrida, Foucault, and Barthes as the Parisian Heideggerians.[19] There is no doubt that Heidegger played an enormous role in these developments in modern criticism, if only because of his place both in the lineage that includes Derrida and in the historical-contextual theories of social-activist critics.

And if one sign of the role he played was the downfall of American higher education, as Bloom thinks, another, less catastrophic sign is the presence of ontology. The theories I'm referring to are not ontological in the same sense that Ingarden's are, that is, their authors are not specifically concerned with something called the mode of being of literary aesthetic objects. Still, there is no disputing that the idea of being plays a role here, and even if it's tied up with political and historical categories, the sort of ontological investigation we saw in Heidegger, Ingarden, and others was a necessary precursor of this kind of criticism.

Once again, of course, the poets appear to have beaten the professionals to the draw. In ontology there is a much clearer connection between at least some of the poets I've discussed and the theories that came later, for, as we'll see in the next chapter, some of the theories were drawn up with these very poets in mind.

CHAPTER ELEVEN

Being in the World
and Being in Structures
in Mallarmé and Valéry

THE "UNIQUE, DIFFICULT BEING" OF LANGUAGE

We are coming full circle. The ontology of literary artworks inevitably gets us back to language. The earlier discussion about language and the fractures that occurred in it led us to the question of the hidden essence and the religious dimension of poetry. But religion was not a stable foundation for much of anything since it was always paired with sacrilege or nothingness. So from religion we turned to the possibility that the essence was a relational structure. Now we find ourselves alone again with the object, the text, or whatever you want to call it, and asking just what it is. And the best course is to go back and confront what it's made of, namely language. Foucault got it right when he talked about Mallarmé's contribution to the modern *episteme*: "Thought was led, and violently so, back towards language itself, back to its unique, difficult being."[1] The importance of having our thoughts turned back to the *being* of language is that language has necessarily become an object of ontological interest. Once language has been fractured and meaning scattered into the realm of the ideal or into the relational space between words, we're forced to take another look at it and the literary works made out of it. Being begins to look like another object of the quest for essence (the word *essence*, after all, has to do with being). Sartre had already tied a number of these factors together. In chapter 4, I mentioned how in Sartre's account the death of God had led Mallarmé to a religion of nothingness (theology), how this religion had become an in-

195

vestigation into being (ontology), and how poetry had been chosen to fill the void (language).

One of the most thoughtful discussions of language theory as it relates to modern poetry is Gerald L. Bruns's *Modern Poetry and the Idea of Language*. Bruns sees his subject as a dialectic of two conceptions of poetry: one Orphic, the other Hermetic. Orpheus was the poet who was torn limb from limb after his death and whose song went into all nature, and so Orphic poets see the world as the horizon of poetry. In the Orphic conception language is "a circle whose circumference is nowhere and whose center is everywhere."[2] In the Hermetic conception, however, language and things made out of it are self-contained, "hermetic" structures. For Bruns, Mallarmé appears at first glance to be the Orphic poet par excellence but turns out to be only a failed Orphic poet. Bruns mentions Mallarmé's line about how everything exists to end up in a book, and he cites the phrase *Orphic explanation of the earth* to illustrate the idea of poetic language (in Mallarmé's view) as in some way encompassing earthly existence (*OE,* pp. 378, 663).

What makes Mallarmé's view paradoxical, as Bruns sees it, is that it is negative and negating. Mallarmé has radically separated language from being, and thus for him the creation of poetry is ultimately an act of annihilation that "establishes the word in the pristine universe of nothingness." Mallarmé is "the poet who seeks to return the world to the original void." His vision, Bruns says at the end of his chapter on Mallarmé, "is of the transcendent word—of language which belongs neither to the world of things nor to the human world of speech but rather to primordial emptiness, in which the splendor of beauty exists as a sheer presence, a pure quality unpredicated of any reality but the word. Mallarmé's, indeed, is the song of Orpheus in his absence."[3] So in Mallarmé's conception language can't really be Orphic (as Bruns defines it). For language to be Orphic, it must in some sense be coterminous with the world, just as in the myth Orpheus's song became infused into nature. But this condition can never be, since language always ends up not in nature or the world but in the void. Mallarmé's theory and practice betray not so much Orphism as a cult of nothingness that results, as the title of his chapter suggests, in the "transcendence of language."

This analysis is fascinating because, without realizing it, Bruns has explained the mechanism by which Foucault's statement about being led back to the unique being of language comes true. If language is separated from being, and poems end up dragging us out into the lonely regions of nowhere, then aren't we forced to come back to those words on the page as the only thing that *isn't* nowhere? Language has already been evacuated of its meaning—as we learned a long time ago when we saw how meaning hid itself in the empty spaces between words. The poet has flown the coop—as we learned when we read of the "elocutionary disappearance of the poet" (OC, p. 366). So what's left besides the words, which now have become hard and objectlike? Here we are truly led violently back to the unique being of language, finally confronting those nasty, obdurate, recalcitrant things called words and asking ourselves, in a more fundamental way than ever before, just what they are. Now we can see the significance of Mallarmé's view, namely that the perspective it forces on us is ontological: what we are facing is the "unique being" of language.

THE "UNIQUE, DIFFICULT BEING" OF THE WORK

The ontology of language is not the whole story. What I've said so far is that Mallarmé makes us think ontologically, not that the content of his writings is ontological. But as it happens, there is ontology in his writings, even though it's not called that. Ontology in Mallarmé has to do with strange questions about boundaries and limits. Mallarmé always joked about the most serious subjects, and this is one of them. I already quoted his remark about cramming stones into a book, a remark designed to illustrate the view that language—that is, poetic language— renders not objects but intangible things (see above, p. 71). The question here is silly but enormously profound: writers are supposed to put things into their books, so how do they fit them in without breaking the bindings? With Mallarmé, though, the answer to a silly question is complicated. Here it involves a kind of dialectic that corresponds to other dialectics in Mallarmé. How do you fit stones into a book? You don't, because . . . well, first we need to say what a book is, and then we need to say what's in it, and that's a spiritual matter. Question and answer imply a dialectic involving two perspectives: literal-physical and spiritual-philosophical.

We can see this dialectic at work in the middle two of the four essays Mallarmé published under the title "Quant au Livre" (Concerning the Book). The first, "Etalages" (Displays [of merchandise]), presents the literal-physical perspective (predominantly), whereas the second, "Le Livre, instrument spirituel" (The Book, spiritual instrument), presents the spiritual-philosophical (predominantly). "Etalages," like any other

Mallarmé essay, is full of tortured syntax that has been wrapped around in a double carrick bend. But here, when we unravel it all, we find that Mallarmé is talking about . . . books. That's right—the things you buy in stores or at those stalls along the Seine in Paris, those piles of printed paper that bear a commercial value just as a tie, a bottle of perfume, or a *tarte aux poires* does. "A piece of news circulated, with the autumn wind, in the market and returned to the bare, solitary trees: might you get a retrospective laugh out of it, equal to mine; it seems there was a disaster in the book business, one might recall the term 'crash'? Volumes were scattered all over the ground if you can believe it, unsold" (*OC*, p. 373). Another of Mallarmé's jokes: if there's been a crash in the book market, it must mean that all the books have come crashing down to the floor. The essay is full of references to physical books and the book trade. In the midst of it we find the poet struggling to uphold the ideal of beauty when all around him books are being marketed and exchanged like dry goods. "As the Poet has his divulgation, so he lives; apart from and without the knowledge of publicity, of the counter weighed down by copies [of books], or of exasperated canvasers: previously according to a pact with Beauty that he has taken it upon himself to perceive with his necesssary and comprehensive gaze, and of which he knows the trans-formations" (*OC*, p. 378).

"Le Livre, instrument spirituel," by contrast, starts out with the Orphic proposition that "everything, in the world, exists to end up in a book" (*OC*, p. 378). Once again Mallarmé evokes the physical dimen-sion of books, but now it is to show the passage from the physical to the spiritual. The act of reading accomplishes that passage: "A solitary tacit concert is given, through reading, to the mind that recaptures, on a lesser sonority, the meaning" (*OC*, p. 380). In a paragraph pregnant with the imagery of pagan sacrifice and sexual conquest, Mallarmé de-scribes the act of cutting the pages of a book, an act by which one takes "possession" of the book (*possession* is a sexual euphemism in French). Mallarmé here and elsewhere is obsessed with the "folds" of a book, which are endowed with a mystical significance as they conceal and reveal its spiritual contents. Mallarmé's descriptions are very physical. In fact, he even compares himself with a cook, knife in hand, slaughter-ing poultry. But the physical book promotes a kind of expansion by which the spiritual is created: "The book, total expansion of the letter, must draw from it [i.e. the letter], directly, mobility and, spacious, by correspondences, institute play, you never know, that will confirm the fiction" (*OC*, p. 380).

Both between the two essays and within each one the dialectic goes on as always in Mallarmé: physical and spiritual, profane and sacred, prosaic and poetic. But the issue is unquestionably ontological. The conflict between the poet with his ideal of beauty, on the one hand, and packets of folded paper, on the other, involves two forms of being: the physical being of signifying objects and the uncertain being of the created world and the meanings associated with those objects. Does Mallarmé resolve the conflict? Of course not; he sees no possible resolution. The important thing is that he explores it.

There is another angle to the ontological question in Mallarmé. We've looked at books and pondered what they are and how we get from them to the spiritual dimension contained in, or associated with, them. How does that spiritual dimension come into being in the first place, and what does the author have to do with it? What is the mode of being of both the author in the work and the world of that work as it materializes? Mallarmé likes to envisage this world as theatre, just as he uses the theatre as the decor for the representation of other spiritual and religious ideas. "The Restricted Action," the first of the four essays on the Book, contains a bizarre passage that describes the coming-into-being of a poetic world—at least that's what it appears to describe:

> The writer, from his ills, dragons that he has coddled, or from a gladness, must set himself up, in the text, the spiritual histrion.
>
> Floor, chandelier, obnubilation of fabrics and liquefaction of mirrors in the real order, up to the excessive leaps of our gauze-enshrouded figure about an intermission, standing, of the virile stature, a Place emerges, stage, over-valuation, in front of everyone, of the spectacle of Self.
>
> (OC, p. 370)

I don't pretend to be able to explain every word in this passage. But it appears that Mallarmé is picturing what it means to "set oneself up" (literally, "institute oneself") as an author in the text. The minute he thinks about that question, a theatre appears to him, with all its trappings—floor, chandelier, mirrors. What is taking place is the "spectacle of Self," as if the author's interior were a place where dramatic performances were put on with the self as hero.

Clearly this passage doesn't go far toward giving us a "serious" answer to the question of what a literary artwork is and where it comes from, since everything in it is highly metaphorical. At least it seems that way. After all, the floors and chandeliers are not real.

Or are they? We have already seen another place in Mallarmé's writings that features a theatre and something like a "spectacle of Self": the manuscript notes for the "Book," edited by Jacques Scherer.[4] The notes contain the same kind of images we find in "The Restricted Action" and some additional ones having to do with theatrical events. There is a performance, there are places for spectators, there is a reading of some sort, there are stage directions, there are the plans to shuffle and distribute pages in the room, there are arrangements for the sale of tickets and the collection of proceeds. Mallarmé repeatedly writes the words *hero, drama, mystery, hymn,* and *theatre* (or abbreviations for them). But in the manuscript notes Mallarmé doesn't appear to be speaking metaphorically, as he does in "The Restricted Action." Rather, he seems to have in mind a real performance of some sort, or at least a performance that could take place in the real world. It is as though he had asked himself how he could perform *in actuality* the "spectacle of Self," the spectacle of his own self, as he had pictured it in his essay. Indeed, how could he? By "instituting himself" in the text, as he had proposed in the essay? But then he'd run into those big rocks, and besides, the book covers wouldn't close on him or them. The joke comes back. By making floors and chandeliers literally spring from his head? No, the only thing to do was to get a theatre, a real theatre, and somehow make the performance there be as much like the one described in the essay as possible. Everything about the room would be set up so as to make it a reflection of the poet's self; in that way, to the extent that such a thing is possible in an atheized and desacralized world, everything could be infused with the poet's real presence, just as the consecrated Host contains the body of Christ. The trouble is, though, that he'd end up having to settle for something mundane, like reading his own poems to a bunch of people sitting in carefully arranged seats and surrounded by sheets of real paper with more poems written on them.

It's no wonder Mallarmé never got far with this project. I don't know whether he seriously thought he could do anything with it. I suspect he didn't. The important thing, however, is the degree to which he explored the limits and boundaries of a category of objects that has always defied precise definition. German romantic artists had done something similar almost a century before Mallarmé by playing with the boundary separating the world of their fictions from the real, historical world of their author. That's why we find all those funny scenes in the works of E. T. A. Hoffmann and Ludwig Tieck, where a character in the story stumbles upon a copy of the story in which he's a character, or where the author suddenly announces a visit he has recently made to a character of his own invention. But Mallarmé has gone farther than this and has given us, if only in a dialectic pondering, the outlines of a metaphysics of aesthetic objects.

I've been saying that Mallarmé probably considered the ontological question unanswerable. Given the idealist tendency we consistently find in him, this is not surprising. If beauty is an ideal and art is meant to contain or embody beauty, then artworks exist at the intersection between a knowable, real world on the one hand and an unknowable, ideal world on the other, and almost by definition their ontology is impossible to specify. There are several places in the manuscript notes where Mallarmé has written things that comment on this state of affairs. For example, here is a curious notation that calls to mind the dialectical nature of the four essays on the Book:

> a book may
> thus contain
> only a certain quantity
> of matter—its
> value—
>   ideal
> not numerical whether
>   it [the value] is
>   more or less
> than what is—to sell it [the book]
> is too expensive and not enough.
>   (39 [A])

The issue here appears to be the impossibility of specifying "matter" and "value" in a book, which is the same as the impossibility of really saying what a book is. In another place a solitary notation reads, "a book neither begins nor ends: at most it pretends" (181 [A]). In still another place the author speaks of "this volume (of whose meaning I am not responsible—not signed as such)" (201 [A]). As we read these passages, the Book starts to look like a wondrously open structure with fluid or nonexistent boundaries. The author isn't there (but then that's nothing new for Mallarmé), and so what *is* there is free to escape into a real-ideal world that perhaps looks like our world and perhaps looks like its own private world.

Mallarmé's idealism leaves him at a hopeless impasse when it comes to distinguishing between the two worlds. But at least he deserves credit for having the imagination to point us in the direction of the other world—whichever one that might be.

VALÉRY AND THE RELATIONAL ESSENCE
OF HUMAN THINGS

For Paul Valéry, more than for any other figure I've chosen, there is an intimate connection between relationalism and ontology. In fact, the two can hardly be separated since Valéry's relationalism is exactly what defines for him the mode of being of artworks. Valéry is a much more satisfying ontologist than Mallarmé, in one sense, because without using the word *ontology* and without offering a carefully elaborated theory of ontology as such, he squarely confronts the issue.

One place where Valéry explored the ontology of art is a modern-day Platonic dialogue that he published in 1923 and called *Eupalinos, or the Architect* (O, 2:79–147). Valéry did not have much of a sense of humor, but this piece is rather amusing. The joke is that Socrates and his friends have died and become shades in the underworld, for, apparently, some time has passed since the great philosopher walked the streets of Athens. And so the characters in the dialogue frequently address each other as Socrates's disciple Phaedrus addresses him in the opening speech: "Why have you wandered off from the other shades, and what thought has united your soul, far from ours, with the borders of this transparent empire?" (O, 2:79). Presumably, if Socrates and his friends are speaking from the underworld, they are freed from their historical connection to ancient Greece and can comment on matters that are relevant to more modern times.

The subject of the dialogue is architecture, and one of Valéry's points is to reverse the traditional nineteenth-century hierarchy of the arts, a legacy from Hegel and Schopenhauer, both of whom believed that architecture, since it was the most material of the arts, was also the lowest. For Phaedrus and Socrates, the materiality of architecture is precisely what makes it the "most complete of arts." Most of man's creations, Socrates explains, are made with a view either to the body, in which case they reflect the principle of utility, or to the soul, in which case they reflect the principle of beauty. A third principle that we seek in our creations but that is often lacking, he says, is solidity or duration. Architecture alone reflects all three, and this capacity makes it supreme among the arts (O, 2:129–30).

The idea is the dual existence of architecture. It exists in the world, like other objects, and yet it owes something of its nature to the human soul. This subject is pursued extensively in *Eupalinos*. Where are works of architecture? What is their space? As Socrates comments at one point, works of architecture (and music, too, for that matter) "exist in the midst of this world, like monuments from another world; or like examples, scattered here and there, of a structure and a duration that are not those of beings, but those of forms and laws" (*O*, 2:105). The peculiar thing about human creations, Socrates says a little earlier (speaking this time about music), is that they dwell in a space that appears to be coterminous with the one we dwell in but contains human characteristics. "Didn't it seem to you," Socrates asks Phaedrus, referring to the experience of hearing music, "that primitive space had been replaced by an intelligible and changing space?" (*O*, 2:102). When we listen to music, Socrates seems to be saying, it is as though the space in which we live had been replaced by one that is coterminous with it but is alive with human content, in short, with meaning. (The word *intelligible*, if Socrates is using it in the standard philosophical way, means accessible to the mind, as opposed to *sensible*, which means merely accessible to the senses.)

Valéry must have enjoyed thinking about this problem, because it turns up frequently in his writings. Dance intrigued him for the same reasons that architecture intrigued his Socrates. Like architecture, dance occupies two spaces. One is real, and the other is something Valéry cannot quite put into words. In a lecture titled "Philosophy of the Dance" Valéry says, "Dance is an art deduced from life itself, since it is nothing more than the set [*ensemble*] of the human body; but an action transposed into a world, into a sort of *space-time* that is no longer entirely the same as that of practical life" (*O*, 1:1391; Valéry's emphasis).

Valéry's interest in the status of human products is perhaps best illustrated in another passage from *Eupalinos*. A great many thinkers in the twentieth century have talked about the difficulty of distinguishing art objects from ordinary objects. The artists themselves have apparently found the subject fascinating since so many have tested the ontological limits of artworks by taking objects from daily life—latrines, Brillo boxes—putting them in museums, and seeing what happens to them. Valéry's very modern Socrates ponders this question, too, because of an experience that has challenged his otherwise facile sense of the distinction between human and ordinary objects. He tells Phaedrus of a day during his life on earth when he had taken a walk by the sea and found what he calls an ambiguous object. In that geographically uncertain region on the border of the marine and the terrestrial worlds, the sea had coughed up an ontologically uncertain thing. It was white, polished, hard, smooth, and light in weight. The problem was what to make of it, and it is clear from the story that Socrates felt compelled—as all of us would—to determine its status. He proposes some possibilities: the bone of a fish, a piece of ivory. Clearly, the most important question, however, is whether it was made by man. "Was it a mortal obeying an idea, who, pursuing with his own hands a goal foreign to the material he was attacking, scratches, cuts apart, reconnects; stops and judges; and finally separates himself from his handiwork,—something telling him that his handiwork is finished?" (O, 2:118). Or was it the product of some other living thing, or quite simply "the fruit of an infinite time," the result of the chance action of water and sand? Unhappily, there is absolutely no means for making a decision, and Socrates ends his story thus: "Whether this singular object was a work of life, a work of art, or a work of time and an act of nature, I couldn't distinguish. . . So I suddenly threw it back into the sea" (O, 2:120).

Valéry obviously has no foolproof and universally effective method for distinguishing between human and nonhuman products. But most human products do not leave the perceiver susceptible to the kind of cognitive impasse Socrates experienced with his smooth, white mystery object. The question, then, is not so much what there is about an object that signals to us that it is a human product and not a thing found in nature (Valéry's Socrates has just demonstrated that we can't always tell) but, once we know that something is a human product, what there is about it that makes it a human product. Valéry's answer is that human products (oeuvres is the generic term he uses) bear the mark of their creators in the form of laws, by which he means the laws of human sensibility. He says this about music and architecture: "But to produce . . . objects that are essentially human; to use sensible means that are not merely resemblances to sensible things and doubles of known beings; to give figures to laws or deduce figures from the laws themselves, isn't this equally the purpose of both [art forms]?" (O, 2:106).

Some types of human products are not likely to give us the problems that Valéry's Socrates has had with his ambiguous object. Literary works serve as a good example here because we have no trouble distinguishing them from objects in nature. Once again, the human origin shows up in the form of laws. In a 1927 lecture titled "Propos sur la poésie" (A few words about poetry) Valéry describes the state in which a poet finds himself at the moment of creation. "The poetic state, or emotion," he says, "seems to me to consist in an emerging perception, in a tendency to perceive a *world,* or complete system of relations, in which beings, things, events, and acts, even if they resemble, one for one, those that populate and make up the sensible world, the immediate world from which they are borrowed, find themselves nonetheless in an indefinable, but marvelously true [*juste*] relation to the modes and laws of our own general sensibility" (*O*, 1:1363). Valéry is talking more about the "world" of the poem here than about the poem itself, but the essential thing is the alignment of world and work with the "laws of our own general sensibility."

What and *where* human products are thus has everything to do with their origin, with *whence* they come. This statement may sound absurdly obvious. If they are human products, and we know that they are human products, then of course their origin is human. But there's more to it than this. Valéry appears to have believed that something gets transferred from the mind of the creating artist into the artwork and that this something remains in the artwork as an inherent quality. The whole process by which artworks in particular and human *oeuvres* in general come into being was always a source of fascination for Valéry. Little notations crop up over and over again in the *Notebooks* about this process, about the transition from one state of existence to another, and about the surviving presence of the author's mind in the resulting product. Here's one example:

> To write: to wish to give a certain existence, a continued duration, to phenomena of the moment.
> But little by little, by dint of work, this moment itself gets distorted, becomes embellished, and makes itself more existent than it ever could have.
>   (*C*, 4:921 [2:998])

In another rambling entry Valéry writes that he and certain other poets "have sought to give the idea of a '*world*' or system of things even more separated from the common world—but made out of its very same elements—the connections alone being selected—and also the definitions" (*C*, 15:248 [2:1116]). And in still another entry he speaks of "phenomenalizing the whole psyche [*psychisme*] and seeking to find for it—(or to give to it)—the *answer*, (at the earliest possible moment) that it is a closed system" (*C*, 20:383).

Valéry resorts to his favorite idea in the last two passages, the idea of systems. When I discussed Valéry in chapter 8, I showed how pervasive the idea of systems is in both Valéry's model of the mind and his model of the artwork. It now seems clear that this notion is the answer to the ontological-aesthetic question in Valéry. What distinguishes the mode of being of artworks (and generally of human *oeuvres*) from that of natural objects is that human *oeuvres* bear the marks of their creator in the form of laws that have their origin in human sensibility. But when Valéry speaks of laws of human sensibility, he invariably reverts to the system or group concept. The reason that both artworks and the human mind operate as systems is that the system is exactly the thing that gets transferred from the mind to the mind's product as that product comes into being. That is Valéry's twentieth-century version of essentialism.

The human product that shows this process in its most obvious form is the geometric figure, something Valéry talks about in a great many places. Socrates and Phaedrus discuss this human creation in *Eupalinos,* noting what me might call the intentional character of geometric figures. Geometry depends for its existence on speech (*parole*), Socrates says, because discursive reasoning (not Socrates' term) is what creates the figure and also what insures that it is not a mere accident but rather the product of a human intention (also not Socrates' term). He and Phaedrus express wonder at how words in the form of propositions can be trans-formed into figures in the outside world, as, for example, when one person orders another to walk in such a way as to remain constantly equidistant from two trees. The person who obeys this order "engen-ders" in the external world a geometric figure that has its origin in the mind of the person giving the order. When this happens, the human mind is made visible (O, 2:109–10). The geometric figure is a particu-larly appropriate Valéryan example because it is a spatial realization of a relational system. Geometry, as Valéry described it in a lecture in 1924, is "the machine of the mind made visible, the very architecture of intel-ligence entirely sketched out,—the temple erected to Space by Speech [*Parole*], but a temple that can reach to infinity" (O, 1:1013).

Valéry did not generally go out of his way to distinguish between human products that were aesthetic and those that were not. That is why human products as a group share the mode of genesis we see in geometric figures. So it is not surprising that Valéry envisages the crea-tion of literary works as similar to the creation of geometric figures. One sign of this view is his tendency to liken literary composition to a form of mathematical activity. Earlier I quoted an entry from the *Note-books* in which Valéry talked about arriving "at the completion of a work by means of formal conditions accumulated like functional equa-tions" (C, 28:468 [1:314–15]). In another place Valéry defines poetry as "the study (more conscious) of verbal trans[formations] that conserve their initial impulses" (C, 9:924 [2:1015]), a definition that suggests a transfer of mathematical operations (transformations of the sort I de-fined in Part III) from the mind into the poetic work. Perhaps the most

telling passage occurs in the writing called "A Few Words about Myself." In a section under the heading "EGO SCRIPTOR" Valéry says:

> Writing (in the literary sense) for me always assumes the form of a sort of
> *calculation*. That is to say that I relate what comes to me, the immediate, to
> the idea of problem and operations; that I regard the proper domain of *lit-
> erature* as a certain mode of combinatory work that becomes conscious and
> tends to dominate and to organize itself on this model; that I distinguish rig-
> orously the given from what the given can become as a result of work; that
> this work consists in transformations and that I subordinate ... the "con-
> tent" to the "form"—always inclined to sacrifice the former to the latter.
>   I justify myself by the example of the musician who deals with harmony
> by means of calculations, develops and transforms.—I get this from working
> on verse, which obliges one to make use of *words* completely differently from
> the way one does in normal usage, that is, under the pressure of a thought
> that sees only itself and that hastens to express itself.
>
>   (O, 2:1515)

But the clearest sign that literary works come into being in the same
way as geometric figures is that literary works are like geometric figures.
All those passages I quoted in chapter 8 showing the literary work as a
relational structure should be proof enough. Works are like minds, and
that is what makes works different from other objects. We might not
always be able to see the system in a work and thus might not be able
to tell that something *is* a work. For all we know, Socrates' white object
was the work of an artist or a craftsman and therefore retained the
relational structure its author transferred to it. The fact that we can't
see this structure doesn't mean it's not there. If the object is a human
oeuvre, then it will contain the remnants of its human origin in this way
whether we see them or not.

It would be silly to call Valéry's musings his ontology of artworks, as
if he had come up with definitive and convincing answers to all these
daunting questions—or as if, for that matter, he had even meant to. For
one thing, Valéry was too busy pretending he was not a philosopher and
was a mathematician to show any such presumption. For another, Valéry's theories almost always have to be gleaned bit by bit from hundreds
of different passages in hugely diverse writings, many of them never
intended for publication. What matters, though, is that he asked the
questions and left us a few thoughts on some possible solutions. And
that at least gives us the satisfaction of knocking the professional philosophers and critics off their thrones by showing that someone else was
there first—or there too.

CHAPTER TWELVE

Into the World of Names
and Out of the Museum

BELY'S SECOND SPACE

In Bely's best-known novel, *Petersburg,* we read this curious passage at the end of the Prologue:

> If Petersburg is not the capital, then there is no Petersburg. It only appears that it exists.
>
> However that may be, Petersburg not only appears to us, it also turns up—on maps: in the form of two circles, one within the other, with a black point in the center. And from this mathematical point, which has no dimension, it proclaims energetically that it is: from there, from this point the swarm of the printed book streams out. From this invisible point the circular rushes out headlong.[1]

The first character we are introduced to is Apollon Apollonovich Ableukhov, whose peculiar feature is that his mind works almost ceaselessly at geometric games. The world for Ableukhov, at least as he would like it to be, is a systematic series of figures, all as regular and orderly as the street plan of the Russian empire's capital city. If Ableukhov likes to play geometric games, the author likes to play ontological ones. The first chapter is subtitled, "in which the story is told of a certain worthy personage, his mental games, and the ephemerality of being." The narrator has explained how Ableukhov's imaginary geometric figures spin off into space and become real. He has told us that when Ableukhov, sitting in his carriage, sees a certain stranger in the street, that stranger exists only because Ableukhov sees him. Things spring from the head of

Ableukhov like Athena from the skull of Zeus. Later in the book we learn of the senator's "second space," a space he sees all the time that is material like the first, everyday space but at the same time spiritual. At the end of the first chapter, we read:

> This shadow [of the stranger] sprang up by chance in the consciousness of Senator Ableukhov and received there its ephemeral being. But the consciousness of Apollon Apollonovich is a shadowy consciousness, because it too is the possessor of ephemeral being and it too is the outgrowth of the author's fantasy. . . .
>
> Once [Ableukhov's] brain has been caught up with the mysterious stranger, that stranger *is*, actually *is*. He will never disappear from the prospects of Petersburg so long as the Senator exists with thoughts like these, because thought too exists.
>
> So may our stranger *be*—he is a real stranger! And may the two shadows of my stranger be real shadows!
>
> And these dark shadows will follow, they'll follow in the steps of the stranger, just as the stranger immediately follows after the senator. And the aging senator will pursue, he'll pursue you, reader, in his black carriage: and from now on you will never forget him![2]

Petersburg is one of those highly self-conscious, early twentieth-century novels that are filled with authorial tricks like this one. But Bely is doing more than just playing games. He's asking the reader to reflect on all these things, all the levels of reality associated with his novel, right down to the physical book the reader is holding. The miracle Bely describes in his playful way is a miracle of language and of being. It's the miracle of how a thing springs into existence because language makes it do so.

Petersburg was not the only place Bely expressed himself on this subject. I mentioned earlier the ontological dimension of Bely's language theory in "The Magic of Words." In that essay he says:

> If words did not exist, then neither would the world itself. My ego, once detached from its surroundings, ceases to exist. By the same token, the world, if detached from me, also ceases to exist. 'I' and the 'world' arise only in the process of their union in sound. . . . Thus consciousness, nature, and the world emerge for the cognizing subject only when he is able to create a designation. Outside of speech there is neither nature, world, nor cognizing subject. . . . The original victory of consciousness lies in the creation of sound symbols. For in sound there is recreated a new world within whose boundaries I feel myself to be the creator of reality. Then I begin to name objects, that is, to create them a second time for myself.
>
> (*S,* 429–30; *SE,* 93–94).

Later in the essay Bely speaks of how creation endows an image with "ontological being independently of our consciousness" (*S*, 446; *SE*, 109).

Most of all, Bely's ontology has to do with the status of signifying objects and the presence in them of a prototype (called *value*). The mode of being of such objects is to a considerable extent determined by the epistemological stance of their observer, something I described when I talked about icons. Like icons in the Orthodox conception, signifying objects inhabit two worlds: the material world, and an invisible world that peers into the material world through the intervening barriers of iconic objects. For Bely, ontology and theology are hardly different.

MORE UNIQUE, DIFFICULT BEING IN
KHLEBNIKOV, AND KHLEBNIKOV'S BOOK

It's striking how similar Khlebnikov and Mallarmé are in some respects. In speaking of Khlebnikov, I could almost repeat what I said in the previous chapter, substituting *Khlebnikov* for *Mallarmé*. Mallarmé's notion of language had led us back to its "unique, difficult being," to use Foucault's expression, because the evacuation of meaning (traditionally conceived) and the disappearance of the author had "yield[ed] the initiative to words," to use Mallarmé's own expression, and left us confronting plain language. Khlebnikov's theories do the same thing. I have talked about the two conceptions of *zaum'* language and about how both had the effect of objectivizing language. The first, "nativist" theory of *zaum'* language saw the poetic word as sharing in the existential autonomy of the object that it ideally designated, whereas the second theory saw the poetic word as existentially autonomous because it was the point of departure from the reality it created. Khlebnikov and Kruchenykh had spoken repeatedly of the word "as such," as if their ideas about poetic language, like Mallarmé's, had left us in the presence of these objects in all their naked existential isolation. (See above, pp. 54–57.)

Khlebnikov was fascinated with numbers, in part because of the comparison he saw between them and words. Much of what he wrote about numbers suggested that he saw them as fulfilling the function that words can never quite fulfill, namely the function of ideally signifying. Khlebnikov was also interested in the mode of being of mathematical entities, as he indicates in a peculiar notation from a series of thoughts collected under the title "Proposals." Each "proposal" is written with its main verb in the infinitive because it is a proposal *to do* something. "Keeping in mind," he says, "that n^0 is the sign for a point, that n^1 is the sign for a line, and that n^2 and n^3 are the signs for area and volume, to look for the spaces of the fractional degrees: $n^{1/2}$ $n^{2/3}$ $n^{1/3}$, where are they?"[3] Tzvetan Todorov quotes this passage in an essay he wrote on Khlebnikov and included in his book *Poétique de la prose*. He, too, sees the movement in Khlebnikov toward a conception of language as independent; and he believes that Khlebnikov's reflections on numbers and words are what led him to this conception. Precisely because words fulfill their function less well than numbers, says Todorov, paraphrasing Khlebnikov, they can "assume the function that really is their own: to be autonomous words."[4] Signifiers of all sorts were thus a source of ontological speculation for Khlebnikov.

Something else is true of Khlebnikov that was true of Mallarmé. Mallarmé's theory of language had a way of forcing us to confront language from an ontological perspective. But this is more a historical comment than it is a characterization of Mallarmé's views. Once again for Khlebnikov, as for Mallarmé, we find that those views themselves are ontological in nature. In the introduction to what used to be the standard English-language anthology of Khlebnikov's works, Edward J. Brown drew a distinction between Khlebnikov's theory of language and the Russian symbolist theory of language. For the symbolists, he says, language was a "vehicle for transcendental experience." For Khlebnikov, however, it was a vehicle "to discover the world." Brown feels that the world, "our own world," is always "vividly present" in Khlebnikov's poetry and prose.[5] I don't agree that language is always a vehicle for discovering the world in Khlebnikov, nor do I think that our own world is always present in his works. Brown's comment applies more to the first of the two versions of *zaum'* than to the second. But he is right to bring the world into the discussion. The theory of language we find in Khlebnikov (and Kruchenykh), with all of its complexities and ambiguities, begins to look a little bit like a pre-Heideggerian ontology. Certainly any investigation of language will bring up questions of the world, but Khlebnikov's theories, like those of many of his contemporaries, blurred the traditional sign-referent conception so much as to lead us and him into a probing of the mode of being of word and world.

Khlebnikov also dreamed of a book not entirely unlike Mallarmé's "Livre." There is nothing in Khlebnikov quite like the essays or manu-

script notes by Mallarmé, but the notion occurs with surprising frequency in short, mysterious passages that show the same ontological
perspective as Mallarmé's writings. Khlebnikov often referred to nature
and the world as a book. Notations he made here and there show him
pondering the idea of the world as a manuscript or poem. He also apparently dreamed of creating a book of nature, or a book of life, like
the Bible or the Koran. One of Khlebnikov's commentators, Raymond
Cooke, has shown with many examples that this was a forceful mystical
aspiration of Khlebnikov.[6] Of course, the book of nature raises the same
issues we find in *zaum'* theory and the same ones Gerald Bruns raises
when he talks about Mallarmé's Book. The view of the poetic work as
coextensive with the world, either because it created that world or because it simply "writes" the world, shows a view of language that, if
nothing else, must be characterized as ontological. Language is con-
fronted with the very idea of being and is made to be identical to it. This
is certainly not the same notion we find in Heidegger, but the orientation
of the thought behind it is quite similar.

BURSTING THE BOUNDARIES OF BEING

Mathematical speculation appears to have given rise to much of Russian
avant-garde aesthetics. Many Russian artists of the period were fond of
producing artworks that belonged to more than one art form. The arts
in Russia seem to have plunged headlong into an examination of their
own ontological boundaries by constantly testing the traditional limits.
The tremendous number of paintings containing printed words shows
the most common attempt in this era to break down the barriers between
two art forms. The effect is to make the reader-viewer wonder exactly
what sort of object a particular artwork is and why. El Lissitzky's "nar-
ratives," formed from a combination of pictures and words and gathered
into a book, force us to ask not only what the nature of El Lissitzky's
painting-books is but also what the nature of painting is and what the
nature of books is.

   One document from this era assigns clearly extraliterary values to the
constituent parts of words. An untitled section of the almanac *Sadok
sudei* (Hutch for judges), signed by David and Nikolai Burliuk, Elena
Guro, Vladimir Mayakovsky, Ekaterina Nizen, Khlebnikov, Livshits,
and Kruchenykh, proposes "principles of artistic creation," including
this: "We understand vowels as time and space, . . . consonants as col-

oring, sound, smell." In fact, the entire document represents an atten-tion-getting attempt to destroy traditional notions about language, writing, and literary texts. "We characterize nouns not only as adjec-tives . . . but also as other parts of speech, such as individual letters and numbers," they say at another point in their proclamation. They go on to say that an author's erasures and doodlings are an inseparable part of a literary work.[7] This text, of course, is not unique. Almost all the manifestos published in the period of the Russian avant-garde contain similar statements. Many appear to be motivated solely by a desire to shock the reader. But it is no accident that the mode of being of artworks is one of the primary subjects that are chosen for their shock value.

If artists of all sorts in this era thought that mixing up genres and forms was shocking, they clearly thought it was even more shocking to mix up art and life. Larionov and *zaumnik* Il'ia Zdanevich published a manifesto in 1913 called "Why We Paint Ourselves." And paint them-selves they did. Larionov and Zdanevich were not the only ones. There is a famous photograph of David Burliuk dressed in formal attire, com-plete with top hat, and sporting on his right cheek a painting of a bird in a tree. The point was to break down the barrier between art and life, something that would become commonplace later in the twentieth cen-tury, when artists started displaying latrines in museums alongside the other *objets d'art*. The artists of the Russian avant-garde, however, were more interested in taking art out of the museum than they were in bring-ing life into it. A young man in public with a painted face—isn't that the perfect way to show that art and being-in-public are really the same thing? And so Larionov and Zdanevich proudly proclaim, "We have joined art to life. After the long seclusion of the masters, we loudly called out to life and life made an incursion into art, now it is time for art to make an incursion into life. The painting of faces is the beginning of the incursion."[8] As the avant-garde movements continue, we find more and more expressions of the desire to take art out of its separate space and put it into "real space." The sculptor Vladimir Tatlin made a special point of working with real space, using recognizable materials from ordinary life to make artworks that would inhabit that space. The whole concept of the object becomes increasingly problematic in the work of artists who were as concerned as these artists were with the margins of aesthetic thinghood. El Lissitzky and Il'ia Ehrenburg (1891–1967), who was to become a central figure in Soviet literary life, founded a magazine in 1922 called *Veshch/Gegenstand/Objet* (Russian, German, and French, respectively, for "thing" or "object"). The purpose of this publication was to promulgate the aesthetics of Constructivism, a movement devoted to producing industrial, real-world, material artworks. The object side of an art object was of primary importance to the artists of this movement; hence the title of their journal.

The Constructivist movement had a political purpose, too. Art in the immediate postrevolutionary era was seen as having a social function: the more concrete, the closer to life it was, the better it could reach out to the masses. The art-into-life aesthetic, which was proposed with such vigor in the years before World War I, ended up serving the postrevolutionary culture in a most convenient way. After the revolution the idea was to bring art to the masses. What better way to do this than to bring them art that didn't look like art, art that no longer lived in its own private, privileged space inside a museum (or a book, for that matter) but lived in *their* ordinary, prosaic, proletarian space and looked just as drab as they and the things in their world did?

I have given only a few isolated examples of a trend that was so large as to overshadow almost everything else in the cultural scene of the years right after the revolution. I'm not interested here in the social and political role of art. I mention the trend because the artists involved in this kind of activity, wild, obstreperous, and unruly as they all were, were showing their own peculiar ontological perspective on art. Their concern with the space not only of truly spatial arts like sculpture but also of nonspatial arts like poetry is a strong indication that they were wondering precisely about the mode of being of art, that they were asking the same questions as the ones I brought up in chapter 10 when I talked about the professional philosophers in the twentieth century who have written about aesthetic ontology.

El Lissitzky wrote about these matters in the 1920s in a number of writings having to do with a familiar subject of ours, the book. In one such writing he muses about the "book-space" and how it must correspond to the content of the book.[9] In another, titled "Our Book," he gives a kind of capsule history of printed books and then surveys the avant-garde movement in Russia. He talks about the linking of painting and poetry in the publications of Futurist poets and painters. He tells how the revolution led to the bursting of the bounds of the traditional book. "The traditional book," he says, "was torn into separate pages, enlarged a hundred-fold, coloured for greater intensity, and brought into the street as a poster." At the end of his essay he says that the book is becoming "the most monumental work of art" because it is reaching out to the masses in an unprecedented way. Illustrated weekly magazines prove this, and so does the rise in publication of childrens' books. For some reason, Lissitzky feels that these books are fundamentally changing the way people relate to the world, and he adopts a quasi-ontological language to express a thought that started out being political: "By reading, our children are already acquiring a new plastic language; they are growing up with a different relationship to the world and to space, to shape and to colour; they will surely also create another book. We, however, are satisfied if in our book the lyric and epic evolution of our times is given shape."[10] Is this just an extravagant way of saying that new books are filled with new ideas that will change the lives of their readers? Given the era when Lissitzky was writing, I don't think so.

CHAPTER THIRTEEN

Rilke's House of Being

Philosophers love Rainer Maria Rilke because his poetry is filled with the issues they always talk about. He was obsessed with *things*—what they are, how we see them, the soul or essence that resides in some of them, how they regard us, and how some of them seem to transcend mere thinghood to inhabit a homey, familiar, human position in our human world. He wondered endlessly about one of the most fundamental philosophical problems: the nature of the interaction between subject and object. He wondered about the position that we occupy in our living, human world. And he wondered about being.

He wondered about all these questions in his poetry without writing overtly philosophical poetry. One of his most brilliant commentators, the German critic Käte Hamburger, thinks this is the quality that makes Rilke unlike any other poet. His poetry, she says, "is constituted in such a way as to be able to respond to philosophical questions—and this precisely because it is not philosophical poetry or poetry of ideas."[1] Rilke's poetry is not classic *Gedankenlyrik* (literally, "thought-lyric") of the sort we find in Schiller and Goethe, not poetry one makes by taking great thoughts and putting them into verse. No, says Hamburger, quoting in turn another Rilke scholar, Rilke's poetry is thought-lyric of another sort because it consists of a kind of "poetically creative shaping of thought" where making poetry and thinking are the same thing.

Rilke could accurately be called the ontologist's poet, if that name didn't have the effect of reducing him to a kind of plaything for tweedy, pipe-smoking academics. From early on, we find him puzzling over the nature of the things we are surrounded by. Things of all sorts occupied his thoughts: art things, home things, living things, indifferent things in nature. He is the author of several collections of poems often referred to as *Dinggedichte*, "thing-poems," in which the poet focuses his vision on a thing and on the interaction between that thing and the subject perceiving it. Often the thing is an art object. Sculptures especially interested him. Hamburger and Paul de Man have both pointed out that Rilke's characteristic trick in these poems is to perform a reversal of subject and object, ascribing selfhood to things, as Hamburger puts it, or locating in the object the inwardness we normally associate with the subject, as de Man puts it.[2] Rilke's interest in the subject-object problem is neither psychological nor purely epistemological. It is deeply ontological. The unusual reversal Rilke operates, his tendency to project the soulfulness of the human subject onto the inert object, shows an impassioned urge to explore the being of both subject and object, the different worlds the two inhabit, and the reasons for their complete separation. Hamburger expresses this eloquently in her book on Rilke. The "effort expended towards overcoming the strangeness, the separateness of man who says 'I' and the being outside of him" is in Hamburger's view the "fundamental problematic" of Rilke's poetry. Rilke's task, she believes, is "to recognize and name what is [*das Seiende*, literally "the being"]." The activity of the self that is described in Rilke's poetry is "grasping the being and being-thus of the 'I.' "[3]

The *Duino Elegies,* which Rilke wrote between 1912 and 1922, offer some of the deepest meditations ever written on being and transcendence, being-in-life and being-in-death. As always, Rilke can write about these things in the most intimate and familiar of tones. "For it appears that everything / makes us at home. See, the trees *are*; the houses / that we dwell in, are still there."[4] "Doesn't the world-space, / in which we dissolve ourselves, taste of us?" (*Sämt.W,* 1:690). "Being-here is magnificent" (*Sämt.W,* 1:710). "Nowhere, beloved, will world be but within. Our / life goes there with transformation. And smaller and smaller / shrinks the outside" (*Sämt.W,* 1:711). The tenth, and final, elegy presents a landscape of what the poet envisions as life, but life that has accepted death as part of it. Rilke, like Heidegger after him, cherished the idea of a human life that tends in the direction of death in a way that blurs the boundary between the two (Heidegger's *Sein zum Tode,* "being-toward-death").[5] His landscape is inhabited by a race of creatures called laments (*Klagen*), and in it we see the same things we see in our own world, except in Rilke's world they are lament-things. The whole vision is extraordinary for its vividly presented dual quality: the poet has taken our world-space and superimposed on it another one with a spiritual dimension that defies exact description but whose presence we feel like a warm breeze. Ontology has to do with the space or world we dwell in, and for Rilke, as for Valéry, ontological questioning involves a questioning of space and world.

In a poem he wrote in 1914, Rilke came up with a name for the realm where the interaction between us and the outside takes place—*Weltinnenraum,* or "world-innerspace":

> Through all beings stretches the *one* space:
> World-innerspace. The birds fly quietly
> through us. Oh, I who wish to grow,
> I look out, and *inside* me the tree grows.
>
> I care, and the house stands inside me.
> I take refuge, and refuge is inside me.
> Lover that I became, on me rests
> the image of lovely creation and weeps and weeps.
>   (*Sämt.W,* 2:93)

This is the place where everything comes together, where those recalcitrant things from the outer world settle within us, where they are *zu Hause,* at home.

So far I've spoken only about the ontological character of Rilke's vision. What about the ontology of artworks? As it happens, there is a place where Rilke talks explicitly about the mode of being of artworks. For six months in 1902 and 1903 Rilke enjoyed an arrangement under which he lived as a kind of disciple of the French sculptor Auguste Rodin, observing the artist at work and talking to him for several hours every day. In December 1902 he completed work on a monograph about Rodin, which was published in March 1903. Later, in 1905 and 1906, he served as Rodin's personal secretary, and in 1907 he supplemented his earlier monograph with a second one. The two pieces were published together and titled simply *Auguste Rodin.* They are often referred to as the Rodin notebooks.[6]

Rodin is sometimes credited with fostering in Rilke his devotion to things. I don't know whether Rodin really deserves this credit or whether Rilke would have come up with the idea on his own, but there is no doubt at all that things are in the forefront of consciousness in the Rodin notebooks. Rilke starts off the second one, which was originally given as a lecture and not intended to be connected with the first one, by inviting his readers (listeners) to ponder things. He tells us to think of a thing from our childhood, a thing we spent a lot of time with, and asks if there was anything "closer, more intimate, more needed" than this thing. He offers a mythical history of human things, speaking of the moment when man first began to make his own things, of how a human thing would suddenly take on "the traces of a threatened, open life," would be "still warm from it," and would then go to take its place among other things in the world, adopting "their composure, their quiet dignity" (*Sämt.W*, 2:210). He moves on to talk about Rodin, always using the word *thing* for the master's artworks. As you look at his works, Rilke says, "you see men and women, men and women, and still more men and women. And the longer you look, the more simplified even this content becomes, and you see: things" (*Sämt.W*, 5:215).

This is the subject of the Rodin notebooks: things and art things, their mode of being in the world and how they are distinguished from one another. As art things take up residence in the midst of ordinary things, they stand out largely for the way they are closed off from the world of nature at the same time as they inhabit that world. Rilke reflects on how Rodin must have come to realize that works of sculpture in this age were no longer associated, as they used to be, with buildings, like cathedrals, that served as a natural habitat for them. In modern times, says Rilke, the work of sculpture has had more and more to stand on its own. "It was a thing that could exist for itself alone, and it was good to give it the essence of a thing, one that people could walk around and look at from all sides. And yet it had to distinguish itself somehow from other things, from the ordinary things that one may confront head-on and touch. It had to become somehow untouchable, sacrosanct, cut off from chance and time, in which it rose up, lonely and wonderful, like the face of a clairvoyant" (*Sämt.W*, 5:149). What makes art things different from ordinary things? Rilke's answer is surprisingly similar to Valéry's. It all has to do with inner laws and relations. He says that people have recently come to see, for painting at least, "that an artistic whole need not necessarily coincide with the wholeness of an ordinary thing, that, independently of ordinary things, new unities arise within the image, new combinations, relations, balances. It is no different in sculpture. It falls to the artist to make one thing out of many and out of the smallest part of a thing to make a world" (*Sämt.W*, 5:164).

Rilke repeatedly stresses the separateness of art things, the way they seem to be closed off from the outside, forming a private world that is different from the space they occupy in the world of ordinary things.

Here is what he says about *The Burghers of Calais,* a Rodin sculpture representing a group of six figures: "Like all groups in Rodin's work, this one, too, was closed on itself, it was its own world, a whole filled with a life that circles around but nowhere spins off and disappears" (*Sämt.W,* 5:193). Describing the way a sculpture gradually takes shape under Rodin's hands, he says this: "To reproduce a thing meant to have gone over every place on it, having concealed nothing, having overlooked nothing, having nowhere been dishonest; to know all the hundred profiles, all the views from above and all the views from below, every point of intersection. Only then did a thing exist, only then did it become an island, detached everywhere from the continent of the uncertain" (*Sämt.W,* 5:217). And here is how Rilke describes Rodin's "acquisition of space": "Once again it was things that looked after him. . . . They repeated to him every time a lawfulness that they were filled with and that he gradually came to grasp. They granted him a glance into a mysterious geometry of space that allowed him to appreciate how the contours of a thing must arrange themselves in the direction of certain mutually inclined planes, so that this thing would actually be accepted by space, so that space, as it were, would recognize it in all its cosmic autonomy" (*Sämt.W,* 5:219–20). Rilke's concluding vision of Rodin's work focuses once again on the notion of worlds: "In a colossal arch he raised up his world above us and set it in Nature" (*Sämt.W,* 5:242).

The closest Rilke comes to an ontology of poetry or literary artworks is in the *Sonnets to Orpheus,* which he wrote in 1922 and which explore something very much like world-innerspace, but specifically in the context of song. Orpheus, the bard who charmed all nature with his song, has become here the bard of being for Rilke, the poet who shapes a world inside us with his song: "There rose a tree. O pure overrising! / O Orpheus sings! O tall tree in my ear!" (*Sämt.W,* 1:731). Orpheus's song has the power to make a world that pervades everything:

> And almost a girl it was and emerged
> from this bliss of song and lyre
> and gleamed brightly through her spring veil
> and made herself a bed in my ear.

> And slept in me. And everything was her sleep.
> (*Sämt.W,* 1:731)

"Song is existence," the poet triumphantly proclaims, using the word *Dasein,* which literally means "being there" (*Sämt.W,* 1:732). Orpheus is a creature who dwells in "both realms." In the myth, when his wife,

Eurydice, died, Orpheus so charmed the gods with his song that he was permitted to seek her in Hades and return to the world of the living with her, provided only that he not look back on the way out. Naturally, he looked back and lost her. But this episode put him in the privileged position of having dwelt briefly in the land of the dead, which for Rilke means that he is one of those beings for whom death has been incorporated into life. "Is he from around here? No, from both / realms his wide nature sprang" (*Sämt.W*, 1:734).

There is something amazingly modern about all this talk of worlds and space and being and existence. Not the least amazing thing about it is that Rilke was not in touch with philosophy, in the academic sense, and yet if we consider the central issues in early twentieth-century thought, they all are there in his work. Käte Hamburger sees the same concern for essences in Rilke's poetic vision as in Husserlian phenomenology, the same desire to penetrate to the inner core of obects—*Wesensschau*, "essence-vision," she calls it. As I mentioned in chapter 6, Husserl sought a method that would allow philosophers to bracket away the presuppositions that naturally accompany an act of perception so as to arrive at the very essence of the contact between consciousness and the phenomenon that presents itself to consciousness. The human subject in Rilke shows the same tendency when he peers into the interior of an object and pretends to see there the soul that is apparently missing in himself.

Hamburger also finds the same structure of consciousness implicit in Rilke's poetry as the one Husserl describes in his writings. For Husserl, consciousness is always intentional, always directed toward something, always consciousness *of* something. Hamburger sees the same notion in Rilke, where the most characteristic situation is one of polarity between the self and what it confronts.

Husserl's pupil, Martin Heidegger, was an admirer of Rilke's poetry; hence any affinities between Heidegger and Rilke are a great deal less surprising than those between Husserl and Rilke. I mentioned the notion of being-toward-death that Heidegger introduces in *Sein und Zeit* (Being and time) and that so closely resembles the idea of death that Rilke advanced in the *Duino Elegies*. The brief outline I gave in Chapter 10 of Heidegger's ontology should make it clear that Heidegger's concerns were close to Rilke's. In 1946 Heidegger wrote an essay about Rilke titled "Wozu Dichter?" in honor of the twentieth anniversary of the poet's death.[7] The title comes from a line in a famous poem by the German romantic poet Friedrich Hölderlin: "und wozu Dichter in dürftiger Zeit," which means something like "and what's the use of poets in needy times?" Needy times for Heidegger has to do with the absence of God in the modern era. Heidegger speaks of "the fault of God" (*der Fehl Gottes*), which means "that no god visibly and unequivocally gathers men and things to himself any more, ordaining out of such a gathering the history of the world and man's sojourn in it" (p. 248). Poets are "the mortals who in all gravity, celebrating in song the god of wine, trace the tracks of the gods who have escaped, stay on their track and thus continue tracking the way for their kindred mortals up to the turning point" (p. 250). Is Rilke such a poet in such a time? Needy times for Rilke meant times when the "unconcealedness of the essence of pain, death, and love were missing." Rilke, according to Heidegger, was able to experience this unconcealedness personally (pp. 253–54).

Heidegger appears to be ascribing to Rilke some sort of religious vision that allowed him to escape the spiritual barrenness of godless times. In doing so, he is pointing to the very crux of the flight from Eden. Heidegger's thought is religious in its origins, as I've said before, and one school of Heideggerian thought actually uses Heidegger as the basis for a modern theology. But Heidegger is careful to avoid anything that sounds explicitly theological, and so he stays with the ontological vocabulary that is characteristic of him. This hesitation between theology and ontology is what makes him a quintessential "twentieth-century thinker," and it is what he claims to see in Rilke. In fact, so strong is Heidegger's desire to see a kindred spirit in Rilke that, in the phrase I just referred to, when he comes to mention the "unconcealedness" Rilke experienced, he doesn't talk about "essence of pain, death, and love," as he had a paragraph before. Instead, he says that Rilke experienced the "unconcealedness of being" (*das Seiende*), a thoroughly Heideggerian phrase. One of the central terminological distinctions in Heidegger— in fact, a distinction that is arguably at the root of his philosophical enterprise—is the one between *Sein* and *das Seiende*. *Sein* (the verb *to be* used as a substantive and usually translated as "Being," with a capital B) is the more embracing term for being in its broadest and most indefinable sense, whereas *das Seiende* (the present participle, "being"— that is, something in the process of performing the action of the verb *to be*—used as a substantive and usually translated as "being," with a lowercase b) refers to that-which-is, to things that, well, *are*. Here is a typical statement Heidegger makes about Rilke: "Rilke names Nature, in as much as it is the foundation [*Grund*] of the being [*das Seiende*] that we ourselves are, the fundamental foundation [*Urgrund*]. This indicates that man reaches farther into the foundation of being than does any other being. The foundation of being has always been named Being [*Sein*]. The relation between founding Being and founded being is the same for man as it is for plants and animals" (p. 257). From here Heidegger moves on to the notion of *Wagnis*, "venture," and the essay continues in the same manner. I'm not trying to make light of what Heidegger says or to pull the classic trick of enemies of culture who cite complicated material out of context so it will sound pretentious and ridiculous. I am neither giving a lesson in Heidegger nor mounting an assault on him. It's merely an effort to show that this prominent reader of Rilke saw ontology as the fundamental issue in Rilke's poetry. But the ontology Heidegger sees sounds like theology (substitute "God" for "Being"). Later on in the essay, after a lengthy passage on the theme of being, Being, and how language is the house of Being (a favorite notion of Heidegger's), he says that "for Rilke's poetry, the Being of being is metaphysically specified as worldly presence, which presence remains connected with representation in consciousness, whether this consciousness has the character of the immanence of the calculating faculty of representing or whether it has the character of an inward turn toward the heartily accessible Open" (pp. 286–87). The "worldly presence" of the "Being of being . . . metaphysically specified"—make a few substitutions and you have the doctrine of the Incarnation.

It has been said about Heidegger, even more than about Rilke, that he is not truly a philosopher but rather someone who thought about philosophical matters and then found an entirely new language in which to talk about them. Once again, I do not want to take a position on a question (whether Heidegger was a philosopher) that is not important for what I'm talking about here. It is beyond dispute, however, that Heidegger used a different language from the one that was traditional in academic philosophy. And it is also beyond dispute that that language has a great deal in common with Rilke's. For both of them, the characteristic gesture was the turn from the heights of speculative abstraction to the most concrete and familiar images of a world that is thoroughly human (and European). The presence of this gesture in Rilke's poetry is obvious. Heidegger is always ready to "ground" his discussion of the Being of being and all his other impossibly cumbersome constructs in the familiarly human with an expression like *the house of Being*. Who would ever expect to find such a phrase in, say, Kant? At the same time, both Rilke and Heidegger show an essentialist vision that, though pretending to flee from the spiritual world of an earlier, Christian Europe, seems ever drawn back to it. When Rilke sought to evoke the "space," the mode of being, of Rodin's artworks, he chose the word *sakrosankt*. This wording can hardly be an accident.

DE MAN AND DE TRUT

We find ourselves coming back to the idea that the poets were there first: if modern criticism has been interested in poets of that era, maybe it's because it got its methods from them and ended up just looking at itself. And looking at itself and knowing that it was looking at itself (remember that phrase of Mr. Head, who, while being, looked at himself looking at himself?) increasingly made modern criticism think that self-referentiality was *itself* a pretty interesting thing to talk about, and so it began to talk about language and how language never does anything but refer back to itself. Which refers *us* back to Part I of *this* book, where we looked at how language became a subject of criticism (which is nothing more than language about other language).

Actually, it refers us back to the very beginning of this book, to the Introduction, where we talked about those modern critics who have made their way into the popular press with the idea that literature is nothing more than subterfuge. After the revelation was made late in 1987 that Paul de Man had written for a pro-Nazi Belgian newspaper during World War II, the popular press for months was full of articles about the great academic scandal. James Atlas wrote an article about the affair in the *New York Times Magazine* in August of 1988. The article contains an amusing story about Paul de Man, amusing mostly because it makes fun of de Man's European accent. One time, after a class with his Yale colleague Geoffrey Hartman, de Man is alleged to have said, "We've had beauty. Now let's have de trut."[8] The master player of the game of subterfuge, the art of concealment and evasion, was Paul de Man. He played it in his writing when he refused to issue an interpretation of a text on the grounds that the text was merely self-referential. He made it the *subject* of his writing when he showed how texts evaded interpretation because they were merely self-referential. And, of course, he played it in his life when he surfaced in this country as a complete unknown after World War II and went on to enjoy a long and brilliant academic career without telling anyone "de trut" about the person he had been before. But I'm not here to talk about "de man." I'm here to talk about his work.

One of de Man's finest examples of the self-referentiality of texts was Rilke. In "Tropes (Rilke)" de Man argues his way from pointing out Rilke's characteristic reversals to claiming that Rilke's poetry is ultimately about language and that it thus asserts the complete failure of language to mean anything. "The determining figure of Rilke's poetry," de Man says, "is that of chiasmus, the crossing that reverses the attributes of words and of things. The poems are composed of entities, objects and subjects, who themselves behave like words, which 'play' at language according to the rules of rhetoric as one plays ball according to the rules of the game."[9] The world Rilke has created "is then explicitly designated as a verbal world" with an "orientation towards the pole of language" (p. 39). De Man analyzes one of the poems from Rilke's *Neue Gedichte* (New poems) called "Orpheus. Eurydice. Hermes." The poem is about Orpheus's ascent from the underworld with Eurydice. The important moment for de Man comes at the end, when Hermes, who has accompanied Orpheus on his journey, leaves Orpheus to return to the world of the living (after Orpheus has looked at Eurydice) and "follows Eurydice into a world of privation and nonbeing" (p. 47). Without any warning, de Man draws this extraordinary conclusion from the scene he has described:

> On the level of poetic language, this renunciation [that is, Hermes's act of renunciation] corresponds to the loss of a primacy of meaning located within the referent and it allows for the new rhetoric of Rilke's "figure." Rilke also calls this loss of referentiality by the ambivalent term of "inwardness" (*innen entstehen*, Welt*innen*raum, etc.), which then does not designate the self-presence of a consciousness but the inevitable absence of a reliable referent. It designates the impossibility for the language of poetry to appropriate anything, be it as consciousness, as object, or as a synthesis of both.
>
> (p. 47)

So everything is language, nothing is determinate, everything is awash in polyvalence, and Rilke proves it. What's more, he seems to believe it. Of course, this is an extravagant thing to say, and anyone other than de Man would be hard put to find this idea in this poem (or "designated" by this poem). Furthermore, as we saw earlier, de Man's worldview is not so polyvalent and indeterminate as he might lead us to think, since it is anchored in a fervent faith in the specificity of poetic language (when it comes to language, de Man calls his private Eden "rhetoricity"). In any case, if we are looking for the idea that de Man sees in Rilke's poem, we will find it sooner in Heidegger and the notion of the *hermeneutic circle*. This concept, which I mentioned in the Introduction, is from Heidegger's *Being and Time,* and it has to do with how, when we interpret something, we must already understand what we are trying to interpret, with the result that understanding and interpretation move in what appears to be a vicious circle. De Man talks about this question early in *Blindness and Insight,* and his intimacy with Heideggerian thought in general is apparent in his writings.

What we do find in Rilke is ontology. We find it in the problematic nature of the interaction between human subject and the subject's world, something de Man has described so well in his analysis of reversals in Rilke's poetry. And we find it in the idea of *Weltinnenraum,* something de Man completely, but predictably, misunderstands (or was blinded to, as he would say). Ontology is one thing that attracted Heidegger to Rilke; it's what they have in common both with each other and with de Man. Once he's convinced that the world is deprived of faith, the Heideggerian can always turn to Being as the object of his essentialist yearning. And Rilke, the most religious irreligious poet that ever lived, is always there to serve as an example.

So what happens is something like this: We begin with Rilke and dwell with him in the "house of Being." This leads us to reflect on ontology. For Heidegger and de Man, ontology is inextricably caught up with hermeneutics and the idea of interpretation. De Man, in fact, declares that the hermeneutic circle is at the basis of *Being and Time.* From the idea of hermeneutics we arrive with de Man at the circularity of language and the indeterminacy and polyvalence of all meaning. And from the idea that interpretation and understanding are circular we arrive at the idea that poetry and criticism are not really so different. This was one of de Man's favorite ideas, and, as it happens, he introduces it, in *Blindness and Insight,* precisely within the discussion of the hermeneutic circle. I quoted from that discussion in the Introduction, and it is worth repeating: "The relationship between author and critic does not designate a difference in the type of activity involved, since no fundamental discontinuity exists between two acts that both aim at full understanding; the difference is primarily temporal in kind. Poetry is the foreknowledge of criticism. Far from changing or distorting it, criticism merely discloses poetry for what it is."[10]

And so here we are, back at Rilke, who gives us the idea that . . . well, it's no use repeating it, because we'll just be starting all over again, with books about books about books. About books.

Notes

ABBREVIATIONS

C	Paul Valéry. *Cahiers.* 29 vols. Paris: Centre National de la Recherche Scientifique, 1957–61.
DI	Saint John of Damascus. *On the Divine Images: Three Apologies against Those Who Attack the Divine Images.* Translated by David Anderson. Crestwood, N.Y.: Saint Vladimir's Seminary Press, 1980.
FI	Sergei Bulgakov. *Filosofija imeni.* Paris: YMCA-Presse, 1953.
O	Paul Valery. *Oeuvres.* 2 vols. Paris: Pléiade, 1957–60.
OC	Stéphane Mallarmé. *Oeuvres complètes.* Paris: Pléiade, 1945.
PG	*Patrologiae Cursus Completus: Series Graeca.* 161 vols. Edited by J.-P. Migne. Paris, 1857–66.
S	Andrei Bely. *Simvolizm.* Moscow, 1910. Reprint. Munich: Fink Verlag, 1969.
Sämt.W	Rainer Maria Rilke. *Sämtliche Werke.* 6 vols. Frankfurt-am-Main: Insel, 1955.
SE	*Selected Essays of Andrey Bely.* Edited and translated by Steven Cassedy. Berkeley and Los Angeles: University of California Press, 1985.
SS	*Sobranie sočinenij* (Collected works).
SU	Pavel Florensky, *Stolp i utverždenie istiny: Opyt pravoslavnoj feodicei v dvenadcati pis'max.* Moscow, 1914. Reprint. Westmead, Eng.: Gregg, 1970.
SW	Roman Jakobson. *Selected Writings.* The Hague: Mouton, 1971–.

INTRODUCTION

1. Paul de Man, *Blindness and Insight* (New York: Oxford University Press, 1971), p. 31.

2. Frank Lentricchia, *After the New Criticism* (Chicago: University of Chicago Press, 1980), p. xii.

3. Robert Greer Cohn, "Mallarmé on Derrida," *The French Review* 61 (1988): 884–89, at p. 888.

4. Paul de Man, *Allegories of Reading: Figural Language in Rousseau, Nietzsche, Rilke, and Proust* (New Haven: Yale University Press, 1979), p. 47. See below, p. 225.

5. De Man, *Blindness and Insight*, p. 185.

6. Terry Eagleton, *Literary Theory: An Introduction* (Minneapolis: University of Minnesota Press, 1983). I review Eagleton's presentation in chapter 4.

7. Lentricchia, *After the New Criticism*, p. 293.

8. Claude Bremond, *Logique du récit* (Paris: Seuil, 1973).

9. Allan Bloom, *The Closing of the American Mind: How Higher Education Has Failed Democracy and Impoverished the Souls of Today's Students* (New York: Simon and Schuster, 1987), p. 379.

10. See below, pp. 222–23.

11. John Macquarrie, *Principles of Christian Theology* (New York: Scribners, 1966), p. 105.

12. *Signs of the Times*, ed. Stephen Heath, Colin MacCabe, and Christopher Prendergast (Cambridge: Granta, 1971), p. 48.

13. See, for example, Robert Greer Cohn, "Derrida at Yale," *New Criterion* 4, no. 9 (May 1986): 82–84. Cohn says that Derrida "leans heavily on Nietzsche, Heidegger, Blanchot, and, not least, Mallarmé" (p. 83).

CHAPTER 1

1. Jean-Jacques Rousseau, *Oeuvres complètes* (Paris: Pléiade, 1964), 3:148.

2. Rousseau, *Essai sur l'origine des langues* (Paris: Bibliothèque du Graphe, 1970), p. 506.

3. Rousseau, *Essai sur l'origine des langues*, p. 505.

4. Eugenio Coseriu, "L'arbitraire du signe: Zur Spätgeschichte eines aristotelischen Begriffes," *Archiv für die neueren Sprachen*, 204 (1967–68): 81–112.

5. Viktor Shklovsky, "Potebnja," in *Poètika: Sborniki po teorii poètičeskogo jazyka* (Petrograd, 1919), pp. 3–6.

6. Jakobson, "Retrospect," in *Selected Writings* (The Hague: Mouton, 1971–), 1:631–33.

7. Shklovsky, "Potebnja," pp. 5–6.

8. Michel Foucault, *Les mots et les choses: Une archéologie des sciences humaines* (Paris: Gallimard, 1966), p. 248; English translation, *The Order of Things: An Archaeology of the Human Sciences* (New York: Vintage, 1973), p. 235. All translations from Foucault are mine.

9. Foucault, *Les mots et les choses*, pp. 309, 315; *The Order of Things*, pp. 296, 304.

10. Foucault, *Les mots et les choses*, pp. 317, 318; *The Order of Things*, pp. 306, 307.

11. Edmund Husserl, *Logische Untersuchungen,* 5th ed. (Tübingen: Max Niemeyer, 1968), 2:105; English translation, *Logical Investigations,* trans. J. N. Findlay (London: Routledge and Kegan Paul, 1970), 1:333.

12. Husserl, *Logische Untersuchungen,* 2:23; *Logical Investigations,* 1:269.

13. Roman Ingarden, *Das literarische Kunstwerk,* 3d ed. (Tübingen: Max Niemeyer, 1965), p. 104; English translation, *The Literary Work of Art,* trans. George G. Grabowicz (Evanston, Ill.: Northwestern University Press, 1973), p. 100.

14. Maurice Merleau-Ponty, *Signes* (Paris: Gallimard, 1960), pp. 112–14; English translation, *Signs,* trans. Richard C. McCleary (Evanston, Ill.: Northwestern University Press, 1964), pp. 89–91.

15. Jacques Derrida, *De la grammatologie* (Paris: Editions de Minuit, 1967), p. 102; English translation, *Of Grammatology,* trans. Gayatri Chakravorty Spivak (Baltimore: Johns Hopkins University Press, 1974), p. 69. All translations from Derrida are mine.

16. Derrida, *De la grammatologie,* p. 104; *Of Grammatology,* p. 71.

17. Derrida, *De la grammatologie,* pp. 96–97; *Of Grammatology,* pp. 65–66.

18. Cleanth Brooks, *The Well Wrought Urn* (New York: Reynal and Hitchcock, 1947).

19. W. K. Wimsatt, Jr., and Monroe Beardsley, "The Intentional Fallacy," *Sewanee Review* 54 (1946): 468–88, reprinted in W. K. Wimsatt, Jr., *The Verbal Icon* (Lexington, Ky.: University of Kentucky Press, 1954), pp. 3–18.

20. Monroe Beardsley, *Aesthetics: Problems in the Philosophy of Criticism* (New York: Harcourt, Brace and Company, 1958).

21. W. K. Wimsatt, Jr., and Cleanth Brooks, *Literary Criticism: A Short History* (Chicago: University of Chicago Press, 1957), 2:664.

22. See especially "Discourse in the Novel" (1934–35), in Mikhail Bakhtin, *The Dialogic Imagination: Four Essays,* ed. Michael Holquist (Austin: University of Texas Press, 1981), pp. 259–422.

23. E. D. Hirsch, *Validity in Interpretation* (New Haven: Yale University Press, 1967).

24. Timothy Clark briefly mentions Derrida's distinction between literary and philosophical texts in "Being in Mime: Heidegger and Derrida on the Ontology of Literary Language," *MLN* 101 (1986): 1003–21.

25. Aristotle, *Poetics,* 1451b.

26. Herder, *Werke,* 5 vols. (Berlin and Weimar: Aufbau-Verlag, 1982), 2:132–33.

27. M. H. Abrams, *The Mirror and the Lamp: Romantic Theory and the Critical Tradition* (London: Oxford University Press, 1953), p. 316.

28. William Wordsworth, Preface to the *Lyrical Ballads,* in *Prose of the Romantic Period,* ed. Carl Woodring (Boston: Houghton Mifflin, 1961), p. 56. The sentence from the footnote is cited in Abrams, *Mirror and the Lamp,* p. 101.

29. Wilhelm von Humboldt, *Gesammelte Schriften,* ed. Albert Leitzmann (Berlin, 1907; rpt. Berlin: Walter de Gruyter, 1968), 7:193–202.

30. Humboldt, *Gesammelte Schriften,* 7:44–46.

31. Humboldt, *Gesammelte Schriften,* 7:86.
32. Humboldt, *Gesammelte Schriften,* 7:90.
33. Humboldt, *Gesammelte Schriften,* 7:93–94.
34. Ernst Cassirer, *The Philosophy of Symbolic Forms,* vol. 1, *Language,* trans. Ralph Manheim (New Haven: Yale University Press, 1955), pp. 161–63. The work was published in German between 1923 and 1929.

CHAPTER 2

1. Victor Erlich, *Russian Formalism: History—Doctrine* (New Haven: Yale University Press, 1955), pp. 23–26.
2. Aage A. Hansen-Löve, *Der russische Formalismus* (Vienna: Verlag der Österreichischen Akademie der Wissenschaften, 1978), pp. 43–58.
3. Some recent articles on Potebnia in the West are Joseph Bya, "Deux précurseurs du formalisme russe: Potebnja et Vesselovsky," *Revue des langues vivantes* 37 (1971): 753–65; Donatella Ferrari-Bravo, "Aleksandr Afanas'evič Potebnja," *Strumenti critici* 42–43 (October 1980): 563–84; John Fizer, "Similarities and Differences in Oleksandr O. Potebnja's Theory of 'Internal Form' and Roman Ingarden's 'Stratum of Aspects,'" *Minutes of the Seminar in Ukrainian Studies Held at Harvard* 5 (1974–75): 32–35; John Fizer, "Potebnja's Views of the Structure of the Work of Art: A Critical Retrospective," *Harvard Ukrainian Studies* 6, no. 1 (1983): 5–24; Renate Lachmann, "Potebnja's Concept of Image," in *Linguistic and Literary Studies in Eastern Europe,* vol. 8, *The Structure of the Literary Process,* ed. Peter Steiner (Amsterdam: John Benjamin, 1982), pp. 297–319; Pirinka Penkova, "The Derivative Semantics of A. A. Potebnja (1835–1891)," *Die Welt der Slaven* 22 (1977): 126–34; Willem G. Weststeijn, "A. A. Potebnja and Russian Symbolism," *Russian Literature* 7 (1979): 443–64.
4. For instance, Oleg P. Presnjakov, *Poètika poznanija i tvorčestva: Teorija slovesnosti A. A. Potebni* (The poetics of cognition and creation: A. A. Potebnia's theory of literature) (Moscow: Xudožestvennaja literatura, 1980).
5. John Fizer, *Alexander A. Potebnja's Psycholinguistic Theory of Literature* (Cambridge, Mass.: Harvard University Press, 1986).
6. Aleksandr Afanas'evich Potebnia, *Mysl' i jazyk* (Thought and language) (Kharkov, 1862; rpt. Kiev: Gosudarstvennoe izdatel'stvo Ukrainy, 1926), pp. 9–22.
7. Potebnia, *Mysl' i jazyk,* pp. 22–38.
8. Potebnia, *Mysl' i jazyk,* p. 11.
9. Cassirer, *Philosophy of Symbolic Forms,* 1:166.
10. Potebnia, *Mysl' i jazyk,* p. 77.
11. Potebnia, *Mysl' i jazyk,* p. 77.
12. Andrei Bely, "Mysl' i jazyk. Filosofija jazyka A. A. Potebni" (Thought and language. A. A. Potebnia's philosophy of language), *Logos* (Moscow) 2 (1910): 240–58. The quoted passage appears on p. 251.
13. John Fizer talks about the analogy Potebnja makes between artworks

and words in *Potebnja's Psycholinguistic Theory of Literature*, pp. 19–23, 36–37.

14. Potebnia, *Mysl' i jazyk*, pp. 149, 143.

15. Andrei Bely, *Meždu dvux revoljucij* (Between two revolutions) (Leningrad: Izdatel'stvo pisatelej, 1934), p. 377–78.

16. Bely, *Meždu dvux revoljucij*, p. 376.

17. Andrei Bely, *Simvolizm* (Symbolism; henceforth *S*) (Moscow, 1910; rpt. Munich: Fink Verlag, 1969), p. 484.

18. Bely, *Meždu dvux revoljucij*, p. 211–12.

19. I have written about Bely's theories in several places. See Steven Cassedy, "Toward a Unified Theory of the Aesthetic Object in Andrej Belyj," *Slavic and East European Journal* 28 (1984): 205–22; "Belyj, 'zaum',' and the Spirit of Objectivism in Modern Russian Philosophy of Language," in *Andrej Belyj pro et contra: Atti del I Simposio Internazionale Andrej Belyj* (Milan: Edizioni Unicopli, 1986), pp. 23–30; "Bely's Theory of Symbolism as a Formal Iconics of Meaning" and "Bely the Thinker," both in *Andrey Bely: Spirit of Symbolism*, ed. John E. Malmstad (Ithaca: Cornell University Press, 1987), pp. 285–312 and 313–35, respectively.

20. English translation in *Selected Essays of Andrey Bely* (henceforth *SE*), ed. and trans. Steven Cassedy (Berkeley and Los Angeles: University of California Press, 1985), p. 95.

21. Aleksandr Afanas'evich Potebnia, *Iz zapisok po teorii slovesnosti* (Notes on the theory of literature) (Kharkov: M. Zil'berberg, 1905).

22. Bely, "Mysl' i jazyk," pp. 248–49.

23. Heinrich Rickert, *Der Gegenstand der Erkenntnis: Einführung in die Transzendentalphilosophie* (The object of cognition: Introduction to transcendental philosophy), 2d ed., rev. and enl. (Tübingen and Leipzig: Mohr, 1904). The book came out in Russian with the title and subtitle curiously reversed, as *Vvedenie v transcendental'nuju filosofiju. Predmet poznanija* (Kiev, 1904).

24. See the translator's introduction to *SE*, pp. 18–52, 64–69.

25. Andrei Bely, *Počemu ja stal simvolistom i počemu ja ne perestal im byt' vo vsex fazax moego idejnogo i xudožestvennogo razvitija* (Why I became a symbolist and why I never ceased being one in all the phases of my intellectual and artistic development) (Ann Arbor: Ardis, 1982), pp. 1–2.

26. Sergei Gorodetsky, "Nekotorye tečenija v sovremennoj russkoj poèzii" (Some currents in contemporary Russian poetry), *Apollon* 5, no. 1 (1913): 46–50, at p. 48.

27. Aleksei Kruchenykh, "Deklaracija slova, kak takovogo" (Declaration of the word as such), in *Manifesty i programmy russkix futuristov*, ed. Vladimir Markov (Manifestos and programs of the Russian Futurists) (Munich: Fink Verlag, 1967), pp. 63–64. The quoted passage appears on p. 63.

28. Velimir Khlebnikov, "O prostyx imenax jazyka" (On the simple names of language), in *Sobranie sočinenij* (Collected works) ed. Vladimir Markov (Munich: Fink Verlag, 1968–71), 3:203–6.

29. Aleksei Kruchenykh, "Novye puti slova" (New ways of the word), in Markov, *Manifesty i programmy*, pp. 64–73, at p. 66.

30. Velimir Khlebnikov, "O sovremennoj poèzii" (On contemporary poetry), in *Sobranie sočinenij*, 3:222–24, at p. 222.

31. Velimir Khlebnikov, "O stixax" (About verses), in *Sobranie sočinenij*, 3:225–27, at p. 226.

32. Raymond Cooke discusses the problem of word and world in Khlebnikov in *Velimir Khlebnikov: A Critical Study* (Cambridge: Cambridge University Press, 1987), pp. 73–74. He also cites Ronald Vroon on the subject. See Ronald Vroon, *Velimir Xlebnikov's Shorter Poems: A Key to the Coinages* (Ann Arbor: University of Michigan Press, 1983), p. 10.

33. Markov, *Manifesty i programmy*, p. 66.

34. The phrase *word as such*, with one variation, appears as the theme or title of at least four important Cubo-Futurist manifestos, all reprinted in Markov, *Manifesty i programmy*: "Slovo kak takovoe" (The word as such), by Kruchenykh and Khlebnikov, pp. 53–58; an originally untitled manifesto by Kruchenykh and Khlebnikov, p. 59, containing the expression *slovo kak takovoe* and later unofficially given this title in the Markov collection and in Khlebnikov's collected works; "Bukva kak takovaja" (The letter as such), by Kruchenykh and Khlebnikov, pp. 60–61; and Kruchenykh, "Deklaracija slova, kak takovogo," pp. 63–64. I cited Bely's phrase above, p. 42.

35. Viktor Shklovsky, "O poèzii i zaumnom jazyke" (On poetry and trans-rational language), first published in *Sborniki po teorii poètičeskogo jazyka* (Collections on the theory of poetic language) (Petersburg, 1916), 1:1–15; reprinted in *Poètika: Sborniki po teorii poètičeskogo jazyka* (Poetics: Collections on the theory of poetic language) (Petrograd, 1919), pp. 13–26, at p. 21.

36. Shklovsky, "O poèzii i zaumnom jazyke," in *Poètika*, p. 25.

37. Viktor Shklovsky, "Potebnja," first published in *Birževye vedomosti*, December 30, 1916; reprinted in *Poètika*, pp. 3–6, at p. 4.

38. *Poètika*, p. 5.

39. Erlich, *Russian Formalism*, p. 23.

40. Daniel Laferrière, "Potebnja, Šklovskij, and the Familiarity/Strangeness Paradox," *Russian Literature* 4 (1976): 175–99.

41. Viktor Shklovsky, "Iskusstvo kak priem" (Art as device), first published in *Sborniki po teorii poètičeskogo jazyka* (Petersburg, 1917), 2:3–14; reprinted in *Texte der russischen Formalisten*, ed. Jurij Striedter (Munich: Fink Verlag, 1969–72), 1:2–35; English translation, "Art as Technique," in *Russian Formalist Criticism: Four Essays*, trans. Lee T. Lemon and Marion J. Reis (Lincoln: University of Nebraska Press, 1965), pp. 3–24.

42. Viktor Shklovsky, "Voskrešenie slova," a brochure (Petersburg, 1914); reprinted in Striedter, *Texte der russischen Formalisten*, 2:2–17; English translation, "The Resurrection of the Word," in *Russian Formalism: A Collection of Articles and Texts in Translation*, ed. Stephen Bann and John E. Bowlt (Edinburgh: Scottish Academic Press, 1973), pp. 41–47.

43. Shklovsky, "Voskrešenie slova," in Striedter, *Texte der russischen Formalisten*, 2:4.

44. Potebnia, *Iz zapisok po teorii slovesnosti*, p. 208.

45. Aleksandr Nikolaevich Veselovsky, "Iz istorii èpiteta," in *Istoričeskaja*

poètika (Historical poetics) (Leningrad, 1940; rpt. The Hague: Mouton, 1970), pp. 73–92.

46. Inge Paulmann, who wrote the footnotes to the second volume of the Striedter collection of formalist texts, has pointed out some of Shklovsky's borrowings from Veselovsky. See Striedter, *Texte der russischen Formalisten*, 2:418n.

47. Veselovsky, "Iz istorii èpiteta," pp. 73–74.

48. Shklovsky, "Potebnja," in Striedter, *Texte der russischen Formalisten*, 2:6.

49. Veselovsky, "Iz istorii èpiteta," pp. 81–82.

50. See, for example, Erlich, *Russian Formalism*, pp. 28–30, and Bya, "Deux précurseurs," pp. 763.

51. For the passage from the *Iliad*, see Striedter, *Texte der russischen Formalisten*, 2:6; Veselovsky, "Iz istorii èpiteta," p. 82; and Potebnia, *Iz zapisok po teorii slovesnosti*, p. 214. For "white hands," see Striedter, 2:6; Veselovsky, p. 81; and Potebnia, p. 213. For "mucky mud," see Striedter, 2:4; Veselovsky, p. 74; and Potebnia, p. 212.

52. Potebnia, *Iz zapisok po teorii slovesnosti*, p. 212.

53. Roman Jakobson, "Two Aspects of Language and Two Types of Aphasic Disturbances," in *Selected Writings* (The Hague: Mouton, 1971–), 2:239–59. See below, p. 123.

CHAPTER 3

1. Stéphane Mallarmé, *Oeuvres complètes* (henceforth *OC*) (Paris: Pléiade, 1945), p. 257.

2. Jacques Michon, *Mallarmé et Les mots anglais* (Montreal: Presses de l'Université de Montréal, 1978), p. 14.

3. Edouard Gaède, "Le problème du langage chez Mallarmé," *Revue d'histoire littéraire de la France* 68 (1968): 54, 56, 57.

4. See Gérard Genette, "Valéry et la poétique du langage," *MLN* 87 (1972): 600–615.

INTRODUCTION TO PART II

1. Terry Eagleton, *Literary Theory: An Introduction* (Minneapolis: University of Minnesota Press, 1983).

CHAPTER 4

1. Jean-Paul Sartre, *Mallarmé: La lucidité et sa face d'ombre*, ed. Arlette Elkaïm-Sartre (Paris: Gallimard, 1986).

2. Foucault, *Les mots et les choses*, p. 317; *The Order of Things*, p. 306. See above, p. 28.

3. Austin Gill, *The Early Mallarmé*, vol. 1, *Parentage, Early Years and Juvenilia* (Oxford: Clarendon, 1979), p. 55. The letter is quoted on p. 54.

4. L.-J. Austin, "Mallarmé et le rêve du 'Livre,' " *Mercure de France* 317 (1953): 81–108.

5. Many critics have commented on Mallarmé's religious upbringing. A review of opinions up to the early 1970s may be found in Michael Danahy, "The Drama of Hérodiade: Liturgy and Irony," *Modern Language Quarterly* 34 (1973): 293 n. 4. Danahy lists several prominent Mallarmé scholars: Henri Mondor, L.-J. Austin, Kurt Wais, and Charles Mauron. A précis of scholarly opinion on Mallarmé and Christianity up to the late 1960s may be found in A. Muller, *De Rabelais à Paul Valéry: Les grands écrivains devant le christianisme* (Paris: Foulon, 1969), pp. 207–9. Paula Gilbert Lewis has written on the role of religion in Mallarmé's aesthetics in *The Aesthetics of Stéphane Mallarmé in Relation to His Public* (Rutherford, N.J.: Fairleigh Dickinson University Press, 1976). She discusses Mallarmé's early religious attitudes on pp. 22–23, referring to some of his juvenile compositions. A few other studies on the subject are Antoine Orliac, *Mallarmé tel qu'en lui-même* (Paris: Mercure de France, 1948), "La cathédrale symboliste," pp. 227–41; Austin Gill, "Mallarmé's Use of Christian Imagery for Post-Christian Concepts," in *Order and Adventure in Post-Romantic French Poetry: Essays Presented to C. A. Hackett*, ed. E. M. Beaumont, J. M. Cocking, J. Cruickshank (New York: Barnes and Noble, 1973), pp. 72–88; and Jewel Spears Brooker, "The Dispensations of Art: Mallarmé and the Fallen Reader," *Southern Review* 19 (1983): 17–38.

6. Mallarmé to Henri Cazalis, June 1866, in Stéphane Mallarmé, *Correspondance,* ed. Henri Mondor with Jean-Pierre Richard (Paris: Gallimard, 1959), p. 220.

7. Mallarmé to Théodore Aubanel, July 16, 1866, *Correspondance*, p. 222.

8. Mallarmé to Cazalis, May 14, 1867, *Correspondance*, pp. 240–41.

9. Mallarmé to Cazalis, May 14, 1867, *Correspondance*, pp. 242–43.

10. *Pour un tombeau d'Anatole*, ed. Jean-Pierre Richard (Paris: Seuil, 1961).

11. Guy Delfel, *L'esthétique de Stéphane Mallarmé*, chap. 3, "Une religion esthétique," (Paris: Flammarion, 1951), pp. 79–109.

12. Delfel, *L'esthétique*, p. 80.

13. Delfel, *L'esthétique*, p. 93: "Je ne crois pas que Mallarmé ait jamais perdu la foi" ("I don't think Mallarmé ever lost his faith").

14. Delfel, *L'esthétique*, p. 88–89.

15. Jean-Pierre Richard, *L'univers imaginaire de Mallarmé* (Paris: Seuil, 1961), p. 412.

16. Cited in Richard, *L'univers*, p. 417. Richard quotes from a text where Mallarmé used the identical passage. See above, p. 72, for my earlier discussion.

17. Mallarmé to Cazalis, May 14, 1867, *Correspondance*, pp. 243–44.

18. Jacques Scherer, *Le "Livre" de Mallarmé: Premières recherches sur des documents inédits* (Paris: Gallimard, 1957).

19. Scherer, *"Livre"* p. 152. The manuscript notes, which form the second part of Scherer's book, are paginated separately by means of a system that includes letters in addition to numbers.

20. Two studies that were written before the publication of Scherer's book are Deborah A. K. Aish, "Le Rêve de Stéphane Mallarmé d'après sa correspon-

dance," *PMLA* 56 (1941): 874–84; and Austin, "Mallarmé et le rêve du 'Livre,' "
81–108. Jean-Pierre Richard devotes a brief section to the *Livre* at the end of
L'Univers imaginaire de Mallarmé, pp. 565–74. A. R. Chisholm feels that there
is no connection between Scherer's notes and Mallarmé's *Grand Oeuvre*, a point
he argues in *Mallarmé's "Grande Oeuvre"* (Manchester: Manchester University
Press, 1962). A few other studies are Marianne Kesting, "Entwurf des absoluten
Buches: Über Stéphane Mallarmé," in *Vermessung des Labyrinths: Studien zur
modernen Ästhetik* (Frankfurt am Main: Fischer, 1965), pp. 31–49; Josef Thei-
sen, "Endzeit des Buches? Betrachtungen zu Mallarmé's Livre," *Die neueren
Sprachen* 18 (1969): 365–72; and Virginia A. la Charité, "Mallarmé's *Livre*:
The Graphomatics of the Text," *Symposium* 34 (1980): 249–59. La Charité
argues more strongly than most against the existence of the *Livre* either as an
unfinished project or as one of Mallarmé's actual texts. The best discussion of
the *Livre* that I know of—one, incidentally, that does not take a position on the
existence or nonexistence of the project, is Gerald L. Bruns, "Mallarmé: The
Transcendence of Language and the Aesthetics of the Book," a chapter in his
fascinating *Modern Poetry and the Idea of Language* (New Haven: Yale University Press, 1974), pp. 101–17. See above, p. 196, for a discussion of Bruns.
I myself have talked about the *Livre* in two articles. See Steven Cassedy, "Mallarmé and Andrej Belyj: Mathematics and the Phenomenality of the Literary
Object," *MLN* 96 (1981): 1066–83; and "Mathematics, Relationalism, and the
Rise of Modern Literary Aesthetics," *Journal of the History of Ideas* 49 (1988):
109–32.

    21. Lentricchia, *After the New Criticism.* Lentricchia makes this point es-
pecially forcefully in chapter 4, "Uncovering History and the Reader: Structuralism," pp. 102–54.

CHAPTER 5

    1. Andrzej Walicki, *A History of Russian Thought from the Enlightenment
to Marxism,* trans. Hilda Andrews-Rusiecka (Stanford, Calif.: Stanford University Press, 1979).

    2. N. O. Lossky, *History of Russian Philosophy* (New York: International
Universities Press, 1951).

    3. Saint John of Damascus, *On the Divine Images: Three Apologies against
Those Who Attack the Divine Images* (henceforth *DI*), trans. David Anderson
(Crestwood, N.Y.: Saint Vladimir's Seminary Press, 1980), p. 16. The Greek
text of Saint John's *Apologies* may be found in *Patrologiae Cursus Completus:
Series Graeca* (henceforth *PG*), ed. J.-P. Migne (Paris, 1857–66), 94:1227–
1419.

    4. *Icon and Logos: Sources in Eighth-Century Iconoclasm,* ed. and trans.
Daniel J. Sahas (Toronto: University of Toronto Press, 1986), p. 178.

    5. Sahas, *Icon and Logos,* p. 179.

    6. Naftali Prat, "Orthodox Philosophy of Language in Russia," *Studies in
Soviet Thought* 20 (1979): 1–21.

    7. Vladimir Solov'ev, *Čtenija o Bogočelovečestve,* in *Sobranie sočinenij*

(henceforth *SS*) (Petersburg, 1877–81; rpt. Brussels: Foyer Oriental Chrétien, 1966), 3:3–181.

8. Vladimir Solov'ev, "Krasota v prirode" (1889), in *SS*, 6:33–74, at p. 41.

9. Vladimir Solov'ev, "Obščij smysl iskusstva," in *SS*, 6:75–90.

10. Andrei Bely, "Emblematika smysla: Predposylki k teorii simvolizma," in *S*, pp. 49–143; English translation, "The Emblematics of Meaning: Premises to a Theory of Symbolism," in *SE*, pp. 111–97.

11. Sergei Bulgakov, *Filosofija imeni* (henceforth FI) (Paris: YMCA-Presse, 1953).

12. Sergei Bulgakov, "Was ist das Wort?" in *Festschrift Th. G. Masaryk zum 80. Geburtstage*, ed. Boris Jakowenko (Bonn: Friedrich Cohen, 1930), pp. 25–70.

13. Pavel Florensky, *Stolp i utverždenie istiny: Opyt pravoslavnoj feodicei v dvenadcati pis'max* (The pillar and ground of the truth: Essay in Orthodox theodicy in twelve letters) (Moscow, 1914; rpt. Westmead, Eng.: Gregg, 1970). Henceforth *SU*. "The pillar and ground" is not necessarily the most accurate translation of Florensky's title, which means something like "the pillar and assertion" or "the pillar and affirmation." Florensky took his title from a phrase in 1 Timothy 3:15, which reads "the pillar and ground" in the King James version.

14. Pavel Florensky, *Sobranie sočinenij* (henceforth *SS*), ed. N. A. Struve (Paris: YMCA Press, 1985–): 1:193–316.

15. Pavel Florensky, "Stroenie slova," in *Kontekst 1972: Literaturno-teoretičeskie issledovanija* (Moscow, 1973), pp. 348–75.

16. Florensky, "Stroenie slova," p. 351.

17. Florensky, "Stroenie slova," p. 355.

18. Florensky, "Stroenie slova," p. 352.

19. Florensky, "Stroenie slova," p. 353.

20. Hansen-Löve, *Der russische Formalismus*, p. 83n.

21. Karl Eimermacher, "Zur Entstehungsgeschichte einer deskriptiven Semiotik in der Sowjetunion," *Zeitschrift für Semiotik* 4 (1982): 1–34, at pp. 4–5.

22. Katerina Clark and Michael Holquist, *Mikhail Bakhtin* (Cambridge, Mass.: Harvard University Press, 1984), p. 85.

23. Clark and Holquist, p. 85.

CHAPTER 6

1. Roman Jakobson and Yury Tynianov, "Problemy izučenija literatury i jazyka," *Novyj Lef* 12 (1928): 36–37. The translation I have used appears in *Readings in Russian Poetics*, ed. Ladislav Matejka and Krystyna Pomorska (Cambridge, Mass.: MIT Press, 1971), pp. 79–81.

2. Jakobson's account may be found in the "Retrospect" to volume 1 of his *Selected Writings* (henceforth *SW*), p. 633.

3. Roman Jakobson and Claude Lévi-Strauss, "«Les chats» de Charles Baudelaire," *L'Homme* 2 (1962): 5–21; reprinted in *Questions de poétique*, ed. Tzvetan Todorov (Paris: Seuil, 1973), pp. 401–19, at p. 414.

4. Roman Jakobson, "Two Aspects of Language and Two Types of Aphasic Disturbances" (1954), *SW*, 2:239–59.

5. Roman Jakobson, "Novejšaja russkaja poèzija," *SW*, 5:299–354. There is a French translation of selected parts of this essay, "La nouvelle poésie russe," in *Questions de poétique,* pp. 11–24.

6. Gustav Shpet, *Vnutrennjaja forma slova* (The inner form of the word) (Moscow: GAXN, 1927).

7. Elmar Holenstein, *Roman Jakobson's Approach to Language: Phenomenological Structuralism,* (Bloomington: Indiana University Press, 1976).

8. Elmar Holenstein, "Jakobson and Husserl: A Contribution to the Genealogy of Structuralism," *Human Context* 7 (1975): 61–83, at p. 75.

9. See above, p. 43. Potebnia uses the term in *Mysl' i jazyk,* p. 134.

10. Holenstein, "Jakobson and Husserl," p. 75.

11. Jonathan Culler, author of one of the principal English-language accounts of structuralism, wrote an essay in which he argued that structuralism has a logical point of departure in phenomenology because it always needs to take the human subject into account, even though its practitioners don't always seem to realize that. See Jonathan Culler, "Phenomenology and Structuralism," *Human Context* 5 (1973): 35–42.

12. Roman Jakobson, "Co je poesie," *Volné smery* 30 (1933–34): 229–39; reprinted in Striedter, *Texte der russischen Formalisten,* 2:392–417; English translation in *SW*, 3:740–50.

13. Roman Jakobson, "Vers une science de l'art poétique," written as a preface to *Théorie de la littérature: Textes des formalistes russes,* ed. Tzvetan Todorov (Paris: Seuil, 1966), pp. 9–13; reprinted in *SW*, 5:541–44, at p. 542.

14. See, for example, a short piece by Jakobson called "One of the Speculative Anticipations: An Old Russian Treatise on the Divine and Human Word" (1955), *SW*, 2:369–74.

CHAPTER 7

1. Many of the ideas in Part III and Part IV have appeared in two of my articles. See Cassedy, "Mathematics, Relationalism"; and "Paul Valéry's Modernist Aesthetic Object," *Journal of Aesthetics and Art Criticism* 45 (1986–87): 77–86.

2. Ernst Cassirer, *Philosophy of Symbolic Forms,* vol. 3, *The Phenomenology of Knowledge,* trans. Ralph Manheim (New Haven: Yale University Press, 1957), pp. 357–405.

3. Immanuel Kant, *Kritik der reinen Vernunft,* "B" edition, p. 75; "A" edition, p. 51; English translation, *Critique of Pure Reason,* trans. Norman Kemp Smith (New York: St. Martin's Press, 1965), p. 93.

4. See Tony Rothman, "The Short Life of Evariste Galois," *Scientific American* 246 (1982): 136–49. The *New York Times* ran an amusing editorial on Rothman's deflation of the Galois story, April 4, 1982.

5. Ernst Cassirer, "The Concept of Group and the Theory of Perception," *Philosophy and Phenomenological Research* 5 (1944): 1–36. This is an English translation of an original French version, "Le concept de groupe et la théorie de

la perception," *Journal de Psychologie* (July–December 1938): 368–414. Cassirer also wrote a shorter and simpler version of this paper as a lecture, which he was working on the morning of the day of his death. The lecture is titled "Reflections on the Concept of Group and the Theory of Perception" and is published in *Symbol, Myth, and Culture: Essays and Lectures of Ernst Cassirer, 1935–1945,* ed. Donald Phillip Verene (New Haven: Yale University Press, 1979), pp. 271–91.

6. Cassirer mentions Poincaré's theory in "The Concept of Group, p. 3.

7. Roman Jakobson, "Verbal Communication," *Scientific American* 227 (September 1972): 72–80. This passage occurs on p. 72.

8. Jakobson, "Verbal Communication," p. 76.

9. Distinctive features are treated in Roman Jakobson and Morris Halle, "Phonology and Phonetics," in Jakobson, *SW,* 1:464–504, and, in the same volume of *SW,* "The Revised Version of the List of Inherent Features," 1:738–42.

10. Ernst Cassirer, "Structuralism in Modern Linguistics," *Word* 1 (1945): 99–120.

11. Jean Piaget, *Le structuralisme* (Paris: Presses Universitaires de France, 1968); English translation, *Structuralism,* trans. Chaninah Maschler (New York: Basic Books, 1970).

12. Michel Serres, *Hermès ou la communication* (Paris: Minuit, 1968).

CHAPTER 8

1. Ginette Mathiot, *Je sais cuisiner* (1932; rpt. Paris: Editions Albin Michel, 1965), p. 13.

2. René Descartes, *Discours de la méthode,* ed. Etienne Gilson (1925; rpt. Paris: Vrin, 1976), pp. 18–19.

3. In fact, the dean of American cookbook authors, Irma S. Rombauer, in the introduction to the *Joy of Cooking,* says, "To live we must eat." She goes on to discuss foods and nutrition, but there is nothing like the step-by-step logical progression of thought that we find in Mathiot. And Fannie Farmer, in *The Fannie Farmer Cookbook,* launches right into a lesson on the basic processes of cooking, without ever stopping to ask why we cook in the first place. See Irma S. Rombauer and Marion Rombauer Becker, *Joy of Cooking* (1931; rpt. Indianapolis: Bobbs-Merrill, 1967), p. 1; and Fannie Farmer, *The Fannie Farmer Cookbook,* 11th ed. (1869; rpt. Boston: Little, Brown, 1965), p. 3.

4. Edmund Husserl, *Die Krisis der europäischen Wissenschaften und die transzendentale Phänomenologie* (The Crisis of European sciences and transcendental phenomenology), ed. Walter Biemel, vol. 6 of *Husserliana: Edmund Husserl, Gesammelte Werke,* ed. H. L. Van Breda (The Hague: Martinus Nijhoff, 1962), p. 75; my translation. There is an English translation, by David Carr, *The Crisis of European Sciences and Transcendental Phenomenology* (Evanston, Ill.: Northwestern University Press, 1970). The quoted passage in Carr's translation appears on p. 73.

5. Husserl, *Krisis,* p. 75; *Crisis,* p. 73.

6. Descartes, *Règles utiles et claires pour la direction de l'esprit en la re-*

cherche de la vérité (Useful and clear rules for the direction of the mind in the search for truth), translated into French by Jean-Luc Marion (The Hague: Martinus Nijhoff, 1977), p. 6.

7. Mallarmé to François Coppée, December 5, 1866, *Correspondance*, p. 234 (Mallarmé's emphasis).

8. Mallarmé to Théodore Aubanel, July 28, 1866, *Correspondance*, p. 225 (Mallarmé's emphasis).

9. Scherer, *Le "Livre" de Mallarmé*, 37–38 (A).

10. Valéry's anecdote is cited in *OC*, pp. 1581–82. It is excerpted from *Variété II* (Paris: Nouvelle Revue Française, 1929), pp. 169–75.

11. James A. Boon, *From Symbolism to Structuralism: Lévi-Strauss in a Literary Tradition* (Oxford: Basil Blackwell, 1972). See especially pp. 155–58.

12. Paul Valéry, *Oeuvres* (henceforth O) (Paris: Pléiade, 1957–60), 2:25. The three periods are Valéry's.

13. For an account of Valéry's education in mathematics, see Reino Virtanen, "Paul Valéry's Scientific Education," *Symposium* 27 (1973): 362–78. Some of the same material appears in Virtanen's book, *The Scientific Analogies of Paul Valéry*, University of Nebraska Studies, n.s., no. 47 (Lincoln: University of Nebraska, 1974). Some other studies of Valéry and mathematics are Albert Gaudin, "Paul Valéry et les mathématiques," *French Review* 19 (1946): 271–78; Jeannine Jallat, "Valéry and the Mathematical Language of Identity and Difference," *Yale French Studies* 44 (1970): 51–64; and Judith Robinson, "Language, Physics and Mathematics in Valéry's Cahiers," *Modern Language Review* 55 (1960): 519–36.

14. Two important books on Valéry's *Notebooks* are Judith Robinson, *L'analyse de l'esprit dans les Cahiers de Valéry* (Paris: José Corti, 1963), and Nicole Celeyrette-Pietri, *Valéry et le moi: Des Cahiers à l'oeuvre* (Paris: Klincksieck, 1979).

15. Valéry, *Cahiers*, 29 vols. (Paris: Centre National de le Recherche Scientifique, 1957–61), 24:762. This edition will be cited in the text as C. The passage is also in the two-volume edition of excerpts from the *Cahiers*, edited by Judith Robinson (Paris: Pléiade, 1973–74), 1:197. Henceforth citations of the Robinson edition will follow in brackets after the main citation. Valéry's punctuation in the *Cahiers* is odd. I've retained it as much as possible in my translations. Emphasis in these quotations is always Valéry's.

16. For a series of perspectives on the System, see the essays collected in *Paul Valéry 3: Approche du «Système»*, ed. Huguette Laurenti, *Revue des lettres modernes* 554–59 (1979).

17. Cited in Jean Hytier, *La poétique de Valéry* (Paris: Armand Colin, 1970), p. 37.

CHAPTER 9

1. Alexander Vucinich, *Science in Russian Culture, 1861–1917* (Stanford, Calif.: Stanford University Press, 1970), pp. 351–54.

2. Vucinich, *Science*, pp. 354–55.

3. Andrei Bely, "Princip formy v èstetike," in *S*, pp. 175–94; English translation in *SE*, pp. 205–21.

4. This figure is given in B. O. Unbegaun, *Russian Versification* (Oxford: Clarendon Press, 1956), p. 36.

5. Roman Jakobson, "On Verse, Its Masters and Explorers," in *SW*, 5:569–601.

6. Jakobson and Lévi-Strauss, "«Les chats» de Charles Baudelaire," pp. 401–19, at p. 414.

7. The standard English-language work on Russian Futurism is Vladimir Markov, *Russian Futurism: A History* (Berkeley and Los Angeles: University of California Press, 1968). See also, specifically on Cubo-Futurism, Vahan D. Barooshian, *Russian Cubo-Futurism 1910–1930: A Study in Avant-Gardism* (The Hague: Mouton, 1974).

8. Gianni Vattimo, *La fine della modernità* (Milan: Garzanti, 1985), p. 10; English translation, *The End of Modernity: Nihilism and Hermeneutics in Post-Modern Culture*, trans. Jon Snyder (Baltimore: Johns Hopkins University Press, 1989), p. 2. This account of modernity is not Vattimo's own; it is the one he finds in Nietzsche and Heidegger.

9. "Poščečina obščestvennomu vkusu" (A slap in the face of public taste), signed by David Burliuk, Aleksandr Kruchenykh, Vladimir Mayakovsky, and Viktor Khlebnikov (Viktor was Khlebnikov's real name; Velimir was a name he adopted). This manifesto was originally published in 1912 and is reprinted in Vladimir Markov, *Manifesty i programmy russkix futuristov* (Munich: Fink Verlag, 1967), pp. 50–51; English translation in *The Ardis Anthology of Russian Futurism*, ed. Ellendea Proffer and Carl. R. Proffer (Ann Arbor, Mich.: Ardis, 1980), p. 179. "Idite k čortu" (Go to hell) also appears in Markov, pp. 80–81.

10. Velimir Khlebnikov, "Vremja mera mira" (Time is the measure of the world), in *Sobranie sočinenij* (Collected works), ed. Vladimir Markov (Munich: Fink Verlag, 1968–71), 3:435–55.

11. Khlebnikov, "Vremja mera mira," 3:446–47. The quotation from Leibniz is actually a paraphrase of a passage in *On the Universal Science: Characteristic (Scientia Generalis. Characteristica)*, section 14; see *Monadology and Other Philosophical Essays*, trans. Paul Schrecker and Anne Martin Schrecker (New York: Bobbs-Merrill, 1965), p. 14; original published in *Die philosophischen Schriften von Gottfried Wilhelm Leibniz*, ed. C. J. Gerhardt (Berlin, 1875–90), 7:200.

12. Khlebnikov, "Vremja mera mira," 3:447.

13. Khlebnikov, *SS*, 3:158; English translation in *Snake Train: Poetry and Prose*, ed. Gary Kern, trans. Gary Kern et al. (Ann Arbor, Mich.: Ardis, 1976), p. 192, and *Collected Works of Velimir Khlebnikov*, ed. Charlotte Douglas, trans. Paul Schmidt, (Cambridge, Mass.: Harvard University Press, 1987), 1:358.

14. Mallarmé, *OC*, p. 364. Tzvetan Todorov wrote about Khlebnikov's theories of numbers, letters, and words in an essay published back when few people were writing about Khlebnikov. See "Le nombre, la lettre, le mot," in *Poétique de la prose* (Paris: Seuil, 1971), pp. 197–211. Todorov also compares Khlebnikov with Mallarmé. Raymond Cooke devotes some pages to Khlebni-

kov's ideas about numbers and words in *Velimir Khlebnikov: A Critical Study* (Cambridge: Cambridge University Press, 1987), pp. 99–103.

15. David Burliuk, "Doitel' iznurennyx žab," in the miscellany *Futuristy: Rykajuščij Parnas* (Futurists: Roaring Parnassus) (Petersburg, 1914).

16. Nikolai Burliuk, "Poètičeskie načala" (Poetic principles), in Markov, *Manifesty i programmy,* p. 78.

17. El Lissitzky, "Pro dva kvadrata," included in reduced reproduction in *El Lissitzky: Life, Letters, Texts,* ed. Sophie Lissitzky-Küppers (London: Thames and Hudson, 1968).

18. Lissitzky-Küppers, *El Lissitzky,* plates 152–56. The project is described on pp. 86, 387.

19. Serres, *Hermès,* p. 33.

20. David Burliuk, "Kubizm" (Cubism), in *Poščečina obščestvennomu vkusu* (A slap in the face of public taste) (Moscow, 1912), pp. 95–101; English translation in the extremely valuable book edited by John E. Bowlt, *Russian Art of the Avant-Garde: Theory and Criticism, 1902–1934* (New York: Viking, 1976), pp. 69–77, at pp. 73, 75.

21. Mikhail Larionov and Natal'ia Goncharova, "Lučisty i buduščniki. Manifest" (Rayonists and Futurists: A Manifesto), in *Oslinyj xvost i mišen'* (Donkey's tail and target) (Moscow, 1913), pp. 9–48; reprinted in Markov, *Manifesty i programmy,* pp. 175–79; English translation in Bowlt, *Russian Art of the Avant-Garde,* pp. 87–91. The quoted passages appear on pp. 177–78 of the Markov edition and pp. 90–91 of the Bowlt translation.

22. Sergei Bobrov, "Liričeskaja tema" (The lyric theme), in Markov, *Manifesty i programmy,* pp. 98–106, at p. 103.

23. Kazimir Malevich, *Ot kubizma i futurizma k suprematizmu. Novyj živopisnyj realizm* (Moscow, 1916), pp. 9, 10, 17, 23, 28; English translation in Bowlt, *Russian Art of the Avant-Garde,* pp. 116–35, at pp. 122, 123, 127, 130, 133.

24. Benedikt Livshits, "V citadeli revoljucionnogo slova," *Puti tvorčestva,* no. 5 (1919); English translation by Vladimir Markov in *Russian Futurism,* p. 403 n. 27.

25. Benedikt Livshits, *Polutoroglazyj strelec* (Leningrad, 1933), p. 49. This book has been translated by John E. Bowlt as *The One and a Half-Eyed Archer* (Newtonville, Mass.: Oriental Research Partners, 1977). The passage I have cited appears in Bowlt's translation on p. 57, although with a misprint. Bowlt's book has "mutual functional independence," undoubtedly for "mutual functional *inter*dependence."

26. Linda Dalrymple Henderson, *The Fourth Dimension and Non-Euclidean Geometry in Modern Art* (Princeton: Princeton University Press, 1983). Chapter 5, "Transcending the Present: The Fourth Dimension in the Philosophy of Ouspensky and in Russian Futurism and Suprematism" (pp. 238–99), is specifically about Russia. Henderson treated the subject in her Ph.D. dissertation, "The Artist, 'The Fourth Dimension,' and Non-Euclidean Geometry, 1900–1930: A Romance of Many Dimensions" (Yale University, 1975). See also her "The Merging of Time and Space: The 'Fourth Dimension' in Russia from Ouspensky to Malevich," *Soviet Union* 5 (1978): 171–203, presenting some of the

same material as chapter 5 of the book; and an early article on a related subject, "A New Facet of Cubism: 'The Fourth Dimension' and 'Non-Euclidean Geometry' Reinterpreted," *Art Quarterly* 34 (1971): 410–33.

27. Aleksei Kruchenykh, "Novye puti slova" (New ways of the word), in Markov, *Manifesty i programmy,* pp. 66, 68. Cited in Henderson, *Fourth Dimension,* pp. 271–72.

CHAPTER 10

1. Roman Ingarden, *Das literarische Kunstwerk,* 2d ed. (Tübingen: Max Niemeyer, 1960), p. 1; English translation, *The Literary Work of Art: An Investigation on the Borderlines of Ontology, Logic, and Theory of Literature,* trans. George G. Grabowicz (Evanston, Ill.: Northwestern University Press, 1973), p. 3.

2. Most of this analysis can be found in the concluding sections (115–17) of Baumgarten's *Meditationes philosophicae de nonnullis ad poema pertinentibus* (Philosophical meditations on several matters pertaining to the poem); English translation, *Reflections on Poetry,* trans. Karl Aschenbrenner and William B. Holther (Berkeley and Los Angeles: University of California Press, 1954), pp. 77–79. Section 116 is where Baumgarten introduces the term *aesthetic* to designate the "science of perception," or science that investigates the lower faculty.

3. Waldemar Conrad, "Der ästhetische Gegenstand: Eine phänomenologische Studie," *Zeitschrift für Ästhetik und allgemeine Kunstwissenschaft* 3 (1908): 71–118, 469–511; and 4 (1909): 400–455. Even the standard history of the phenomenological movement makes no mention of Conrad. See Herbert Spiegelberg, *The Phenomenological Movement: A Historical Introduction,* 2 vols. (The Hague: Martinus Nijhoff, 1960). The standard full-length book on phenomenology and literature also contains no reference to Conrad. See Robert R. Magliola, *Phenomenology and Literature: An Introduction* (West Lafayette, Ind.: Purdue University Press, 1977).

4. Conrad, "Ästhetische Gegenstand," 3 (1908): 76.

5. Conrad, "Ästhetische Gegenstand," 4 (1909): 452–54.

6. See Roman Ingarden, "Phenomenological Aesthetics: An Attempt at Defining its Range," *Journal of Aesthetics and Art Criticism* 33 (1974–75): 257–69. Ingarden talks about Conrad on p. 258.

7. Ingarden, *Literarische Kunstwerk,* pp. 121–33 (secs. 20–21); *Literary Work of Art,* pp. 117–27.

8. Roman Ingarden, *Untersuchungen zur Ontologie der Kunst* (Tübingen: Max Niemeyer, 1962).

9. René Wellek, "The Mode of Existence of a Literary Work of Art," *Southern Review* 7 (1942): 735–54.

10. René Wellek and Austin Warren, *Theory of Literature* (London: Jonathan Cape, 1949), chap. 12, "The Analysis of the Literary Work of Art," pp. 139–58. The discussion of Ingarden is on p. 152.

11. Stephen Pepper, *The Work of Art* (Bloomington: Indiana University Press, 1955); George Dickie, *Art and the Aesthetic: An Institutional Analysis*

(Ithaca, N.Y.: Cornell University Press, 1974); Nelson Goodman, *Ways of Worldmaking* (Indianapolis: Hackett, 1978); Arthur C. Danto, *The Transfiguration of the Commonplace: A Philosophy of Art* (Cambridge, Mass.: Harvard University Press, 1981).

12. Martin Heidegger, "Der Ursprung des Kunstwerkes," in *Holzwege* (Frankfurt-am-Main: Klostermann, 1950), pp. 7–68.

13. Heidegger, "Ursprung," p. 39. See below, pp. 222–23, for the distinction between Being and being.

14. Heidegger, *Sein und Zeit* (Halle: Niemeyer, 1927), p. 227.

15. Heidegger, "Ursprung," p. 59.

16. Heidegger, "Ursprung," p. 60.

17. The phrase is featured, for example, in "Das Wesen der Sprache," in *Unterwegs zur Sprache* (Pfullingen: Neske, 1959), pp. 157–216.

18. Heidegger, "Ursprung," pp. 61–62.

19. See Bloom, *Closing of the American Mind.*

CHAPTER 11

1. Foucault, *Les mots et les choses*, p. 317; *The Order of Things*, p. 306. See above, p. 28.

2. Bruns, *Modern Poetry*, p. 101. See above, p. 234, n. 20.

3. Bruns, *Modern Poetry*, pp. 101–2, 117.

4. Scherer, *Le "Livre" de Mallarmé*; see above, pp. 94–95, and p. 234 n. 19 for an explanation of references to this book.

CHAPTER 12

1. Andrei Bely, *Peterburg* (Petrograd, 1916; rpt. Letchworth: Bradda Books, 1967), p. 2.

2. Bely, *Peterburg*, p. 55.

3. Khlebnikov, *SS*, 3:158.

4. Todorov "Le nombre, la lettre, le mot," pp. 209–10.

5. E. J. Brown, Introduction to *Snake Train: Poetry and Prose*, ed. Gary Kern and trans. Gary Kern et al. (Ann Arbor: Ardis, 1976), pp. 11–26, at pp. 11–12.

6. Cooke, *Khlebnikov*, pp. 176–83.

7. The document appears in Markov, *Manifesty i programmy*, pp. 51–53.

8. Markov, *Manifesty i programmy*, p. 173; English translation in Bowlt, *Russian Art of the Avant-Garde*, p. 81.

9. Lissitzky-Küppers, *El Lissitzky*, p. 359.

10. Lissitzky-Küppers, *El Lissitzky*, p. 362–63.

CHAPTER 13

1. Käte Hamburger, "Die phänomenologische Struktur der Dichtung Rilkes," in *Philosophie der Dichter: Novalis, Schiller, Rilke* (Stuttgart: Kohlhammer, 1966), pp. 179–275, at p. 179.

2. Käte Hamburger, *Rilke: Eine Einführung* (Stuttgart: Klett, 1976), p. 15. Paul de Man, "Tropes (Rilke)," in *Allegories of Reading,* pp. 20–56, at p. 36.

3. Hamburger, *Rilke,* pp. 18, 16, 17.

4. Rainer Maria Rilke, *Sämtliche Werke* (henceforth *Sämt.W*) (Frankfurt-am-Main: Insel, 1955), 1:690.

5. Being-toward-death is the subject of the first chapter of the second part of Heidegger's *Sein und Zeit,* pp. 235–67. George Steiner, among others, has made the comparison between Rilke and Heidegger on this point. See George Steiner, *Martin Heidegger* (New York: Viking, 1978), p. 104.

6. Rainer Maria Rilke, *Auguste Rodin,* in *Sämt.W,* 5:139–280. The work has been translated into English as *Rodin,* trans. Robert Firmage (Salt Lake City: Peregrine Smith, 1979). This edition includes black-and-white photoplates of many of Rodin's sculptures.

7. Heidegger, "Wozu Dichter?", in *Holzwege* (Frankfurt am Main: Klostermann, 1950), pp. 248–95.

8. James Atlas, "The Case of Paul de Man," *The New York Times Magazine,* Aug. 28, 1988, p. 69.

9. De Man, *Allegories of Reading,* p. 38.

10. De Man, *Blindness and Insight,* p. 31.

Index

Compositor:	J. Jarrett Engineering, Inc.
Text:	10/13 Sabon
Display:	Sabon
Printer:	Maple-Vail Book Mfg. Group
Binder:	Maple-Vail Book Mfg. Group